Gentleman Jim Corbett

Also by Patrick Myler
and published by Robson Books

A Century of Boxing Greats

Gentleman Jim Corbett

The Truth Behind a Boxing Legend

Patrick Myler

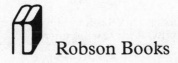 Robson Books

To my daughter Gillian,
with thanks for her support and patience

First published in Great Britain in 1998 by Robson Books Ltd, Bolsover House,
5–6 Clipstone Street, London W1P 8LE

Copyright © 1998 Patrick Myler
The right of Patrick Myler to be identified as author of this work has been
asserted by him in accordance with the Copyright, Designs and Patents Act
1988

British Library Cataloguing in Publication Data
A catalogue for this title is available from the British Library

ISBN 1 86105 212 X

Typeset by Columns Design Ltd., Reading
Printed and bound by WBC Book Manufacturers,
Bridgend, Mid-Glamorgan

Fight one more round

When your feet are so tired that you have to shuffle back to the centre of the ring, fight one more round.

When your arms are so tired that you can hardly lift your hands to come on guard, fight one more round.

When your nose is bleeding and your eyes are black and you are so tired that you wish your opponent would crack you one on the jaw and put you to sleep, fight one more round.

Remember that the man who always fights one more round is never whipped.

James J. Corbett

Contents

Contents

Acknowledgements

Writers, like fighters, need commitment, stamina, and a good team in their corner. Whenever my enthusiasm and energy showed signs of flagging, I knew I could depend on the help and encouragement of some marvellously dedicated people to keep me going. Without them, I wouldn't have lasted the distance.

I owe a particular debt of gratitude to Tony Gee, who unselfishly spent many hours conducting research on my behalf at the British Newspaper Library. I am glad to see his meticulous attention to detail and insistence on correcting long-established myths now finding an outlet in his own boxing writings.

Special thanks, too, to Niels Thorsen, in Denmark, who delved deep into his huge collection of boxing books to find any mention of James J. Corbett, and was always willing to follow up on a request for further research. Bill Schutte, of Wisconsin, provided a copious amount of newspaper cuttings, as well as Gentleman Jim's own scrapbook of his early boxing career.

Richard T. Corbett, of Plainsboro, New Jersey, a descendant of the west of Ireland Corbett family which included the champion's father, was foremost in providing information on the wider Corbett clan. I thank, too, the many other distant relatives who, along with other interested readers, answered my appeal in the *San Francisco Chronicle* for information.

On my visit to San Francisco I was kindly given a tour of the Olympic Club, which launched Corbett on his illustrious career, by general manager Paul Kennedy. The club's formal dress code went unsullied thanks to sports writer Jack Fiske, who lent me his blazer and tie to hide my inappropriate summer shirt.

Robert Soderman was an enthusiastic supporter of my project and supplied lots of material from US sources, especially the Chicago newspapers. Luckett Davis, recognised as one of the leading authorities on boxers' records, unselfishly shared his findings on Corbett with me. Robert G. Russell, of El Cerrito, California, told me about serving on the World War 2 Liberty ship, the *James J. Corbett*.

Other American help was freely given by Don Scott, editor of *Boxing Collectors' News*; Michael T. Isenberg, author of the definitive biography of John L. Sullivan; Miriam Marseu of *Sports Illustrated*; Bill Cayton of The Big Fights Inc.; Robert J. Chandler of the Wells Fargo Historical Services; the San Francisco Public Library; California State Library; California Historical Society; California Genealogical Society; Bayside Historical Society, New York; New York Public Library; the National Archives; Dyer Memorial Library, Abington, Mass.; University of Wisconsin; Van Pelt Library at the University of Pennsylvania; and Catherine Ann Curry, assistant archivist, Catholic Archdiocese of San Francisco.

Information on Corbett films, in which he either appeared or was represented, was found through diligent research by John Exshaw. Kristine Kruger turned up a mine of useful data at the Margaret Herrick Library, US Centre for Motion Picture Study, California. Dan Streible, Professor of Film Studies at the University of South Carolina, also helped in this regard. I look forward to the publication of his book, *Fight Pictures 1894–1915*.

Luke McKernan, of the National Film and Television Archive, British Film Institute, was extremely helpful in tracing references to Corbett movies in published works, and answered all my queries with remarkable patience. I also thank him for arranging my attendance at the unforgettable *Battles of the Century* film night at the BFT in 1997, when I was privileged to see the entire Corbett-Fitzsimmons fight.

Derek O'Dell, ever willing to help with research or share his expert knowledge on boxing, came up trumps as usual. Other much appreciated British help came from Fred Snelling, Barry Hugman, Roy Hudd, Brian Atwood (editor of *The Stage*), Brian Doogan, Jim Crichton, C.D. Paramor, Cyril Stansfield, who dug into the newspaper files to trace Corbett's English music hall appearances, and the US Information Service at the American Embassy, London.

Paul Hennessy, from New South Wales, told me of his visit to the site of the Corbett-Sullivan fight in New Orleans, where, sadly, there is nothing to mark the historic spot. Arnold Thomas provided useful details of Gentleman Jim's trip to Australia.

In Ireland, I was given valuable information on the Corbett family by the South Mayo Family Research Centre in Ballinrobe. I am also grateful to the *Tuam Herald*; the staffs of the National Library and Mayo County Library; the library staff of Independent Newspapers;

as well as Alan Loughrey (whose mother is a west of Ireland Corbett), John Courtney and Denis Morrison.

I wish to thank the Putnam Publishing Group, New York, for permission to publish extracts from Corbett's autobiography, *The Roar of the Crowd.*

I am extremely grateful for the use of photographs from the private collections of Bill Schutte, Don Scott and Jack Fiske, as well as those supplied by the Margaret Herrick Library and the Bayside Historical Society. I was especially pleased to come across the only photo I ever saw of Corbett with his first wife, Olive. It was taken during the couple's Irish visit in 1894. Thanks to Tricia Forde, photographer in Claremorris, County Mayo, for the print. I also thank Edmund Burke, publisher, for permission to use the photo of Jim's uncle, the Rev. James Corbett.

Thanks to Barry McGuigan for writing the foreword, to Kate Mills, editor at Robson Books, and to my agent David O'Leary.

Finally, this book would never have been completed without the support of my family. I especially wish to thank my wife Frances, who only occasionally complained about the missed outings and undone jobs.

Foreword

by Barry McGuigan

When I was growing up in Clones, County Monaghan, there were always boxing magazines around the house. My father, Pat, was a real fight fan.

I remember seeing photographs of this tall, upright, handsome Irish-American, James J. Corbett, and reading about his exploits.

Later, as I took a deeper interest in boxing history, I learned what a significant part Gentleman Jim had played in changing the course and image of the game. Before him fighters were typecast as big, thick-set brawlers who owed their successes to power and endurance above all else.

Then along came Jim Corbett.

Here was someone who showed that you could win fights with skill and dexterity, rather than just brute strength. He wrote the original boxing textbook for the others to follow.

In beating John L. Sullivan to become world heavyweight champion, Corbett was the matador against the bull. He just frustrated Sullivan with his speed and cleverness and wore him out. It was a triumph for brain over brawn.

The only time I have seen Corbett on film was his loss to Bob Fitzsimmons, but he looked such an elegant boxer. Tall, athletically built, boxing from an upright stance, he was a master craftsman with a beautiful left jab.

They say Gentleman Jim was aloof, but he attracted a whole new audience, including women, to boxing. He brought an air of respectability to what had been considered just a blood-thirsty sport.

People often ask me how fighters from Corbett's era would fare against their modern counterparts. It's an unfair question. There is just too much of a time gap.

Boxing has evolved so much. Fighters of today are bigger, stronger, better all-rounders. The old-timers didn't have the benefits of modern training techniques, dietary control and all the rest.

One of the great things they had back then was endurance. Corbett, at thirty-three, was able to last twenty-three rounds with a much heavier and stronger James J. Jeffries. And just imagine going sixty-one rounds, as he did with the great Peter Jackson, only to find the referee declaring it 'no contest'!

I fought in some of the last fifteen-round world title fights, before the limit was reduced to twelve, and they were tough enough, believe me. I was known as a hard trainer and had good stamina, but the idea of fighting for over three hours is just mind-boggling.

I am honoured to have been asked to pay my own small tribute to one of boxing's scientific masters and outstanding personalities.

Barry McGuigan is a former World Boxing Association featherweight champion. Now a TV commentator and fight analyst with Sky Sports, he also writes a boxing column for the Daily Express. *He is chairman of the Professional Boxers Association.*

Introduction

Most fight fans, though they might not care to admit it, get their thrills from seeing a fighter transport another into dreamland with a perfectly timed and delivered pay-off punch.

It's sudden. It's dramatic. It leaves them wide-eyed, breathless, expressing their appreciation with an inadequate 'Wow'.

But boxing is not just about knockouts. It's about the men whose success in the ring is due to highly developed skills, who can nullify their opponents' power with a tactical master plan designed to frustrate, outwit and ultimately outscore the aggressor.

Is there not something quite beautiful in the balletic grace of a Muhammad Ali, the masterful counter-punching of a Gene Tunney, the art of picking off an opponent's punches in mid-air as mastered by Jack Johnson?

James J. Corbett, the subject of this book, was the first boxing master. He showed the rest how it was done. He was the pioneer, the innovator, the deep thinker who worked on his strengths, disguised his weaknesses, and singlemindedly set out to prove to the world that brain can conquer brawn.

Quickly realising he lacked the physical bulk and the natural hitting power to take on the top heavyweights at their own game, he used fast footwork, a tight defence, clever feinting and precision punching to conquer many of the most feared ringmen of his day. His left jab was as unerring as a guided missile. When he injured his knuckles, he turned the jab into a left hook, a punch that was unknown up to then, and which would, in time, be perfected by the likes of Jack Dempsey, Joe Louis, Rocky Marciano, Joe Frazier and Mike Tyson.

In becoming the first world heavyweight champion under Marquis of Queensberry Rules by toppling the mighty John L. Sullivan on 7 September 1892, Corbett showed extraordinary concentration and patience as he systematically softened up his rival over twenty-one rounds, only moving in for the kill when he knew Sullivan no longer posed a threat.

Overnight, the former San Francisco bank clerk had transformed the character of boxing. He had turned a brutal test of strength and endurance into a scientific art.

Although Bob Fitzsimmons found a gap in that seemingly impregnable guard to land his renowned 'solar plexus punch' and take the title – a defeat that hit Corbett so hard he was suicidal – the Californian proved his courage and endurance in an epic bid to regain the championship from James J. Jeffries. After dazzling the lumbering Jeffries for twenty-three rounds, he succumbed to a knockout blow. Despite its outcome, this fight is looked upon by many historians as Corbett's best performance.

My admiration for Corbett stems from a boyhood fascination with the giants of the ring. From well-worn books and magazines picked up in second-hand shops, I learned all about the fighting champions while my pals were feasting on the escapades of Captain Marvel, Rockfist Rogan, and Wilson, the athlete who never grew old. My heroes had their frailties, but they were real flesh and blood.

Corbett stood out as a glamorous figure, a handsome, elegant, well-mannered man – a 'damned dude' in the scornful words of John L. Sullivan – who had lifted an uncivilised sport onto a new, more acceptable, plane.

He wasn't universally loved for destroying an icon, but the legend that he was never forgiven for beating Sullivan is an exaggeration. Most fair-minded people accepted that he had won the title fairly and squarely, and applauded him for his steely determination to beat the odds.

Corbett was the first champion to appreciate the value of being cleverly marketed. With the aid of his enterprising manager, William A. Brady, he exploited his success in the ring by building a success-ful career as an actor. His confidence before the spotlights, allied to his impressive appearance, clear voice and ability to adapt to his new role, made him into a popular stage and screen performer. Boxing contemporaries like Sullivan, Fitzsimmons and Jeffries had tested the same waters and all but drowned. Jim was equally at home as a lecturer and broadcaster.

All the nice things one can find to say and write about Corbett, however, must be balanced by the often unflattering picture that emerges when one looks at the complete man. There is more than ample evidence that the 'Gentleman Jim' tag he rejoiced under was something of a misnomer.

Moody, arrogant, quick-tempered, inconsiderate, an adulterer, a racist, a bully: he was all of these. A gentleman wouldn't twist a fellow professional's nose when a friendly greeting was offered, or snub his great rivals at their funerals, or berate the great Jack Johnson as 'the black man with the yellow streak', or torture his wife with a lighted cigar and threaten to kill her. On all these charges, Corbett was guilty.

Previous biographies, all but one written while he was still alive, showed him in too glowing a light. Nat Fleischer, the last to chronicle his life story, in 1942, admitted that Corbett was no plaster saint, but insisted he was 'a rather modest soul'. This conclusion is contrary to all the evidence. Although Gentleman Jim was nine years dead before *The Ring* magazine's founder and long-serving editor penned his words, it is clear that Fleischer had no desire to highlight the faults of a friend.

Corbett's popular autobiography, *The Roar of the Crowd*, published in 1925, is a complete whitewash. Not only did he hardly take a punch in his entire career, if you believe his account, but he draws a veil across most of the unhappy events of his life. The tragic deaths of his parents – his father murdered his wife before turning the gun on himself – are ignored. His marriage to Vera Stanwood is depicted as bliss all the way. He fails to mention the scandal that followed her disclosures to the press about her 'brutal' husband, although she later dropped her divorce plans. Corbett's previous marriage to Olive Lake also gets lost in his self-glorifying recollections.

The book was ghost-written by Robert Gordon Anderson, but the views were Corbett's own. John Arlott, the well-known cricket commentator, contributed a foreword to a British edition of *The Roar of the Crowd* in 1954, in which he wrote '... the man who told this story was an intelligent, decent chap – and Champion of the World; the man who set it down for him was an experienced journalist with a genuine admiration for his principal.'

That said it all. Yet, in attempting an honest appraisal of Corbett's life, it would be unfair to totally debunk the 'Gentleman Jim' image. For all his imperfections, he could be a man of considerable charm and compassion. He made enemies, but he made many long-lasting friendships. Generous with his money, he set up his brother Harry in a restaurant called Corbett's, which was a popular landmark in San Francisco for many years. He cleared off his father's mortgage on his livery business and sent his parents back home to Ireland on a holiday. He was also known to pay for friends' weddings and funerals.

Neighbours in the Bayside area of New York where Jim and Vera made their home knew him as a courteous man who was always ready to help a local event, especially if it was for a charitable cause. Having no children of his own, there was nothing he enjoyed more than playing ball or exchanging banter with the local kids who gathered around him. Vera, who knew his dark side more than anyone, forgave his indiscretions and remained by his side for thirty-eight years, right up to his death in 1933.

Ultimately, of course, it is as a world heavyweight champion that James J. Corbett is judged and remembered. In terms of aggression, punching power and ability to withstand a solid shot, he doesn't match many of those who succeeded him to the throne. On his mastery of the scientific side of the sport, he rates ten out of ten.

This was the man who truly epitomised the Manly Art of Self-Defence.

In the words of Gene Tunney, 'He had the keenest and most analytical brain that ever graced a prize ring'.

CHAPTER 1

Dress Rehearsal

John L. Sullivan was in a bad mood. For someone with such a volatile personality as the reigning heavyweight champion of the world, this was hardly unusual. What got his goat on this occasion was the newspaper article asking when the Boston Strong Boy was going to be seen back in the ring.

He crumpled up the paper and flung it to the floor. How dare anyone try to tell him who and when he should fight? Hadn't he proved himself, over and again, the best fighting man in the world? Why, then, were constant demands being made for him to put his superiority to the test?

The reason, which he was reluctant to admit, was that it was almost three years since he had last fought, thwarting the challenge of Jake Kilrain in a bitter bare-knuckle encounter that had lasted into the seventy-fifth round. He had insisted that would be his last bare-fist fight. From now on, he would adhere to the Marquis of Queensberry Rules, which stipulated the use of gloves.

But he was in no hurry to strip off for action again. Not for fear of any of his persistent challengers, more the dread of what was required to get his bloated body into fighting shape. Years of idleness, over-eating and heavy drinking had left him fat and unfit. It would be sheer hell working off those unwanted pounds. But the clamour for his return was growing daily. There was only one thing to do.

In March, 1892, while on a theatrical tour with the play *Honest Hearts and Willing Hands*, in which he had the leading role, the

1

champion turned challenger. His dispatch to Joe Eakins, editor of the *New York World*, was printed the following day.

> I hereby challenge any and all of the bluffers who have been trying to make capital at my expense to fight me either the last week in August or the first week in September this year at the Olympic Club, New Orleans, Louisiana, for a purse of $25,000 and an outside bet of $10,000, the winner of the fight to take the entire purse ... I insist upon the bet of $10,000, to show that I mean business ... I give precedence in this challenge to Frank P. Slavin, of Australia, he and his backers having done the greatest amount of bluffing. My second preference is the bombastic sprinter Charles Mitchell, of England, whom I would rather whip than any man in the world. My third preference is James Corbett, of California, who has achieved his share of bombast. ... The Marquis of Queensberry Rules must govern this contest, as I want fighting, not foot racing, and I intend to keep the championship of the world where it belongs, in the land of the free and the home of the brave.

It was a clever ploy by Sullivan. He knew the contenders would find it very difficult to raise the $10,000 sidestake. Thus, if no-one was able to accept his challenge, he could sit back and say he had made the effort, but no-one had responded. He could then get on with his theatrical career, complete his autobiography, which was due out later in the year, and still bill himself as 'undefeated heavyweight champion of the world'.

Sure enough, neither Slavin or Mitchell could meet Sullivan's requirements. His third preference, Corbett, was not prepared to give in so easily. In a newspaper announcement, Corbett said he would be willing to meet Sullivan under the latter's terms. As a guarantee of his good faith, Corbett's manager, William A. Brady, deposited a cheque for $1,000 with the editor of the *New York World*. Now all that was required was the small matter of raising the other $9,000.

'Where in hell can we dig up that sort of dough?' Brady asked his fighter.

Everyone considered Sullivan unbeatable. Who was going to throw away good money? They arranged a meeting with a leading New York horse-racing figure, Colonel Frederick McLewee. Corbett told him he had no doubt he could beat John L.

'My boy, I don't think you can whip Sullivan,' said McLewee, 'but you certainly have a lot of nerve and you can put me down for $5,000.'

Brady and Corbett tried their salesmen's pitch with several other sporting people and came away with the requisite guarantee. The challenge for the championship was secure. Sullivan could not dodge the issue any longer.

The fighters and all other interested parties met up at the offices of the *New York World* and contracts were signed. The contest would take place at the Olympic Club, New Orleans, on 7 September 1892. It would be fought under Marquis of Queensberry rules. The gloves would be 'the smallest that the club will allow'. The purse would be $25,000, plus the stake money of $10,000. All the money would go to the winner, as the champion had insisted.

While Sullivan went away to contemplate how best to get rid of the unsightly spare tyre that encircled his waist, the challenger had no such worries. He was young, he was in his physical prime and he knew in his heart that his time had come. Nothing and no-one would prevent him from achieving his goal. He would dislodge the mighty John L. from the championship throne and earn his place in ring history.

★

Out with the old, in with the new.

With the dawn of the new century on the horizon, the prevailing mood in America was of hope and promise. Although workers still faced a stiff battle for their rights, and life down on the farm entailed long hours of back-breaking drudgery with primitive implements, the wheels of industry were going at full pelt. More and more people were moving to the cities, where rapidly increasing electrification was proving a metaphor for the bright future.

Another giant leap forward was achieved when residents of one city were enabled to speak directly to those of another through the miracle of the telephone. By the end of the nineteenth century the first long-distance lines were established. The motor car began to appear less of a novelty on the streets and the horse was less given to panic at the sight of one of these menacing contraptions disputing its domain. Some 300 companies were already engaged in car manufacture, though many failed to prosper and the number had dwindled to 109 by 1900.

For the social underclass, recreation as an escape from the long, hard hours of work was found largely in cheap saloons, gambling halls and sleazy, smoke-filled sporting arenas. Much of the sports followers' time was spent dodging the attentions of the law as they flocked to some illicit promotion. Even though a police raid might bring the proceedings to a halt almost as soon as they started, and perhaps result in spectators, as well as contestants and organisers, ending up in jail, it was a risk they were quite prepared to take. It was all part of the thrill.

Bare-knuckle boxing, particularly, drew the odium of the authorities throughout the country. It was not so much the sport's brutality and frequent consequence of severe injury, even death, that caused it to be outlawed in most states, but because it attracted rough elements who looked for, and often found, the flimsiest excuse to start a riot. Heavy betting was a natural part of prize-fighting and if one of the boxers looked set for defeat, it was not uncommon for his backers to start a commotion, making it impossible to continue the fight. All bets would thus be off – and then the real trouble would start.

Change was imperative if the sport was to survive the growing opposition. Salvation came in the form of the Marquis of Queensberry rules. Drawn up in England in 1867 by John Graham Chambers, an accomplished oarsman who played a key role in organising Britain's Amateur Athletic Association, they received the support of John Sholto Douglas, 8th Marquis of Queensberry. The two men, who had met at Magdalen College in Oxford, shared an interest in boxing. Douglas agreed to sponsor the new rules in return for giving them his name. With some modifications over the years, the Queensberry rules still prevail.

The new code revolutionised the sport and gave it at least a modicum of respectability. Principally, it banned many of the former rough-house tactics, such as wrestling and head butting, and replaced rounds which ended only when a man was knocked down with fighting periods confined to three minutes. A fallen fighter was given ten seconds to rise before he was declared 'out'. The rules also specified that 'fair-sized boxing gloves of the best quality, and new' must be worn.

As in Britain, the Queensberry rules found favour in the United States over the old London Prize-Ring Rules. It was not an overnight transition, however. Bare-fist pugilism continued in tandem with gloved combat for quite some time, until more and more boxers opted for the new statutes. Eventually, bouts without gloves became so rare as to be regarded as oddities. Boxing, in keeping with so many other popular activities, had moved with the times.

★

As excitement built up in the weeks leading to the Sullivan vs. Corbett showdown, the cocky challenger advised anyone who would listen that they should bet on him. Jim was convinced his youth, speed and guile would be too much for the fat, ageing titleholder. If evidence was needed, he issued a reminder of how, a year earlier, he had scored an important psychological victory over Sullivan. He had learned at first hand what were the weak points in the champion's fistic armoury when facing him in a bizarre exhibition bout – with both men wearing dress suits!

The occasion was a benefit night for Corbett at the Grand Opera House on Mission Street, San Francisco, on 26 June 1891. Jim had only received half of his promised $5,000 for enduring sixty-one rounds with Peter Jackson, of Australia, a titanic struggle that had ended in the referee declaring 'no contest'. Corbett's supporters, claiming he had been robbed of certain victory as well as his full payment, arranged the testimonial to help make up the loss. As it happened, Sullivan was in town with *Honest Hearts and Willing Hands*. What better attraction for the benefit night than a sparring match between the heavyweight champion and one of his leading contenders?

On the opening night of John L.'s play, Corbett had booked a private box. It didn't please the Boston Strong Boy one bit when Jim arrived late, acknowledged the cheers of the locals, and sat down. Jim later insisted he had not wanted to interrupt the champion's performance and had not wished to show himself off at Sullivan's expense, but that was a bluff. He clearly intended to rattle the short-fused John L.

After the first act, Corbett went to the leading actor's dressing room and put to him the plan for an exhibition bout. Sullivan, still fuming at the Californian's apparent effort to upstage him, eventually cooled down after Jim convinced him they could both make good money out of the affair. They shook hands on the deal.

The night before the benefit, Sullivan made the astonishing statement that he would not enter the ring unless both men boxed in full evening dress. Corbett, rightly insisting that this would make them look ridiculous, nevertheless conceded that the world champion was the one calling the shots. Sullivan's ploy was to show that he didn't take the young Californian seriously as a challenger. More importantly, it was the best way to hide his beer belly.

The crowd's laughter turned to boos and jeers when the fighters took off their top-coats and commenced sparring in their dress suits.

They looked more like a couple of well-heeled guests who had got into a row at a formal dinner and decided to sort out their differences there and then.

The four rounds passed tamely, with neither man exerting himself. John L., slow and short of breath, made a joke of the affair, boxing carelessly and frequently turning away to engage in banter with the audience. Corbett, obviously the much fitter man, could have used his speed to make the corpulent champion appear even more leaden-footed and clumsy than he was, but he contented himself with sizing up Sullivan's style of fighting. He discovered that John L. was 'a sucker for a feint'.

At the conclusion of the farce, Corbett whispered to Billy Delaney, his trainer: 'Billy, I know I can whip this fellow.'

Sullivan scornfully remarked that the only preparation he needed to face 'the damned dude' was a haircut and a shave.

While John L. and his pals adjourned to the nearest bar, Gentleman Jim headed off to enjoy a treat of strawberries and ice-cream.

CHAPTER 2

'No' to the priesthood

James John Corbett made his mind up early.

He was not prepared to take the path to the priesthood laid out for him by his Irish-born, devoutly Catholic parents. The attainment of a permanent, pensionable job in the bank was equally unappealing.

Jim was an adventurer, a risk taker. He wanted to find out how far his ambitions, backed by steely self-assurance, could take him. Fame and fortune were his goals. His fists were the tools he would use to follow that destiny. Success in the ring, once achieved, would open the doors to further opportunities to exploit his talents.

To his parents Patrick and Catherine Corbett, the idea of his shedding blood and risking serious injury as a prizefighter, while mixing with the riff-raff of society, was anathema. They wanted Jim to be someone they could be proud of. Boxing would bring only shame and humiliation.

As with most large Catholic families, it was expected of the Corbetts that one member, at least, should devote his or her life to the service of God. James was singled out as an ideal candidate for the priesthood for a special reason. He was named after Patrick's brother, James, a parish priest in Ireland. No prouder honour could come the family's way than seeing young Jim follow his uncle's vocation.

The Corbetts of Ballycusheen, a townland at Kilmaine, near Ballinrobe, in County Mayo, were a much respected family in their local community. They were a pretty healthy bunch, with a record of longevity. At a time when most Irish people were lucky to see forty, the future world champion's grandfather, Patrick Corbett Snr, was sixty when he died in 1850. His widow Mary survived to her eighty-eighth year.

It was a nice boost to the family's social standing when one of Patrick Snr's sons became a priest. No docile cleric who spent his time reading his breviary and catering to the simple needs of his parishioners, Father James Corbett was a life-long campaigner for the rights of downtrodden Irish tenant farmers and a perpetual thorn in the side of the authorities. It was said that Gentleman Jim got his fighting spirit from his Uncle Jim.

Another of old man Corbett's sons who made a bit of a name for himself was his eldest boy Francis. After running a small farm in the townland of Carrownagarruan, Francis became a spirits dealer, with premises in High Street, Ballinrobe. On moving to nearby Tuam, in County Galway, he was a successful merchant for many years before taking the prestigious post of Town Clerk. He was still acting in that capacity when he died, aged seventy-eight, in 1893.

Patrick Junior, the future world champion's father, set his sights much further. He was only eighteen when he sailed for America in 1854.

Though he knew the chances of ever seeing his family again were remote, he had experienced too much misery over the past decade to have any doubts about his decision. The terrible ravages of the Great Hunger (1845–9) might be over, but its legacy was a deep and permanent scar on the heart of every Irish person who followed the emigration trail.

Those who set off for the New World took with them their meagre belongings, together with the harrowing memories of successive food famines caused by potato blight. For the poor (one-third of the population) the potato was the only source of food. When it failed, so did they. The wheat and other vegetables they grew had to be sold to pay the rents on their land. If they didn't pay up, they were evicted by agents of the detested absentee landlords.

When, for season after season, nothing appeared in the soil except blackened, soggy, inedible potatoes, the results were catastrophic. Between death from starvation and the diseases cholera and typhus, together with emigration, the population of Ireland declined by almost two million in the ten-year period up to 1851.

America, whatever its distance and its uncertainties, had to be better than what the desperate emigrants were leaving behind.

Pat Corbett joined his brother John, who had settled in New Orleans. Whatever elation he might have felt at finding a home in a land where survival didn't depend on the humble spud was soon shattered. A yellow fever epidemic struck the state of Louisiana. Pat lost two brothers and two sisters to the outbreak.

Numbed by his loss and his disenchantment with life in the

Crescent City, he took off after three years for California. There, he found the climate to his liking and the opportunities plentiful for a young man anxious to get on. He settled in San Francisco and, after several years as a hack driver, built up a successful livery stable and undertaking business.

Pat married another Irish immigrant, Catherine McDonald, in November 1858. Kate, as she was known, was three years younger than her husband. Born in Dublin, her father ran a stagecoach business at Barrack Gate, Islandbridge, next to the city's Phoenix Park. Pat and Kate would have twelve children, two of whom would die in infancy. Those who survived to adulthood were, in order of birth, Frank, Edward (Harry), Esther, James J., John (Jack), Theresa, Mary (Mamie), Katie, Joseph and Thomas.

The San Francisco of that time was not the Golden Gate attraction of today's glossy travel brochures. It was a principally a collection of shacks and saloons, populated by gold prospectors and speculators with little knowledge of or respect for law and order. Dominated by Boss Broderick, the diamond-studded overseer of the Barbary Coast, it provided ample scope for men to gamble, drink and sample the fare at the countless brothels, where girls could be hired at twenty cents for twenty minutes.

Pat Corbett, a man of deep religious convictions, was initially shocked at the huge culture change from his old home in the quiet, green hills of County Mayo. However, as he later observed, 'if Daniel could live in a lion's den, I could certainly do my best to live in San Francisco.'

At least Pat had plenty of Irish company to prevent him growing too homesick. In a city undergoing massive population growth due to the influx of immigrants, the Irish were the most numerous of those born abroad. By 1880 one-third of the city's inhabitants were Irish-born or the sons and daughters of Irish settlers. The predominant religion was Catholic, with two small branches of the Loyal Orange Institution and a Scotch-Irish Society getting limited support.

The district where the Corbetts set up home was known as 'South of the Slot' after the city's cable-car system was introduced in 1873. It was an area renowned for turning out good fighters. As well as Jim Corbett, it produced world champions in Jimmy Britt, Willie Ritchie and Frankie Klick.

Jim was born on 1 September 1866. No official record of his birth exists, owing to the massive destruction caused by the 1906 earthquake and fire, but the San Francisco Directory for 1865–6 shows that Patrick J. Corbett, hackman, lived in Perry Street, between Harrison and Bryant streets. This is clearly the future champion's father. Perry Street, which was in the predominantly Irish Ward Ten, today lies buried beneath the James Lick Skyway. By 1875, when Jim was nine, the family had moved to 518–20 Hayes Street.

Jim did recall that, when he was a young boy, the family migrated across 'the Slot'. It was such a traumatic experience for the sensitive youngster that, in his sixties, he still recalled vividly his humiliation as he led the family cow to their new home in Hayes Street. He wept all the way there.

Of his early dwelling place, he said it was 'a dirt road, lined with saloons and filled with drunks. Because of our loose surroundings, I got a strict upbringing. My parents taught me the value of a clean collar, a clean suit of clothes and a clean reputation. I've always been grateful to them.'

Once Patrick's livery stable at Hayes Street was established, it bustled with the comings and goings of the Corbett horses and hacks hired for christenings, weddings and funerals. The business had its difficulties, but the parents' dream of providing a good education for their children was fulfilled in the main. In Jim's case, however, his dislike of authority and his rebellious nature was to result in his education coming to a premature halt.

Enrolled at Saint Ignatius Parochial School soon after his sixth birthday, Jim was a fair to average student. A school report revealed that he 'wrote a good, angular hand' but that, although he read a lot, he was not a good speller. It concluded, 'James J. Corbett is an exceptionally well-mannered, friendly boy, with an aptitude for mathematics. However, he is too free with his fists and often involves himself in street fighting.'

Jim later maintained that he never started fights, but sought to run away from trouble. This was not the case. He relished showing off how he could handle himself in rough-and-tumble escapades. Tall for his age, he would sneak into the 'big yard' at lunchtime to play handball and other games with the older boys. His first big scrap occurred when he was twelve years old.

The bully of the 'big yard' was Fatty Carney. One of Jim's pals accidentally bumped into Carney and got a thump for being so careless. Corbett took his friend's part and got into a fight with Carney. The mêlée was broken up by a teacher and Jim was ordered back to the 'little yard'. As he was going, Fatty called after him, 'I'll see you after school.' The bully was waiting as school broke up for the day. In his autobiography, *The Roar of the Crowd*, Corbett recalled:

> My first intention was to run away. Then it suddenly occurred to me that if I ran away, all the boys would laugh at me and I would be looked upon as a coward. My pride was now aroused and I said to myself, 'I will go out and get a licking'. That afternoon an idea came to me that has stood me in good stead – to avoid trouble, if possible, but if it lay ahead of me, to be the aggressor and not let the other fellow think I was afraid. In my heart, I was afraid of Carney, but I marched right over to him and said 'Are you waiting for me?' He said 'Yes'. We went around to a lot opposite the United States Mint, called the Mint Yard, and the whole school followed. He was a big strong fellow. I had never had a boxing lesson, but occasionally had watched my brother box. He was six years older than me and I remembered a few of his tricks, such as looking at the stomach and hitting in the face, just the crude principles of the boxing art.
>
> 'Fatty' started to rush me and, as he was stronger and older, I began to jump out of his way, instinctively using my head, even at that age, though I didn't realise it. After a few minutes, the police came and scattered us, but by that time I was sure I could whip 'Fatty'. We came to the Circus Lot, used for circus performances in those days. I had no supporters with me, just two or three of the boys from my own neighbourhood, while 'Fatty' had his whole gang at his back. We started fighting and he realised I was getting the better of him when he grabbed hold of me and started to wrestle. Being much stronger, he threw me down and proceeded to punch me while I lay underneath him. An old man who had been watching us stepped in and hit 'Fatty' on the back with his cane. He told him he should fight boys of his own age and size. I went home with a black eye.

Jim was scared of what his father would say when he saw the 'souvenir' of the fight. When he explained that he had got the bruise in a fight with Fatty Carney, the surprisingly mild riposte was, 'Carney down on Howard Street? Hmm, what do you think of that?'

When Jim returned to school the next day, he found he was the centre of attention. 'You ought to have seen him yesterday,' said one boy, 'this kid was shifting and using judgement the way professionals do.'

Not so enamoured with the reports of the fistic encounter was the headmaster. He called the would-be pugilists to his office and told them they had brought shame on the school. Both were expelled.

The scrap, whatever its unwelcome consequence, was a useful

experience for young Corbett. 'I learned a lesson that lasted me all my life,' he said, 'that the size of a man does not count and that, by using my head and feet, I could lick a man much stronger than myself.'

The following year, Jim enrolled at the Sacred Heart College in Ellis Street. He soon showed how smart he was – at finding means of ducking classes. A boy who was subject to epileptic fits looked to Corbett as his protector. Jim decided to use his pal's affliction to their mutual advantage. He would get him to feign a fit, so the teacher would say, 'Corbett, take him outside.' The young rascals would have a great time, fooling around in the schoolyard for an hour, before returning to class. The ruse worked so well that it was employed at least once a week to earn time off.

Jim got into lots of fights with other pupils. One eventful day, a boy who sat behind him in class made an abusive remark. When Corbett turned around to remonstrate with his tormentor, the Christian Brother in charge of the class called him forward. The teacher took a window pole, broke it in half and told him to hold out his hand. The pole crashed down on his palm, causing him to cry out in pain. When Jim was asked to take similar punishment on his other hand, he refused and walked back to his seat.

When the class was dismissed, the Brother asked Corbett to remain behind. The youngster caught a glimpse of the big stick under the teacher's gown and made a bolt for the door, pursued by the teacher. He was on the fourth floor of the building that had galleries on each level surrounding an open court. On each successive gallery, which he reached in his descent, the chase was taken up by other Brothers. By the time he arrived at ground level, seven grim-faced Brothers were lined up to trap him. Corbett picked out the biggest target, 'a big fat fellow looking like Friar Tuck', and delivered his version of the solar plexus punch – with his head. The recipient went over, rolled on the floor and out into the street.

It was the end of Jim's schooldays.

Pat Corbett, realising it would be fruitless trying to enrol his troublesome son in another college after two expulsions, helped him get a job in a mercantile establishment. Jim, who started work at fourteen, became a very efficient clerk with a reputation for being unusually quick at figures. It was not long before the opportunity arrived to better himself in the commercial world. One of his father's customers at the livery stable was J. S. Angus, a cashier at the Nevada Bank's branch in San Francisco. A recommendation by

Angus secured a job for Corbett as a messenger boy at the bank. He worked there for six years, rising to the post of assistant receiving teller.

'At the bank,' he said, 'I had my first look at the good life – the high silk hats, the gold watch chains, the refinement that comes with money. I swore that some day these things would be mine, though at the time I had no idea how I would get them.'

CHAPTER 3

Banking and boxing

Jim seemed to settle down well at the new job, to the delight and relief of his parents. If he had disappointed them with his unruly conduct at school and his refusal to become a priest, he at least held a respectable position at the bank. Had they known, they would have been horrified at their boy's secret yearning – to swap his neatly pressed suit and starched shirt collar for the 'long johns' of a prize-fighter.

During lunch breaks, Jim would engage in harmless sparring sessions with his fellow clerks. He would practice jabbing with his left hand, while guarding his chin with his right. Later, at home, he would shoot out his left hand into a cushion, trying repeatedly to hit the same spot. He would also try out his footwork and feint for an opening in an imaginary opponent's guard. He didn't know it then, but he was learning the basic moves that would develop him into a world-fêted boxing master.

'I did not know I had any natural boxing ability,' he said later, 'but I tried to put into practice certain things I had seen the professionals do. However, a pal of mine named Lew Harding saw in me things I didn't see in myself – quickness of the eye and feet and a natural understanding of and instinct for the game.'

Joe Donoghue, Corbett's one-time trainer, used to tell of how Jim developed the accuracy and striking power of his left jab. 'Prior to Corbett's advent,' said Donoghue, 'good left-hand ring performers were scarce, especially among the heavyweights. Jim perfected his left to an extent never excelled and seldom equalled as a weapon of offence and for counter hitting.

'He told me that, when sitting at his desk in the bank teller's cage, he noticed that the muscles of his left hand, which he had rested all afternoon on an accounts book, ached badly. They were experiencing a strain which had not been apparent with the right hand, with which he had been writing.

'He clenched his left, making a fist, but found it not so easily done as with the right. He saw that, like most other people, he had developed the right hand muscles while ignoring those of his left. He made up his mind to practise constantly hitting with the left and making it strong.'

A couple of sets of boxing gloves were kept at the Corbett livery yard and Jim, along with his brothers Frank and Harry, would spar with some of the hack-drivers. Jim found he could hold his own with any of the others, with the exception of Billy 'Forty' Kenealy, a tough scrapper who had given Joe Choynski, another local favourite, a terrific battle before being knocked out in four rounds. Kenealy was a good deal heavier than Corbett and had a dangerous right-hand punch. The word got around that Jim was afraid of Kenealy.

One night, the two men showed up, unaware of each other, at a show featuring gymnastics and sparring exhibitions. Corbett was invited to go four rounds with Kenealy. He hesitated, knowing that the ill-feeling between them would turn it into a real fight, not an exhibition. Besides, what would his father say? Old man Corbett was constantly urging his boys to 'be gentlemen and keep out of trouble'.

Kenealy settled the issue by remarking that Corbett was afraid of having his pretty face spoiled. Jim snapped, 'Give me the gloves.'

Kenealy stormed out at the first bell, intent on a knockout. Corbett, knowing it would be foolish to slug it out with the bigger man, concentrated on using his left jab and nipping smartly away when his rival got too close. Kenealy, growing more wild and desperate, swung a right from the hip. Corbett ducked beneath it, then, as he came upright, his head caught his opponent under the chin. Kenealy dropped to the floor for a count. It had happened so quickly and unexpectedly that most spectators thought Jim had scored the knockdown with a left hand punch. He was declared the winner, and saw no point in enlightening the back-slappers as to what really happened.

Lew Harding, without Jim's knowledge, devised a scheme to put his friend's fistic development to the test. He took him to gatherings of some of the roughest young men of the town and organised matches. Looking back in later years, Corbett said, 'I had a good many fights in those places, some of them pretty tough ones. At first they used to sneer at me and look upon me as a dude, for, being a bank clerk, I naturally took pains with my personal appearance. However, I fought myself into their estimation and soon they forgot to call me this withering name and made no more remarks about my white collar or kid gloves.'

Harding, too, remembered those tough encounters: 'The bruisers who filled the Barbary Coast pool-rooms were Jim's favourite game. I never saw him lose one of those fights – and he had dozens of them. Jim wasn't a trouble maker or a wise-guy. Fighting just came naturally to him, the way laying eggs is for a hen.'

Corbett's first real step on the path to ring success came when he joined the famous Olympic Athletic Club in San Francisco. He was introduced by Denny Dillon, who lived around the corner from the Corbett livery stable and was a leading middleweight boxer at the club.

Initially, the club officers encouraged him as a promising baseball player. Jim was a good, all-round athlete in his young days. He was a fast sprinter and a good gymnast, as well as excelling at ball games. He played baseball for the Alcazars, competing against clubs that had players like Ed Morris and Fred Carroll, who became famous with the Pittsburgh Nationals, George Van Haltren, for many years centre-field of the Giants, and Tom Brown of the Washingtons.

A bad injury suffered during a game – his right hand was split between the little and third fingers – finished off his hopes of a base-ball career. It was not the end of the Corbett family's involvement in the game, however. His younger brother, Joe, became a noted pitcher with the Washington Senators, the Baltimore Orioles and the Saint Louis Browns. In 1897, while playing for the Orioles, he helped the team compile a record of 24 victories against six defeats in the National League. But he quit the sport, complaining he couldn't stand the rowdy tactics and foul language. Joe later ran a bar and betting shop in San Francisco. He died on 2 May 1945, aged 70.

As for Jim, he maintained his interest in baseball long after he had hung up his boxing gloves. He was a familiar figure at New York's Polo Grounds, occupying a box right over the dugout of his favourites, the Giants, during the season.

Thwarted in his baseball ambitions, Jim devoted his energies at the Olympic Athletic Club to boxing. The club's boxing instructor didn't know what to make of the brash young man who, on meeting him for the first time, insisted on getting into the ring with him. Asked if he had ever boxed, Corbett, thinking of his many unofficial bouts against the town's roughnecks, cockily replied, 'Oh, yes, hundreds of times.'

The coach saw that the brash young man needed taking down a peg or two. He proceeded to show Corbett that there was still a lot to be learned about the fight game. Jim saw so many boxing gloves coming at him that he thought he had run into a shower of leather.

The next day, his conceit undiminished, Corbett set eyes on a big fellow with a huge growth of beard. "Blackbeard', as he called him, was sparring around with a friend, but didn't look too impressive. Jim asked the instructor if he could go a few rounds with the bearded one. The coach grinned to himself and put the gloves on Corbett. He neglected to tell him that 'Blackbeard' was the heavyweight champion of the club and a terrific puncher. Jim found out the hard way.

He woke up to find himself sitting in a chair, with someone throwing water over him, another rubbing his legs and a third man holding smelling salts under his nose. To show the members he was all right, Corbett tried to jog around the gym, but, still groggy, he fell flat on his face. 'It then dawned on me that I had really been knocked out for the first time in my life,' he said. 'I think it was the greatest blow to my pride I ever experienced. I saw then that I needed boxing instruction.'

Twelve months after this salutary lesson, Corbett met for the first time a man who was to have a major influence on his future. The Olympic Club took on Professor Walter Watson, a middle-aged Englishman, as the new boxing instructor. Jim and the professor hit it off right away. Watson saw real promise in his young pupil and gave him special attention. An advocate of the English style of boxing, the professor taught him the art of straight punching, as well as footwork, feinting, slipping blows and correct hitting.

His pupil would take note of what Watson told him, then go home and practise feints and shifts in front of a mirror. He soon felt confident enough to try out his progress with his brother Harry.

Harry, the second eldest of the family, had always been able to cuff his younger brother about as he pleased. This time, he found himself knocked back against the livery stable wall. Angered, Harry tried to get his revenge, but Jim was able to duck and slip out of harm's way. Harry called on their oldest brother, Frank, to see if he could do any better. He, too, had to admit defeat. Harry and Frank ran to their father to tell him Jim was going to be a prize-fighter. Pat Corbett laughed heartily. Who could believe such nonsense?

Professor Watson had a score to settle with the middleweight champion of the Olympic Club, Dave Eiseman, who had taken unfair advantage of the much older man when they sparred on the day of Watson's arrival. He swore then he would find a club member within three months who would give Eiseman 'the worst licking of his life'. He now believed he had found his man.

Corbett got ready for the bout with Eiseman on the understanding that it was an exhibition. He was surprised when, just before the opening bell, Watson told him, 'Go for that fellow with all you've got.'

Eiseman had been told it was to be a real fight and launched an immediate attack. Corbett met him in the centre of the ring and the two slugged it out for the full three minutes. The spectators, used to seeing tame sparring matches, loved the furious action. They cheered lustily when the young novice, who had been kept pretty much a secret by Watson, landed a solid right-hander that sent Eiseman sprawling clean out of the ring. The chastened champion was unable to continue and the new hero was rushed off his feet trying to cope with the numbers anxious to congratulate him.

Professor Watson displayed his protégé on the regular 'boxing nights' at the Olympic Club. Corbett's progress impressed the members. His stamina was good, equipping him well for the lengthy contests that lay ahead. Watson realised that the youngster, although strong, would never be a powerful puncher. His reflexes were exceptionally fast and the Englishman advised him to concentrate on becoming an expert counter-puncher. The words of wisdom were well heeded.

Corbett's victory over Eiseman earned him recognition as the club's middleweight champion. By the time he was eighteen, he was also heavyweight champion and had won seven silver cups. Though still an amateur, he made it a point that whenever a prominent professional arrived in San Francisco, he would spar with the visitor. The professional would be paid for appearing, but Jim, so it was said, got nothing – except invaluable experience. He became so proficient that eventually he was the only entrant for the club's heavyweight competition. No-one thought they had a chance against him. Corbett agreed to withdraw and let the competition be fought out by the rest. A special medal was struck to present to the club's star, in gratitude for his sacrifice and in recognition of him as undisputed champion.

Continuing the odd arrangement of amateur versus professional contests, Jim got the better of noted pugilists James C. Dailey, Martin 'Buffalo' Costello and Mike Brennan, billed as the Barbary Coast champion. Dailey, like Corbett a San Franciscan of Irish parentage, predicted a brilliant future for his conqueror. 'Corbett is a wonder,' he said. 'He is strong, quick and courageous. In seven or eight years, he will be in his prime. If he doesn't knock out every man that faces him, I'm no judge.'

On one memorable occasion, Corbett enjoyed a useful workout with the original Jack Dempsey, the one they called 'the Nonpareil'. Dempsey, no relation to the Jack Dempsey (real name William Harrison Dempsey) who was world heavyweight champion from 1919 to 1926, was actually John Kelly, born near Clane, in County Kildare, Ireland. He was taken to America as a child and won recognition as the first middleweight champion of the world. He reigned for seven years until suffering an unmerciful beating from English-born Bob Fitzsimmons, who was to figure prominently in Corbett's fighting career at a later date. Dempsey, one of the greats of his era, was only 33 when he died from tuberculosis.

'The Nonpareil' was given guest privileges at the San Francisco Olympic Club and frequently exercised there. With him on one occasion was Mike Cleary, a heavyweight who had often worked out with Corbett. After a sparring session with Jim, Cleary still had a sore mouth the following day and declined an invitation to spar with Dempsey. He beckoned towards Corbett, saying, 'There's a young fellow who'll box with you.'

'Hell,' snorted Dempsey, 'I want a sweat.'

Cleary grinned and said, 'Oh, he'll give you a sweat all right.'

Dempsey and Corbett had been sparring for half an hour when the middleweight champion used one of his sneak tricks, a blow with the wrist to Jim's nose. The Californian shed blood for the first time as a boxer. His temper aroused, he was about to go after his antagonist when Dempsey held up his glove and said, 'Boy, that's enough for today.'

Corbett thought no more about the encounter until the following day, when he attended a minstrel show. He was recognised by the box-office cashier, who shouted, 'Hey, here's the kid who gave Dempsey a tough go yesterday.' Within seconds, Jim was surrounded by well-wishers who complimented him on his showing.

Dempsey, apparently, had been spreading the word about the promising youngster in the Olympic Club. Jim was satisfied that he had given the great man his 'sweat'.

The first 'big name' on Corbett's record was Jack Burke, born in Killarney and known as 'the Irish Lad'. The hugely experienced Burke had held Dempsey to a ten rounds draw and had twice drawn with the highly regarded Englishman Charlie Mitchell. He had met world heavyweight champion John L. Sullivan two years earlier, losing in five rounds. Burke's greatest claim to fame, however, was the 110 rounds he fought with Andy Bowen in New Orleans on 6 April 1893. It was the longest fight on record, either with bare fists or gloves. After seven hours and nineteen minutes, the referee had declared it 'no contest'.

Corbett, mindful of Burke's reputation, boxed cautiously. After eight rounds, it was declared a draw. The opinion of the audience was that if Jim had been more enterprising, he would have won handily.

Joe McAuliffe, who had gone forty rounds with Mike Brennan, lasted only four with the rapidly improving Californian. According to Corbett, he then dispatched George Atkinson and Frank Glover in two rounds apiece. But his accounts of his early fights are sometimes at variance with the findings of historians. Some list his bout with Glover, for instance, as a three-round draw, while Tracy Callis, a meticulous compiler of boxers' records, could trace only a four-round exhibition between the pair.

While Corbett maintained his amateur status throughout this period, it is unlikely that he left every arena empty-handed. It was not unknown for a good amateur who was a popular drawing card to be given 'expenses' for his efforts. Jim, even at that early stage of his career, pulled in the crowds. It was not until the Amateur Athletic Union took control of amateur boxing in the United States that the practice of handing over 'expense money' was stopped.

One of Jim's opponents, Joe Choynski, gave the game away after they boxed four rounds at the Olympic Club. Billy Brown, an official at the club, wanted Corbett to have the honour of beating another professional. Choynski was an amateur, but he was per-suaded by Brown to take ten dollars before the fight, which Corbett won. A few weeks later, Choynski applied to enter an amateur tournament. He was challenged by Brown, who said he had been paid for his last fight. 'That's all right with me, Mr Brown,' said a quick-thinking Choynski, 'but I had to split that ten dollars with

Corbett.' Brown had no more to say. Choynski turned professional shortly afterwards.

Corbett, by now, was sure that his future lay as a professional fighter. Part of his motivation was to see his parents get rid of their financial burdens. During his time at the bank, Jim often helped his father at night in keeping his books. He realised how hard it was to keep up payments on the $6,000 mortgage on their home and the livery stable. Seeing his father worry about the feed bills for the horses and other problems made him understand why the old man was so often depressed.

On happier occasions, his parents would take delight in singing a song or dancing an Irish jig at a party. They had often stated their greatest desire was to see Ireland again before they died. Jim vowed that, if he ever had the means, he would grant them their wish.

CHAPTER 4

'A mad act of youth'

'You could always tell where Jim's cage was,' said a worker at the bank. 'It was the one with all the girls crowded around in front.'

Corbett had grown into a tall, well-built young man with dark, neatly groomed hair, a pleasant manner and a ready smile – especially for the ladies. He could have had the pick of the bunch, but in June 1886, when he was not yet twenty, he took off on what he later described as 'a mad act of youth'.

He got married to Olive Lake.

Jim and a friend, Herman Eppinger, had fallen for a couple of girls who were pals. Each knew their parents would not approve of their getting hitched, so they threw up their jobs and eloped to Utah. They lied about their ages to a Justice of the Peace, who conducted the double wedding ceremony.

According to Corbett in *The Roar of the Crowd*, the marriages were later annulled, when it was found that all four were under the legal age. His version of events seems doubtful. Most probably, he was playing down what turned out to be an unhappy union that ended in divorce after nine years. In his book he didn't even have the grace to give his wife a name.

Olive, or Ollie, as she was better known, said at the time of the divorce that the marriage took place in Salt Lake City on 28 June 1886. But the *San Francisco Monitor*, the official newspaper of the city's Catholic Archdiocese, shows they were married in San Francisco on 21 August of that year by Father James Connolly. The church where the ceremony took place appears to have been the old

St John's at 1122 Eddy, although the parish register is now missing. The most likely explanation is that the couple did get married at a Salt Lake City registry office, but Jim's devoutly Catholic parents would have insisted on a 'proper' wedding in church.

Had Ollie been less the dutiful stay-at-home wife and insisted on accompanying Jim on his frequent out-of-town trips, he would have had less opportunity to enjoy flings with other women. Ollie's patience with his numerous infidelities would finally run out.

After the runaway double marriage, the four lovebirds spent their honeymoons in Salt Lake City. In the blissful ignorance of youth, they thought the $500 they had between them would sustain their living needs for ever. After six weeks, they learned something about the harsh realities of life. Love doesn't buy food or pay the rent. They had to find some way of earning money.

Corbett saw a story in a local newspaper stating that Frank Smith, the heavyweight champion of Utah, was looking for opponents. Jim, though hardly in a proper mental or physical state for boxing, decided the fight would pay the rent of the quartet's cottage for a while. With Eppinger accompanying him as 'manager', Corbett went to the newspaper office and told the sports editor he wanted to take up Smith's offer. He signed his acceptance 'Jim Dillon', not wishing to reveal his whereabouts to the folks back home if a report of the fight got into the California papers. The subterfuge worked, although it had an amusing consequence.

The Utah champion, on the night of the fight, confronted Corbett and said, 'I'm on to you, Charlie.' Jim wondered what his opponent was getting at, until he realised that Smith thought he was Charlie Mitchell. Mitchell, a prominent English pugilist, had fought many of the world's leading heavyweights and had only recently held the great John L. Sullivan to a draw. No wonder Smith was worried.

Corbett couldn't believe his luck. He had convinced himself that, as a newly-wed, he would not have the energy to engage in a tough fight with the Utah titleholder. Now he could bluff his way to certain victory. He warned Smith that if he didn't play ball, he, 'Mitchell', would give him the hiding of his life. The plan worked perfectly. According to Jim, Smith collapsed, on schedule, in the second round. Little did Smith know that his 'conqueror' was so weak that he could barely stand up as the referee raised his hand. Only when his 'manager' Eppinger came to the dressing room an hour and a half later and handed over his $460 purse did Corbett, aka 'Mitchell/Dillon', manage a smile of satisfaction.

Corbett's claim of a second round win is not borne out by the four-line report in the *Police Gazette* on 31 July, 1886: 'A weak attempt at a glove fight took place at Salt Lake City on the 3rd inst. between Dillon, of San Francisco, and Frank Smith, of Salt Lake. Smith had to be coaxed to put up his hands. Dillon was awarded the fight after four light rounds.'

A week later, Corbett received an offer of a contest in Evanston, Wyoming. A local miner, who supposedly 'couldn't fight a lick', was nevertheless backed for $1,000 by an eccentric businessman. Corbett, accepting the challenge, was less than two hours in Evanston when rumours spread that he was not who he said he was. This time, it was alleged, he was the world middle-weight champion, Jack 'Nonpareil' Dempsey, posing as 'Jim Dillon'.

Corbett saw no reason to spoil anyone's fun and allowed himself to be billed as Dempsey. The world champion's name on the notices would ensure more box-office money than 'Dillon'. Jim was enjoying his good fortune until he heard that some of Dempsey's home-town followers from Brooklyn had arrived in Evanston. They had to be avoided at all costs. He managed to find enough dark corners to hide in until fight time. When he was announced as 'Jack Dempsey', he expected a thousand voices to cry out 'You liar'. But there was just a sprinkling of jeers. Only the real Dempsey's closest associates knew what he looked like. Newspaper photography was only in its infancy and, with only line drawings to go by, it was easier to get away with a deception.

The miner originally slated to appear in the top-liner did a quick flit when he heard he would be facing Dempsey. Instead, Corbett/Dillon/Dempsey boxed with Duncan McDonald, who had refereed Jim's previous bout at Salt Lake City. Some accounts credit Corbett as winning the decision after six rounds. McDonald insisted it was declared a draw.

Jim revealed little about the affair in *The Roar of the Crowd*, merely stating that he was in better condition than he was in Salt Lake City and that his 'exhibition' pleased the audience. In his earlier auto-biography, *My Life and My Fights*, Corbett ignored the occasion completely. If it was a draw, the result would earn McDonald a unique place in ring history. Born in Scotland, raised in Canada and based in Butte, Montana, he would be the only man who fought both Corbett and John L. Sullivan without conceding defeat. He had drawn with a grossly unfit Sullivan in a four-rounder that John

L. was lucky not to lose, according to Nat Fleischer, founder and editor of *The Ring* magazine.

On his return to Salt Lake City, Corbett had a surprise caller. His father, though angry at his disappearance, threw his arms around him and begged him to return home. Jim wanted to comply, but he was too proud to admit he was broke. It was Duncan McDonald who saved the blushes of Corbett, Eppinger and their brides by pawning his gold watch and chain to ensure they travelled back to San Francisco first class.

Not wishing to cause his parents further anguish, as well as having a wife to support, Jim got a clerical job with the Anglo-Nevada Insurance Company for $100 a month. The routine work bored him and he quit after two years.

'That's the way it is with Jim,' sighed his father, 'you can lead him, but he won't be driven. He's a bit pig-headed, like myself. Once he made up his mind to pass up a job, there was no use in arguing with him. But thank God he has given up the idea of becoming a professional boxer.'

Not quite. Jim's secret yearning was temporarily kept in check while he acted as instructor at the Olympic Club, in succession to Professor Watson. He did put on the gloves, but only in exhibition bouts with club members or stars of other athletic clubs in the Bay District.

The big decision, however, would not be long delayed. He wanted to be a full-time professional fighter and no one was going to stand in his way.

CHAPTER 5

Battle on a barge

While Corbett was biding his time before turning professional, another San Francisco fighter was building up a strong following. Joe Choynski never emulated his rival by becoming world champion, but he developed into one of the outstanding heavyweights of the era.

Jim and Joe had grown up within a few blocks of each other in the Hayes Valley district. Their brothers, Frank Corbett and Herbert Choynski, worked together as clerks in the auditor's office at City Hall and frequently argued as to which of their brothers was the better boxer. Each fighter had his band of supporters and the rivalry was drummed up into a bitter grudge by local sportswriters. Choynski, fed up with the debate, said he would take a punch at Corbett the next time they met.

That settled it. Corbett announced that he was ready for a show-down.

The two fighters agreed on a 'fight to the finish', meaning there was no set number of rounds. The contest would end only when one man was unable to continue, or they agreed to a draw. Each was backed for $2,000, on a winner-take-all arrangement.

The newspapers played up the angle that Corbett was Irish and Choynski Jewish. Competition between fighters of different ethnic backgrounds was always certain to keep the turnstiles clicking. Also, Corbett, the former bank clerk, had the backing of the wealthy businessmen at the Olympic, while Choynski, a labourer in a candy factory, drew the working-class fans.

Corbett would now devote himself fully to the professional ring. He left behind an amateur career of just one defeat, a four-round decision he dropped to Billy Welch. He gained emphatic revenge by dispatching Welch in the first round of their return match.

When he told his father of his decision, the old man was furious. 'Jim, I don't want you to fight for money,' he exclaimed. 'Go out in the hills and fight him for nothing, if you must. I just don't want you to be a prize-fighter. That settles it.'

But the matter had gone too far for Jim to back down now. As the date for the fight, 30 May 1889, drew near, the sporting columns were filled with reports of how each man's preparation was going. One rather insensitive headline read, 'Jews and Gentiles prepare for battle, as Corbett and Choynski get ready to fight for the heavy-weight championship of California.'

The emphasis on ethnic differences alerted the authorities. Fearing a riot, they ordered the police to stop the contest from taking place. This was easier said than done, as no venue had been decided. The fact that it was a 'finish fight' meant it could not be staged in a club. A remote barn near Fairfax, in Marin county, fifteen miles north-west of San Francisco, was chosen. Only those 'in the know' were able to find their way there, but the boxers were surprised to discover several hundred spectators on hand when they arrived.

Corbett was a bit put out to find that Jack 'Nonpareil' Dempsey, whom he considered a friend, was to act as his opponent's chief second. When Jim confronted Dempsey, the middleweight champion told him he was only doing it because he was getting paid $1,000 for his services. 'Would you care to bet half of that on Joe?', invited Corbett. Dempsey declined, as did Choynski when Jim offered him a $500 side-bet.

It was the third time Corbett and Choynski had faced each other in the ring. The others had been amateur encounters. The first lasted just one round, when Choynski quit. (This is, rather oddly, given as a one-round 'no decision' in several record books). Jim won the return match on a three-round decision. He was certain he would win his professional debut without too much bother.

His confidence seemed justified when he shot across a right hand to send Choynski tumbling to the floor in the opening round. The knockdown surprised Joe's supporters. They knew Corbett was a clever boxer. They did not consider him a heavy puncher.

Choynski got to his feet at the count of five and fought back furiously. The exchanges continued at a hot pace. Then Corbett, attempting another right like the one that had floored his rival, caught Choynski high on the head. He felt his thumb go out of joint, but did his best to hide his discomfort. He faced a crisis. How could a virtually one-handed fighter carry on in a contest with no agreed time limit? Luckily for him, fate intervened in the form of the local sheriff. Obviously a fight fan, the lawman stepped into the ring just after the fifth round began and announced, 'I'm sorry, gents, but I'll have to stop this fight. If you go over to the next county, I'll be glad to go over with you and see the boys scrap. But you've got to leave here.'

Before they left the ring, the referee, Patsy Hogan, advised the boxers to take their gloves with them. The gloves had to be made to order to fit a fighter's hands and new ones could not be secured at short notice. This was to prove a major point of controversy when the fight was re-scheduled.

It took the promoters a week to secure a new location. To avoid the possibility of the law again intervening, it was decided to stage the fight on the deck of the *Excel*, a grain barge moored off Benicia, on the north shore of Carquinez Strait, an arm of San Francisco Bay. The logic was that the location of the barge, near the boundary dividing Solano and Contra Costa counties, would confuse the local sheriffs as to whose jurisdiction it was.

The logistics of getting the spectators to the barge proved to be a difficult and hazardous business. One tugboat got stuck in the mud and its passengers jumped onto small fishing boats which were also heading for the fight venue. An overcrowded boat overturned, spilling its occupants into the bitterly cold water. A man nearly drowned when another stood on his shoulders and drove him deep into the soft mud. Fortunately, he struggled free and swam back to the boat. By 5.30 a.m., a crowd of 257 was on board the *Excel*. Just over an hour later, the contestants entered the ring. Corbett, at 180 pounds, had a weight advantage of eight pounds.

A row broke out when it was discovered that Choynski had 'forgotten' his gloves. Corbett had his two-ounce gloves from the aborted meeting. Jack 'Nonpareil' Dempsey, Choynski's chief second, suggested they fight in bare knuckles. Corbett, who had never fought a bare-fist battle, would not hear of it. He quickly realised what the opposition was up to. They had got wind of Corbett's injured thumb and knew that, without the protection of gloves, he would be at a disadvantage. Jim offered a compromise. He would wear gloves and let Choynski fight with bare knuckles. This was not acceptable to the Choynski side.

It was then that a spectator 'came to the rescue' by offering Choynski the use of his driving gloves. Corbett, cold and fed up with the delay, agreed that the fight should go ahead. Too late, he realised that he had been the victim of a cruel trick.

The 'helpful' onlooker, a rancher from Sonoma county, was part of a Choynski plot. The action had commenced before Jim noticed that Joe's gloves had three thick seams along the knuckles. Every time Choynski landed to his body, it left a huge welt. Corbett used his skill to avoid most of the punches aimed at his face, but enough got through to leave their mark. Jim's darting left jab did even more damage, however. 'After the first two rounds, I had his face looking like a piece of liver,' he said later.

Wary of using his right hand, damaged in the earlier aborted match, Corbett was in real trouble in the third round when he hurt his other hand. To add to his agony, his feet were badly blistered from the heat of the boards exposed to the scorching sun. His thin canvas shoes proved totally inadequate protection. It was now that the man derided as 'the Dude' was called upon to show he was made of tougher stuff than the tag implied.

Despite the intense pain, Corbett continued stabbing his onrushing rival with hard jabs. Choynski bled so much that time was called in the sixth round for the boards to be sanded to prevent the fighters slipping on the gore. By the fourteenth round, Corbett's right eye was almost closed.

For round after round, the brutal battle waged on. Some spectators were so sickened by the spectacle that they turned their faces away. When Frank Corbett looked for his brother Harry to discuss how the fight was going, he found him at the stern of the barge, crying. 'That's a hell of an attitude when Jim needs you,' he yelled, and smacked him on the face. The pair started to scuffle, but quickly broke up when they realised they were missing the real action.

The referee, seeing that neither Corbett or Choynski were prepared to concede defeat, wanted to call a halt and declare a draw. Neither contestant would hear of it. They had agreed on a fight to the finish, had they not?

Late in the fifteenth round, Corbett scored with a hard left and felt the pain from his damaged hand shoot right through his arm. He almost fainted on his feet. Choynski saw his agonised expression, but thought he might be foxing. Joe lost his big chance. Corbett ducked and held until his head cleared, then resumed peppering his opponent's much-abused face, all the time trying to ignore the agony it caused him every time fist met head.

Corbett took up the story of the concluding rounds in an interview many years later with Nat Fleischer for *The Ring*.

> In the twenty-fifth round, Joe was fairly masked in blood and seemed to be fading fast from the heat and many injuries. I was but little better off. My blistered feet, my broken thumb, the strained tendon in my left hand, my bruised body and the steady suffering caused by the burning sun, formed a combination of agony, almost beyond human endurance. Sorry looking sights we were as we came out for the twenty-sixth round. Still, in that session and the following two, I had by far the better of the going.
>
> In the twenty-eighth frame, which proved to be the finale, I could do little but hit with my wrists and forearms, for both of my hands were out of commission for striking purposes. I could scarcely close my right hand, so I determined to let one desperate wallop go with my left, in a dying bid to finish up matters. As luck had it, I got that punch home. It crashed squarely on Joe's jaw. Over he keeled and lay prostrate. I stood like a man in a dream while the referee counted him out. Actually, I was almost out on my feet and could scarcely realise it was all over. I was dazed when I collected my senses, so much so that I asked Billy Delaney, my trainer, who was by my side, what had happened. 'You knocked him out, Jim', said Delaney exultantly.

Throughout boxing history, a code of mutual respect has existed between bitter rivals. Opponents who have battered each other without mercy usually embrace at the final bell and often become good friends. That was how it was with Corbett and Choynski. After leaving the barge, they spent seven hours together in a Turkish bath, their blistered feet in pails of hot water and their hands encased in ice buckets. They shook hands, delicately, and tried their best to smile and talk through their mis-shapen mouths. A friendship was formed that would last for life. When Choynski became an instructor at the Pittsburgh Athletic Club, Corbett was a regular visitor.

It was in the battle on the barge that Corbett is credited with 'inventing' the left hook, a punch that was unknown up to then. His action was brought about by sheer necessity. So intense was the pain from his left hand – the damaged tendon was between the third and little fingers – that he took to throwing the punch in a arc, so that it landed with just the inside knuckles. More often than not, it was his wrist or forearm that hit the target rather than his fist.

Even when the hand healed, Corbett would alternate between jabs and hooks when he fought or sparred in the gym. 'My sparring partners, expecting only a jab, would not pay much attention to my left leads,' he said. 'I floored a few with left hooks when they were expecting a jab on the nose, and they asked me what I called the punch. I named it a "hook". They wanted me to explain it and demonstrate it, which I did. And so the left hook was added to the attacking equipment in boxing warfare.'

It might have been thought that Corbett and Choynski had suffered enough, but they were at it again within a month. This time, however, it was a much less strenuous four-rounder, at Corbett's domain, the Olympic Club. Jim earned the decision.

Thus, in five meetings, Choynski was unable to claim a win over his great rival. Yet Joe was to progress to a fine career, lasting sixteen years, which included bouts with some of the top ringmen of his era. He drew with Bob Fitzsimmons, James J. Jeffries, Tom Sharkey and Kid McCoy, but topped the lot with a sensational third round knockout of Jack Johnson in 1901. That was seven years before Johnson won the world heavyweight title. Choynski finally managed to beat Corbett – by outliving him by ten years. He was 74 when he passed away in Cincinnati, Ohio, in 1943.

CHAPTER 6

'Fight Jackson and you'll disgrace family'

Corbett resigned as boxing instructor at the Olympic Club in December 1889 and took off on an exhibition tour of Pacific Coast cities. Stopping off in Portland, Oregon, he entered into an extraordinary pact with local heavyweight Dave Campbell. They would box for ten rounds and if both men were still on their feet at the end, it would be declared a draw. Jim had the better of his opponent but failed to knock him out. So Campbell, who later became chief of the Portland Fire Department, took an honoured place in the record books as having held James J. Corbett to a draw.

Whatever his growing reputation on the west coast, Corbett's name meant nothing to boxing followers in the east of the United States. Newspapers were the only way the public learned about sporting events, and the Californian's progress was not considered important enough to merit mention outside his domain. This was about to change dramatically.

A new weekly newspaper, the *California Illustrated World*, featured an illustration of Corbett on the front page of its first edition. The caption labelled him 'the coming champion of the world', adding the advice: 'Pin this to your hat.'

A copy of the paper was picked up in New Orleans, a stopping-off place for William Muldoon's boxing and wrestling troupe. The star of the company was Jake Kilrain, who, seven months earlier, had lasted seventy-five rounds with John L. Sullivan in the last bare-knuckle heavyweight championship bout. Kilrain was looking for someone who would box six rounds with him during the city's

Mardi Gras week. A telegram was sent to Corbett asking if he would be willing to take on Kilrain. The winner of the bout would be guaranteed $3,500 and the loser $1,500.

Without hesitation, Corbett cabled back his acceptance. When word got out, friends expressed their apprehension. Jim, with his very limited professional experience, was about to face one of the most formidable heavyweights of the day. Kilrain, from Greenpoint, Long Island, was aged thirty-one and had been boxing for ten years. Two years before losing to Sullivan, he had fought Jem Smith for the championship of England on an island on the river Seine, in France. Falling darkness had forced the bare-fist battle to a halt. It was declared a draw – in the 106th round!

Before he left San Francisco, Corbett asked Jack 'Nonpareil' Dempsey what he thought of his chances. 'Kilrain won't lay a glove on you. You'll make a sucker out of him,' laughed the middleweight champion. That was just what he wanted to hear. 'Dempsey said it as if he meant it,' wrote Jim in his memoirs. 'Whether he did or not, I fully agreed with him. I was that confident.'

Though he had not yet acquired a manager, Corbett was smart enough to ensure no-one took advantage of his inexperience in handling the business side of things. In his dressing room at the Southern Athletic Club, he rejected the Kilrain side's choice of referee. After some argument, he accepted E.R. Violett, a local cotton dealer and amateur boxer, as the official. It turned out to be a sound choice. Violett was an honest man who called the fight as he saw it.

On the day of the fight, 18 February 1890, Corbett's weight was announced at 183 pounds and Kilrain at 201. Jim, looking at his rival's brawny figure, shouted, 'If Kilrain only weighs 201, then put me down as 170.' The sarcasm of his remark caused merriment among ringsiders, while Kilrain glared across the ring at the cheeky Californian.

At the first bell, Corbett emerged from his corner with a wide smile, in contrast to Kilrain, whose bushy moustache made him look even more grim. Jim feinted twice and planted three sharp jabs to the face before Kilrain could get his guard up. The younger man continued to confuse Jake throughout the six rounds with the speed of his attacks and his ability to nip smartly away from attempted counter-punches. At the conclusion, Kilrain was cut and bruised, whereas his opponent was completely unmarked. Referee Violett announced that the result would be decided on scientific points scored, not on the strength of blows. He declared Corbett the winner. As soon as Jim was dressed, he was whisked away by his new-found admirers to a champagne celebration at the posh Pickwick Club.

Kilrain proved a sore loser. He complained that only five rounds had been completed and demanded an extra round be fought. When he got nowhere with this line of argument, he moaned that Corbett had hit him with his elbow. Years later, Kilrain was still bitter, dismissing his conqueror as 'a jabbing runner who wouldn't stand up and fight like a man'.

Now it was time for the New York papers to take note of the promising young San Franciscan. They reported his convincing win over Kilrain and speculated on his possible takeover of the world heavyweight throne if Sullivan retired. Not many people, however, would back him to beat John L., they suggested.

Invited to New York by Phil Dwyer, a leading racehorse owner, Corbett was introduced to many of the big city's top sporting figures and impressed them with his good manners and his self-confidence. He boxed a three-round exhibition with Professor Mike Donovan, boxing instructor with the New York Athletic Club, but was called upon to show his prowess in a real fight. Dominick McCaffrey, from Pittsburgh, was the chosen opponent at the Casino Rink, Brooklyn, on 14 April 1890.

McCaffrey, like Corbett, had spurned his parents' ambitions for him to become a priest, in favour of a prize-ring career. Noted as a clever boxer, he had beaten English champion Charlie Mitchell, lost a ten-rounder to Jack 'Nonpareil' Dempsey, and had been outpointed over six rounds by John L. Sullivan. Some ring historians suggest the Sullivan vs McCaffrey bout in 1885 was the first for the Queensberry rules heavyweight championship, but most accept the Sullivan vs Corbett contest seven years later as the first time gloves were used in a heavyweight title fight. Diligent researcher Barry J. Hugman, author of the *British Boxing Board of Control Yearbook*, maintained the Sullivan-McCaffrey meeting could only loosely be described as being for the vacant Queensberry rules title. Sullivan, he said, was never anything other than a bare-knuckle champion.

Corbett outclassed McCaffrey, who ended up doubled over the ropes at the end of the fourth round, imploring the referee to 'Take him away'. The decision was awarded to Corbett. McCaffrey, in an interview with noted journalist J. B. McCormick, was glowing in his praise of his conqueror: 'I was as helpless as a baby in Corbett's hands. He is the greatest boxer I have fought. If he ever meets John L. Sullivan in a finish fight, he'll lick the big fellow as easy as breaking sticks.'

While McCaffrey's comments were laughed off by most experts, there was no denying the impression Corbett had made on his first sojourn east. His name now figured prominently in the sports pages, even reaching as far afield as England and Australia. On his return home, he resumed his job as instructor at the Olympic Club at $3,000 a year, and reaped the benefits of his new-found fame by appearing in regular exhibition matches, for which he got paid extra. In one sparring session at the club, Corbett was a bit too vigorous in showing John D. Spreckles, the sugar magnate, how foolish it was to play around with professionals. A spirited exchange ended with Jim landing a right that broke Spreckles' nose.

When he wasn't busy at the club, Jim spent time helping a local blacksmith. The heavy work helped build up his arm and back muscles, as well as increasing his weight.

In the meantime, he found another outlet for his already ample ego. He got his first acting role. The seed that would grow into full bloom as a national footlights favourite, and later as a movie star, was sown on the stage of the Baldwin Theatre, San Francisco, in August 1890.

A benefit was being staged for a crippled actor and Corbett, as a local personality, was enticed to join a star-studded assembly. It was only a small part, as Count De Varville in a burlesque version of *Camille*, but Corbett was nervous about making a fool of himself before a large audience. He asked the leading actor, Maurice Barrymore, for advice.

Barrymore, a member of the famous acting family and father of movie stars John, Lionel and Ethel, told him, 'Young man, all the other actors will be wearing burlesque dress and make-up. You go out on the stage in your full evening dress and be deadly serious. You'll make such an impression that you'll be the hit of the show.'

'I was,' Corbett later recalled.

It was his first taste of wearing fine clothes, and it didn't harm his self-esteem to be told how handsome and elegant he looked. Gentleman Jim was on his way.

The Olympic Club officials, anxious to showcase their boxing star, cabled Frank 'Paddy' Slavin, who was on an English tour. Slavin claimed the Australian heavyweight championship and was a leading contender for Sullivan's world title. He made such extravagant cash and conditions demands for a match with Corbett, however, that the club's matchmaker looked elsewhere for an opponent. Overtures were made to Peter Jackson, who disputed Slavin's claim to the Australian title, and who was in America when the offer came.

Jackson accepted readily and articles were signed for the contest to take place at the California Athletic Club in San Francisco on 21 May 1891. Each fighter posted a forfeit of $500 and the club agreed to put up a $10,000 purse. The winner would receive $8,500 and the loser $1,500. Apart from the Jack 'Nonpareil' Dempsey vs Bob Fitzsimmons world middleweight title fight three months earlier, when the purse totalled $12,000, no other contest up to then had generated such a financial outlay. Much credit was accorded to Corbett for taking on a man considered by many as the best heavyweight in the world – bar none. Potential rivals, champion Sullivan included, found an easy excuse for avoiding Jackson – he was black!

Racial prejudice was as rampant in boxing as in every other walk of American life, and John L. was strongly backed for his stand in refusing to meet Jackson, or any other black boxer. Sullivan bluntly told Corbett, 'You shouldn't fight a nigger.' Support for the world champion's view came from a most unexpected quarter – Jim's father. In a hysterical outburst, Pat Corbett wrote to the editor of the *San Francisco Morning Call* that his son would bring disgrace on his family if the fight was allowed to take place in his home town.

'I would rather see Jim in a coffin than in a ring with Peter Jackson,' said Pat in a follow-up interview. 'If he persists in disobeying his father's wishes and goes into training for the battle, I shall go before the grand jury, have him indicted and bound over to keep the peace.'

Relishing the opportunity to sound off about his son's chosen profession, he went on, 'As I have often told him, I would rather see him carrying a hod for a small salary and earning an honest living than making thousands as a boxer. From the very first, I was opposed to him becoming a pugilist. Jim was always an industrious, dutiful son until his powers as a boxer began to develop. Since the mania seized him, he can talk and think of nothing else. I don't blame John L. Sullivan for drawing the colour line, but it is not because Jackson is a negro that my son must not do battle with him. It is because I am opposed to his becoming a member of a class that is largely composed of ruffians and the scum of civilisation.'

The attack surprised and embarrassed Jim. He told a *Call* reporter, 'My father is very foolish and hot-headed in acting this way. I'm in the pugilistic business and making my living from it. No disgrace or odium whatever is cast upon my family by my profession. I am ranked as one of the leading pugilists in the world and I am in the business to stay. If my father is so foolish as to try to stop the fight here, I will go to any place on earth to meet Jackson, even Australia.'

Though his father's threat to prevent the bout taking place didn't materialise, Jim could have done without the distraction. He needed his total concentration on the difficult task ahead. Indeed, many of his friends thought he was crazy to take the fight.

Corbett's refusal to follow Sullivan's example was less a sense of fair play, but more a quest for experience. 'I have sparred plenty of white men, but here I am soon to crawl through the ropes to fight to the finish with a Herculean black, and I do not know how it seems to stand in front of one of them. There may be something in a dark opponent that is not found in a light one and, if so, it behoves me to find out.'

The leading heavyweights were well justified in avoiding Jackson, a highly skilled boxer and strong puncher. His speciality was a destructive 'one-two', a stiff left followed by a pile-driver of a right. Born on the island of St Croix, in the West Indies, he moved with his family to Australia when he was six. Working on ships from the age of fourteen, he was given credit for quelling a mutiny by knocking out several rebellious seamen. He was taught to box by Larry Foley, founder of the Australian school of boxing, and won the national heavyweight title by beating Tom Leeds in thirty rounds. Eager to prove his worth on the world stage, he travelled to America and scored impressive wins over leading heavyweights George Godfrey, Joe McAuliffe and Patsy Cardiff, before a trip to Europe saw him flatten Irish champion Peter Maher in two rounds in Dublin and win on a foul over British titleholder Jem Smith in London.

Historians admire Corbett for his refusal to bow to the pressure to withdraw and for taking on Jackson when Sullivan and others were reluctant, or afraid, to do so. Certainly, he showed courage in tackling such a dangerous opponent. It was a risk – but a calculated one. By beating Jackson, the 'uncrowned' champion, Jim would be entitled to claim he was the best heavyweight in the world. Sullivan, who guarded his status as king of the ring jealously, would then be shamed into a showdown with Corbett.

The consequences of defeat were not entertained by the cocky Californian.

As for his apparent lack of racial prejudice in taking on Jackson, this is a myth. He was as much a bigot as the average white person of the period, as he showed the first time he met Jackson. He upset the polite, modest Australian by his lack of courtesy. Jackson, on his first visit to San Francisco, met Corbett and then asked for directions to Charlie Mitchell's house. Jim seemed to be heading that way and the visitor suggested they walk together. Corbett then said he was going the opposite way. He was embarrassed, some time later, to meet Jackson coming towards him and claimed he simply 'forgot' he was heading towards Mitchell's place. Corbett denied a snub, but Jackson refused to believe him.

Jackson was further incensed on hearing that Corbett considered him over-rated. They ignored each other whenever they met and declined to shake hands when re-introduced at a gathering of the California Athletic Club. On one occasion, when details of the upcoming contest had to be discussed, Jackson respectfully addressed his opponent as 'Mr Corbett', while Jim referred to him as plain 'Jackson'. In the context of the period, it was simply a case of a black man and a white man each knowing his place.

CHAPTER 7

Sixty-one rounds and no winner

Before getting down to serious training for the Jackson bout, Jim took a trip to New Orleans to see his friend Jack 'Nonpareil' Dempsey take a fearful beating in losing his world middleweight title to Bob Fitzsimmons. Little did he realise what a bad omen this was for his own clash with Fitzsimmons six years later.

Corbett journeyed on to Chicago to see John L. Sullivan performing in *Honest Hearts and Willing Hands*. On arrival at the theatre, he was surprised when word came to the box office that he was to be given a private box as Sullivan's guest. After the first act, the heavyweight champion invited him to his dressing room. Sullivan took his hand and squeezed it so hard that Jim thought he would break it. It was a common trick of Sullivan's to try to intimidate a prospective opponent.

When the show was over, John L. offered Corbett a lift down town in his hack. On the way, they stopped off at several saloons. At each one, Sullivan, already half-drunk after imbibing backstage, would order drinks for the house, slap the bar with his fist and roar, 'I'm John L. Sullivan, and I can lick any son-of-a-bitch in the house.' He would then introduce his guest: 'This young fellow is Jim Corbett. He's going to fight that nigger, Jackson.'

It was obvious to Jim that he was included in the 'son-of-a-bitch' slur and he tried to find an excuse to get away. His patience finally exhausted, he looked John L. straight in the eye and said, 'Mr Sullivan, you have made that remark several times in my presence this evening. You are the champion of the world and everyone is supposed to think you can whip anyone in the world, but I am in the same profession as yourself and it's hardly courteous. I don't want to hear you say it again.'

Taken aback, Sullivan shut up. Though he wouldn't admit it, he had a new-found respect for this level-headed young man who had the nerve to call his bluff.

Corbett returned to the west coast in March and immediately set up training camp at the seaside resort of Sausalito, on the Marin county shore. There, at the Ross Villa, he began the task of getting into fighting shape under the careful guidance of Professor John Donaldson. Later he was joined by the veteran trainer Billy Delaney and gradually attained the degree of physical perfection described as 'fit to fight for his life'.

The Jackson camp was pitched at Dives' hostelry, on the road leading to San Leandro, Alameda county, the same quarters he had used for his fights with Joe McAuliffe and George Godfrey. The Australian, a month behind his rival in getting down to serious training, had the misfortune of being thrown from his buggy while out driving. He suffered a strained ankle ligament, forcing him to lay off roadwork for a couple of weeks. His manager, Charles E. Davies, known as 'the Parson' for his sombre black apparel, was sufficiently worried as to suggest a postponement of the fight, but Jackson would not hear of it. 'I could lick Corbett if I had only one leg to stand on,' he boasted.

Despite the interruption to his training, Jackson was in prime condition by fight time.

The newspapers published comparisons of the boxers' measurements, noting that both were six feet, one inch in their socks. Corbett's chest was forty-one inches, to forty for his opponent, but the Australian had bigger shoulders and a greater chest expansion. Jim's biceps measured fourteen and a half inches, half an inch more than Jackson's. Corbett, aged twenty-four, was by five years the younger man.

The great excitement generated by the battle was shown by the large number of prominent sportsmen from all over the United States, as well as journalists from home and abroad, who attended. The contest was the biggest ever staged by the California Athletic Club, on New Montgomery Street, between Mission and Howard. Corbett had devised a scheme, accepted by the club directors, whereby only members could view the fight. Anyone could join the club, but would have to pay the annual membership fee of $66.50. Existing members whose subscriptions were fully paid up would be charged a nominal fee for a seat. It was announced the day before the bout that every seat had been sold. Hundreds of disappointed fans who had travelled from all over the country were turned away.

Today, it seems incongruous that fighters should have a say in how the referee should do his job. That's the way it was back then. Just before the contest, referee Hiram Cook called both boxers to a room.

'First of all, gentlemen,' he asked, 'do you want to hit in the clinches?'

'I'll leave the choice to Mr Corbett,' said Jackson.

Jim, anxious to show that he cared little about such matters and only wanted to get on with the main business, snapped back, 'You can have it any way you like, Jackson, it makes no difference to me.'

Corbett's apparent indifference to what seemed a major point of debate surprised Jackson. With a sixteen pound weight advantage, the Australian knew his extra strength would be to his benefit at close quarters. But the first round of the psychological battle had gone to Corbett. He had shown such confidence of success that trivialities didn't concern him.

Next came the question of selecting corners. Corbett again coldly dismissed any debate, suggesting, 'Let him have any corner he wants.'

To which the still polite Australian replied, 'Thanks, Mr Corbett, I'll take my usual lucky corner.'

'Go ahead, you'll need all the luck you can get,' sneered Gentleman Jim.

Jackson said he had only one request, that he be allowed to enter the ring last. This had been his custom in previous fights and no-one had objected. Corbett, seeing another opportunity to get one over on his rival, demanded, 'You can't have everything your own way, Jackson. This is one time you'll go first under the ropes.'

For forty-five minutes the argument continued, with the crowd growing restless, until it was agreed that both men should enter the ring together. When they got to the ring apron, Corbett nodded to his opponent and put his head through the ropes. Jackson climbed through, but Corbett slyly slipped back and was last to enter. He stood, grinning broadly, in his corner while the black man's irritation was plain for all to see.

The fighters donned the five-ounce gloves over their bare fists. The use of hand bandages for protection was still some years away. In Corbett's corner were John Donaldson and Billy Delaney, with his brother Harry as bottle-holder. Jackson's seconds were Sam Fitzpatrick and Billy Smith, and Billy Fields was bottle-holder.

Jackson was favourite to win, at odds of two-to-one on. Even many of Corbett's staunchest supporters thought he had taken on too big a task and limited their cash outlay to how long he would survive. Most bets were on how many rounds the contest would last. It was a designated 'fight to a finish', so it would go on as long as either man was still standing. No-one suspected the fight would last into the sixty-first round, with no winner and all bets declared off!

The bout began at nine o'clock in the evening and lasted through the first hour of the following morning. In a supreme test of skill and endurance, both men came through with great credit, even though the referee's declaration of 'no contest' was a most unsatisfactory verdict. For the first couple of hours, spectators marvelled at the brilliant scientific show put on by both men. It then lapsed into an endurance contest, with each trying to outlast the other.

Jackson later claimed that the ankle injury suffered in the fall from the buggy had badly handicapped him. If so, there was little evidence of it in the early stages as he went all out to score a knockout. Corbett's speedy footwork frequently got him out of danger and earned him sustained applause. His effective ducking under the Australian's terrific right-handers was 'nothing short of phenomenal' and he impressed everyone with the way he came back with strong counter attacks. This Corbett was no mere 'Fancy Dan', as his critics had tagged him.

One of Jim's most effective punches was a left hook to the stomach, which he landed frequently. Jackson's much-feared right to the heart was less successful, though it did hurt when it was on target. The Australian, for the most part, relied on straight punching, but found it difficult to land cleanly on his elusive rival. While Jackson did most of the forcing, he failed either to corner Corbett or lure him into a test of strength.

The fight earned a niche in history as the first time an automatic timekeeper was used. It not only timed the three-minute rounds, but sounded the gong at the beginning and end of each round. Up to then, it had not been unusual for seconds of a fighter who was taking a battering to 'accidentally' step on the bell and cut a round short. The automatic device took a while to become generally accepted throughout California, and it wasn't until 1925, when the new Madison Square Garden opened, that it was used in New York.

Corbett was severely hurt for the first time in the sixteenth round. A Jackson left to the face stung him, and it was followed by a jolting right to the body. He felt a chill running up and down his back. Showing great courage, he survived his toughest round of the fight. In the twenty-eighth round it was Corbett who came close to a dramatic victory. After being stunned by a hard right to the head, Jim unleashed a barrage of punches to drive his rival across the ring. The onslaught left Jackson nearly helpless, but Corbett was in too much of a hurry to punch with the necessary accuracy. The bell saved Jackson and Corbett cursed the impetuosity that cost him a knockout win.

As the bout dragged on, Jackson's legs lost their spring and he regularly dropped his hands by his sides for a rest. Corbett's arms also felt like lead and his hands were so numb and sore that he couldn't punch with his full weight. The padding in his gloves had become loosened and only by working the horsehair into a ball and clenching it in his palms was he able to tell if his hands were closed. His now almost bare knuckles meant he risked further damage to his hands every time he hit his opponent's head.

Those who had wagered that Corbett would not last ten rounds had then bet he would not go twenty – then thirty, forty and so on. As the exchanges between the two tired fighters grew more infrequent, there was often more activity outside the ring as gamblers argued about the odds.

Jackson later claimed that his left shoulder had 'given out' in the twenty-fifth round and he was barely able to use that arm after that. Corbett's body blows didn't bother him, he said, but this was a lie. He was later found to have two broken ribs. What caused him most concern, he admitted, were the left hand smashes he took in the face. The blood from his nose went down his throat and almost choked him.

Corbett said he also hurt his left forearm in that eventful twenty-fifth round. 'I thought it was broken at first,' he said afterwards, 'and after two more rounds I couldn't strike a blow with my left. I just used it to protect my body.'

Some of the audience had actually fallen asleep by the start of the sixtieth round, when referee Cook told both men that they must try to end the battle or else they wouldn't get their purse money. Still hardly any punches were struck. Corbett's hands were so painful that they were practically useless. His legs were still strong, however, and he was able to step away from his opponent's attempted blows. Jackson's mobility was badly affected by tiredness and his nagging leg injury.

The referee addressed both men: 'You've walked around long enough. We want more action.'

Corbett replied, 'I've countered all his leads and I'll continue to do so.'

Jackson said, 'I'm too tired to do all the leading, and I don't propose to leave myself open so he can hit me.'

When the contestants came up for the sixty-first round, it was plain that only their sheer courage and determination not to concede defeat kept them going. Jackson swung a right and missed. It was all he could do to keep from toppling over. Corbett attempted to counter, but reeled around the ring.

Before the round was two minutes old, Cook suddenly called a halt and sent the fighters to their corners. He then addressed the crowd: 'Gentlemen, this contest is becoming very unsatisfactory to you and the directors of the club. Both men have admitted they cannot go on to a satisfactory conclusion. You have ample evidence that they cannot go on except as walkers. I therefore declare the entertainment ended and that it is no contest. All bets are off.'

Despite his exhaustion, Corbett had enough energy to go across the ring to Cook and protest about the verdict. Jackson's cornermen put up no argument. Corbett claimed he was robbed, as he was willing to go on whereas Jackson showed no such inclination. His argument was reinforced when he saw Jackson fall flat on his face on the way back to his dressing room and had to be carried the rest of the way.

Jim also claimed the referee acted illegally in leaving the ring to consult with the club directors before announcing his verdict. The fairest outcome would have been to call it a draw. Indeed, many record books list it as a drawn contest, but this is a misleading interpretation of what actually happened. In the final analysis, Cook had no right to declare 'no contest' unless the fighters were faking, which they certainly were not.

To the Corbett family, who had round-by-round progress of the fight relayed to their home by telephone, there was no doubt that Jim was the victor. Pat, unable to check his excitement, made his way to the club, threw his arms around his son and kissed him. His earlier opposition to the fight was now forgotten. When Jim noticed his father's watch chain hanging loose, he asked what had happened to the watch. Pat, momentarily upset that he had been robbed, then broke into a huge smile and said, 'To hell with the watch, you whipped the nigger.'

However unsatisfactory the verdict, there was an even greater shock in store for Corbett and Jackson when they went to collect their purse money the following day. They were told that, instead of the $5,000 each should have received, they would get only half that amount because the bout had ended in a 'no contest' decision and had not been fought to a finish.

The club maintained that the $10,000 purse had been offered only if the fight went to a satisfactory conclusion. 'If the contestants – one too tired to fight and the other afraid to make him – preferred to save their friends from chances of loss in the betting, rather than continue the fight until somebody won it, that was their own look-out,' said an official.

Jim wanted to sue, but was advised against taking the issue to court. The law was unlikely to be sympathetic to his argument. The California papers unanimously denounced the club's cheap action. Many prominent members, admitting the fighters got a raw deal, resigned. The internal row finally broke up the organisation and the California Athletic Club passed out of existence.

At least the marathon battle served to ensure the boxers' lasting respect for each other's ability. When they met in a Turkish bath a few hours after the fight to ease their aching muscles, Jackson said, 'Mr Corbett, you were a great man tonight, the quickest I ever saw in my life. It was just like boxing a ghost.'

'Well, Jackson,' came the reply, 'I'm glad it's all over and I hope I'll never have to fight a man as good as you again. All those things I said about you that were published in the papers, and my conduct during the whole affair, I apologise for. I was just trying to annoy you as much as I could.'

In his 1925 autobiography, Corbett had some rare words of praise for someone apart from himself: 'That night I thought Peter Jackson was a great fighter. Six months later I thought him still a great one. And today, after thirty-three years, I still maintain he was the greatest fighter I have ever seen.'

After Corbett became world champion, efforts were made to re-match him with Jackson. But it never happened. Frustrated at his failure to get his well-deserved break, Peter grew increasingly melancholy and took to drinking heavily. It was only a shadow of the once-great fighter who returned to America in 1898 to meet an up-and-coming James J. Jeffries. Jackson was knocked out in three rounds. Within three years, he was dead from tuberculosis. He was buried in a pauper's grave in Queensland, Australia.

CHAPTER 8

What's wrong with being a dude?

Although not in the Rudolph Valentino league, Corbett was quite handsome and cut a dashing figure when dressed to the nines, which he was at every opportunity. He especially enjoyed showing himself off in full evening dress, complete with top hat, tails and silver-topped cane. Gentleman Jim was undoubtedly the best-dressed boxer in history.

While he took his nickname as a compliment, others used it as a term of abuse. A fighter was supposed to look like a fighter, not a 'damn dude', as Jake Kilrain – and later John L. Sullivan – tagged him. Corbett's answer to that was, 'Maybe I look too nice to be a fighter, though why a fighter can't be careful about his appearance I don't understand. If I had arrived for my fight with Kilrain wearing a blue flannel shirt, two days' growth of beard and a lot of scars on my face, he'd have said I was a real gladiator. But I've always been fond of my toothbrush and clean linen, and I like to shave every morning. I had a good tailor long before I began to fight. Why should I give him up because I'm fighting?'

'Pompadour Jim' was another appellation he picked up. This was because, at that time, he wore his hair cut short on top and brushed back high from his forehead. It followed the style set in the eighteenth century by the Marquise de Pompadour, mistress of Louis XV of France. But it was the 'Gentleman Jim' tag that stuck.

Corbett was not the first boxer to be honoured, or burdened, with the 'Gentleman' label. A century earlier, John Jackson, bare-knuckle champion of England, had been known as 'Gentleman Jackson' for his fine clothes, polished manners and charitable deeds. He mixed with the nobility, taught Lord Byron how to box and was recruited by the Prince Regent to assemble a guard of eighteen pugilists for the prince's coronation as King George the Fourth. Jackson rather spoiled his reputation in his last fight, however, by holding Daniel Mendoza's long hair in one hand while bopping him with the other. Hardly the act of a gentleman.

While Corbett could never be accused of resorting to such tactics in the ring, he was a master at upsetting opponents to gain an advantage. In his private life, he was generally well-mannered and considerate. But Gentleman Jim didn't always live up to his name. The disclosures which would be made by both of his wives, especially, caused widespread shock. Elliott J. Gorn, in *The Manly Art*, suggested that 'the reality of Corbett's life was less attractive than his public image, for he was a deeply moody and even brutal man'.

Jim's prestige as a ringman enjoyed an enormous boost from his performance against Jackson. Even though he had not won, he had shown great skill, courage and endurance in the marathon encounter. Considered not much more than a novice up to then, he had proved a match for the man many experts regarded as better than John L. Sullivan. Now, if he was to lure Sullivan into a show-down, he would need all the help he could get. Above all, he needed a good manager.

He dumped Charlie Stenzel, who had been looking after his affairs. Corbett was annoyed at his manager's failure to persuade the California Athletic Club to pay his full purse. He claimed that, after paying his training expenses and giving Stenzel his share, all he had to show for his four hours of bruising battling with Jackson was $850.

Enter, William A. Brady. The very epitome of the term 'promoter', Bill Brady was a quick-thinking, fast-talking theatrical agent, manager and producer, a discoverer and developer of talent, and manager of the wrestler Yousouf 'the Terrible Turk'. He was a sharp operator who never missed a trick when it came to getting good publicity for his protégés, or putting one over their rivals.

The son of a Dublin-born freelance newspaperman, whose income fluctuated as he picked up good stories or his 'scoops' dried up, young Brady had soon learned ways of augmenting the family income. As a boy in San Francisco, he had met Jim Corbett and they had sold newspapers together. On moving to New York, Brady lived in the Bowery, where he developed into a proficient hustler.

One of his ventures was to collect discarded fruit and vegetables from the markets and sell them to theatre queues. An average two dollars income per day was enough encouragement for the budding entrepreneur.

While he was still a teenager, his sense of adventure led to his taking a job as a 'peanut butcher' on trains travelling between east and west. Peanuts were not the sole commodity he had to sell. What he operated was more of a travelling general store, carrying candy, tobacco, books (mainly dime novels), and even bedding for the hard wooden boards that passengers slept on. As he recalled in his auto-biography, *Showman*, he was able to shift lots of useless junk on well-off drunks. 'The prices were as much as you dared ask over the company's book-keeping prices. The difference went into your pocket,' he wrote.

A row with a Chinaman, who pulled a knife when Brady tried his 'disappearing coin' trick, got him sacked from the train job. He settled back in San Francisco and found an outlet for his theatrical aspirations, first as an actor and later as a manager and producer. Brady purchased the rights to Dion Boucicault's play *After Dark* and took it on the road. In New York, the melodrama was playing to reasonable audiences at the Bowery Theatre. But Brady wanted to see 'house full' notices. He needed a 'name' in the cast. It was when he picked up a newspaper and saw the report of his old pal Corbett's fight with Jackson that he got his brainwave. He cabled Jim, offering him $150 a week to appear in a scene, which included a sparring match, at the end of the play. Jim readily accepted and had a few lines specially written for him.

'You only had to see Corbett walk on a stage to see that he was a natural actor,' said Brady. 'He had already been a big hit as an amateur in *Camille* and it was no surprise to me when, on his first real stage appearance – singing "Ta-ra-ra-boom-de-ay" in a very pleasant baritone, as cool as any old-timer born in a prop-box – he showed he could have got over without his pugilistic prestige to excite curiosity.'

It was the beginning of a great team. Corbett and Brady were good for each other. Their mutually rewarding partnership lasted many years. Brady not only guided Jim into a successful acting career but was the driving force behind a boxing link-up that set the pattern for other famous fighter-manager pairings, like heavy-weight champion Jack Dempsey and Jack 'Doc' Kearns, Georges Carpentier and François Descamps, Jimmy McLarnin and 'Pop'

Foster, and Floyd Patterson and Cus D'Amato. In his later years Corbett, looking back over forty years' involvement with boxing, said he never knew a smarter manager than Brady.

Corbett and Brady had met up again, for the first time since boyhood, when Jim was working at the Nevada Bank and boxing as an amateur. While Corbett was courting Ollie Lake, Brady was going out with her sister Georgie. The girls lived in Santa Cruz, California. Brady was doing his 'peanut butcher' job on the train from San Francisco to Santa Cruz and, every weekend, Jim would take the train to be with his girlfriend. The two men always found time for a chat during the journey. Even though Brady thought his girl was the prettier of the sisters, he was aware that Corbett was the one who gained most females' attention.

'Few women could resist the temptation to turn around and take another look at his long, straight back and the easy swing of his shoulders,' he said. 'If Corbett had picked my girl, I'd have been out of luck.'

Though Ollie accepted Jim's marriage proposal, her sister's romance didn't last. Brady later married stage dancer Maria Rene. Their daughter, Alice Brady, became an accomplished movie actress, first as a 'vamp' in silents and then, in talkies, usually playing a fluffy society matron or a drab housewife. She won an Academy Award in 1938 as best supporting actress in *In Old Chicago*, playing Molly O'Leary, the Irishwoman whose cow was said to have kicked over a lantern and started the great fire that destroyed the city. A year later Alice died from cancer at the age of forty-seven. Bill Brady, who lost his only son in a fire (he fell asleep with a lighted cigarette), later divorced Maria Rene and married the actress Grace George.

From the start of their business partnership, Brady dreamed up highly imaginative schemes to bring Corbett's name to wider public attention. After the success of Jim's appearance in *After Dark*, his manager commissioned a play to be specially written for Corbett. And what better way to keep him in the boxing limelight than by securing a match with the world heavyweight champion, albeit only a four-round exhibition. This was the occasion, already described, when John L. insisted they box in full evening dress.

Apart from disguising his lack of fitness, the charade was Sullivan's way of showing his contempt for the brash young contender. 'John L. did not like Corbett,' wrote Nat Fleischer. 'One could go further and not err by saying that Sullivan actually hated him. Not only because he was a boxing rival who cherished serious title aspirations, but also because Jim Corbett was in every way the very antithesis of bluff, roaring John. Sullivan was a bar-room king. Corbett, while no stranger to the saloon atmosphere, didn't mix with the rowdy element, and prided himself on being somewhat socially select as regards his immediate associates. The two men were as far apart as the North and South Poles.'

Shortly after the tame set-to with Corbett, Sullivan set off for a less-than-triumphant tour of Australia. Jim, in an apparent act of courtesy before the boat set sail, sent a messenger with a box of cigars. The world champion accepted the package, took a look at the signature on the card and tossed it – and the cigars – into San Francisco Bay. On hearing what happened, Jim chuckled to himself. Once again, he had succeeded in getting the goat of the easily-roused Bostonian.

Brady, while waiting for a response to the regular challenges to Sullivan, took his man on a boxing tour, offering $100 to anyone who could stay four rounds with Corbett. Sullivan had done this sort of thing successfully, though his offer went as high as $1,000. He was so powerful a hitter that only one man, Tug Wilson, had lasted the distance, and then only by hugging and repeatedly falling to the floor. It was different for Corbett. He had remarkable skills, but he wasn't in Sullivan's class as a puncher. Though he outclassed Ed Kinney in Milwaukee, he wasn't able to put him away inside schedule and Brady had to pay up.

The showman's imagination was really working overtime. When the tour reached New York, he advertised that Corbett would fight three men on the same night at Madison Square Garden. It was a great publicity stunt, but it nearly backfired. Although Jim, billed as 'the California Wonder', easily dispatched Bill Spilling and Bob Caffrey, both in the first round, he was taken the full three rounds by a grossly unfit Joe Lannon. Worse, he hurt his delicate hands. There would be no more of these rash three-in-one affairs.

Jim was back in San Francisco when Sullivan made his bombastic newspaper announcement that he was prepared to meet any of the top contenders who could put up the required $10,000 sidestake. Brady and Corbett, having managed to meet the champion's demand, met with all the other interested parties and the deal was done. The fight was set for New Orleans on 7 September 1892.

The announcement that Sullivan would have his first fight in over three years, with the young Californian in the opposite corner, caused great excitement throughout the sporting world. There had been fears that the last had been seen of 'the Boston Strong Boy' in the ring. He had grown fat and lazy, and it would take an enormous effort to get into anything like fighting fitness. Yet, it was widely assumed, even a half-fit John L. was more than a match for any of the current 'bluffers'.

After completing his theatrical engagements, Sullivan visited New York for a final good-time spree before knuckling down to the dreaded training grind. He set up camp at the Canoe Place Inn, Bay Head, Long Island, a quiet spot away from his adoring fans, who always wanted to 'shake the hand of the man who shook the world'. Liquor was strictly forbidden at the camp and there wasn't a saloon within fourteen miles. This was exactly what John L. needed, even if it took him some time to lose his grouchiness and knuckle down to the serious business of shedding those excess pounds.

In a thorough physical check-up by Dr Dudley A. Sergent, director of the Harvard College gymnasium in Cambridge, Massachusetts, Sullivan was pronounced 'an excellent example of the brawn and sinew that conquers both opponents and environments and sustains the race'. His power came from his exceptionally thick trunk, hips and thighs, observed the medic. The champion's breathing was his main problem, however, and, for a man of his height (five feet, ten and a half inches) he carried too much weight. Vigorous bouts of skipping and fast games with international handball champion Phil Casey enabled him to trim down from 229 pounds to 218, his weight ten days before the fight.

Corbett, meanwhile, needed no big stick to get him prepared for the opportunity of his life. Always a diligent trainer, he enthusiastically got down to work at Bill Brady's beautiful summer home, Loch Arbour, near Asbury Park, New Jersey. Rowing, swimming, handball, roadwork, horse-riding, sparring, bag-punching, and the use of pulley-weights to build up strength were the principal training methods. Billy Delaney, his regular trainer, was in charge of the camp, assisted by Denny Dillon. Jim Daly, from Philadelphia, was the chief sparring partner. So determined was Corbett to achieve peak fitness that he even had a small gymnasium installed in the private railroad car that would take him to New Orleans.

Enormous amounts of newspaper space were given over to the most minute details of the two fighters' preparation. Every line was lapped up by enthusiastic readers, who counted the days leading up to the encounter. Though Jim had no doubts about his upcoming triumph, he was well aware that few others gave him the remotest chance of toppling the mighty Sullivan off his throne. He knew, too, that far from being acclaimed a hero, he would be despised for demolishing a national icon. In *The Roar of the Crowd*, he said:

> I don't think a fighter ever lived, or ever will live, who was as popular with the masses, and especially with the Irish, as John L. Sullivan. Many of our Irish citizens hated me just because I had the insolence to fight him. One night, not long before the match, I was boxing an exhibition at Miner's old Eighth Avenue Theatre, and someone shouted from the gallery, "So you're the guy who thinks he can lick John L. Sullivan." A bottle sailed clear across the orchestra, just grazing my head, and smashed into a thousand pieces on the stage. My unpopularity with the Irish struck me as rather peculiar, for everybody that belonged to me, as far back as we could trace, was Irish through and through. Sullivan, like myself, was born in the United States of Irish parents. Of course, this attitude was due to Sullivan's disposition, which was just the right mixture of good nature, aggressiveness and temper for a fighter, so people thought. I was always more controlled and a little too businesslike, perhaps, to vie with him in popularity. Then, though I entered saloons occasionally, I did not care to waste a lot of time standing up against the bars of any city I happened to be in. To me, it was the most boring thing in the world to be mauled around by a lot of drunks, while John L., in the same circumstances, was on his native heath, as they say.

A week before the big fight, exhibition bouts were arranged for the combatants. It gave the fans a chance to see the two leading heavy-weights stripped off into their ring gear and to find out how well prepared they were for active service. Corbett appeared at Madison Square Garden, while the champion sparred at the Claremont Rink in Brooklyn. Sullivan would have preferred the Garden, but Brady, knowing this, had got in ahead and booked it. Another one up for the challenger!

The Sullivan supporters, who packed the venue as hundreds more were unable to gain admittance, gave their hero the customary rousing reception, but there were more than a few mutters about his bulging paunch. It was noticeable, too, that his closely-cropped hair was streaked with grey and there were deep furrows in his brow. Nevertheless, they cheered every half-hearted effort of the great man. At the end of the sparring session, John L. told the gathering, 'I thank you with my whole heart for this grand reception. Next week I hope to show you that I'm still the champion of old, and not the sort of passed-by fighter that some of my bluffing enemies would have you believe.'

Corbett's appearance at the Garden was also a huge success. He showed what fine shape he was in by working out with the pulleys and skipping rope, playing handball, wrestling, punching the bag and boxing three fast rounds with Jim Daly. Whatever doubts many of the spectators might have retained about the challenger's ability to defeat Sullivan, they were convinced Gentleman Jim couldn't be better prepared for the fight of his life.

After his daily training sessions, Jim often visited a local ice-cream parlour. Sullivan supporters, mindful of their own man's hard-drinking reputation, guffawed loudly and made sarcastic remarks as they watched the Dude enjoying nothing more naughty than a couple of plates of ice-cream.

Maybe it was a deliberate bid to dispel that unflattering image, but Corbett, having lunch with a friend in a posh restaurant, was seen drinking champagne. The newspapers got hold of the story and soon word got about that the challenger had gone on a 'bender'. It got to the stage that Jim's backers threatened to pull out, but Corbett was assured by Phil Dwyer, the stakeholder for the fight, that no money would be refunded. Another of his patrons' worries was that he would be too light for Sullivan. He agreed to a public weigh-in and satisfied his doubters by scaling 197 pounds. What they didn't know was that he had several lead weights from his training pulleys in his overcoat pockets as he stepped on the scales. He was actually twenty pounds lighter.

To get his mind off the big event, Corbett spent some time rehearsing for his lead role in the new play Brady planned to launch soon after the fight. Not too imaginatively entitled *Gentleman Jack*, it had been written at Brady's behest by Charles T. Vincent, a competent hack playwright of his acquaintance. Vincent was also the author of *Sport McAllister*, in which Corbett had appeared a few months earlier. *Gentleman Jack*, with its obvious play on the fighter's nickname, had no pretensions to great artistic merit, and was blatantly aimed at cashing in on Corbett's renown. So confident of Jim's victory over Sullivan was his manager that he had advertising posters put up *before* the fight announcing the star of the drama, Corbett, as champion of the world. The outrageous publicity stunt was to pay off handsomely. Indeed, Brady frankly admitted that he saw Jim's ascent to the heavyweight throne more as a vehicle to a successful theatrical career than an end in itself. It turned out to be a valid judgement. Though he is remembered as a great boxing champion rather than a talented thespian, Corbett earned much more from stage and film work than from his ring career.

As the great day drew near, the crowds flocked to New Orleans. From New York, Boston, Chicago, Cincinnati, Cleveland, St Louis and San Francisco, special trains rolled to the scene of the greatest fight festival ever put on. To celebrate Mardi Gras week, the Olympic Club had arranged three world championship fights, to follow one another on successive nights. The first was between George Dixon and Jack Skelly for the featherweight title. Next was Jack McAuliffe and Billy Dwyer for the lightweight prize. The climax was the one the entire country, indeed the world at large, was waiting for: the first contest for the world heavyweight championship under Marquis of Queensberry rules.

CHAPTER 9

Champion of the world

Some boxing historians have done John L. Sullivan an injustice by refusing to recognise him as the first world heavyweight champion. They maintain that he was merely the ring ruler who saw out the old bare-knuckle era and that Corbett, in defeating him under Queensberry rules, was the initial heavyweight title-holder. The Boston Strong Boy deserves better. If champion of the world, taken in its literal sense, signifies the best fighting man of his class, then Sullivan was it. Maybe his claim was diluted by his drawing the colour bar against Peter Jackson, but for the complete decade of his championship reign (1882–92) John L. towered over the heavyweight scene like no man before, and only the likes of Jack Dempsey, Joe Louis and Muhammad Ali have managed since.

Nat Fleischer acclaimed Sullivan as 'a symbol of national glory, a manifestation of America's greatness. The Bostonian occupied an altogether unique position in the emotional structure of America's working millions. They swore by him, condoned his faults, admired his very human frailties, loved him'.

Contrary to common belief, Sullivan much preferred boxing with gloves to bare-knuckle combat. In fact, he did much to advance the cause of the Queensberry rules long before Corbett gained widespread popularity for the new code. Though John L. became champion by knocking out Paddy Ryan under London Prize Ring rules and defended it twice in bare-fist fights, these were the only occasions in his forty-seven contests that he boxed without gloves.

Two of his early bouts were under London Prize Ring rules, but the contestants wore kid gloves.

John Lawrence Sullivan was born in Boston, Massachusetts, on 15 October 1858. Like Corbett, he would have become a priest if his Irish immigrant parents had had their way. But the powerful youngster – he got his strength from his mother, who weighed thirteen stone, against his father's nine stone, four pounds – found a natural outlet for his energy in fist fights. His exceptional punching power, supreme self-confidence and ability to intimidate his opponents took him to the championship heights and earned him an aura of invincibility. The myth was finally shattered by Corbett, but that was the only time he suffered defeat in a career that spanned twenty-seven years.

Gilbert Odd, long-time editor of *Boxing News* and author of many books on the sport, said that Sullivan's chief asset was 'his ability to put the fear of God into his opponents long before the starting bell of a contest. John L. developed a deep growling, intimidating voice, brusque and belligerent manners, and an ominous glare from his steel-blue eyes that had his opponents devoured by apprehension long before they felt the weight of the Bostonian's mighty fists'.

Sullivan wrapped up preparations for the Corbett fight and set off from his Long Island training camp for New Orleans on 1 September. Wherever the train stopped en route, he was greeted by bands and huge crowds who cheered him to the echo. To his adoring fans, there was only one, all-conquering 'Jawn L'. Those close to the champion, however, noticed that he seemed a trifle gloomy and disinclined to return his loyal admirers' frenzied greetings.

Corbett arrived at the fight scene a few days later. The journey was completed quietly, except for one stop at Spartanburg, South Carolina, where he barely escaped arrest for daring to exercise on a Sunday. This was not one of his manager's usual publicity stunts. The time for ballyhoo was over. It was now down to the serious business.

In an interview, Corbett boasted that Sullivan 'can't hit me in a week, and he'll be the worst licked man you ever looked at'. He didn't care if the champion weighed 200 pounds or half a ton. 'I am 500 per cent stronger than when I fought Jackson.'

Sullivan stayed at the Young Men's Club of New Orleans, while Corbett settled in at the Southern Athletic Club, where he had beaten Jake Kilrain. Thousands turned out to watch both men sparring at their respective quarters. On Jim's arrival in town, the betting was 3/1 in favour of the Bostonian. The odds lengthened to 4/1 by fight time. Corbett's manager even bet $1,000 dollars on Sullivan – just in case. 'Naturally, I was with Jim all the way,' Brady later explained, 'but after all, there is only one John L. Sullivan.'

Never had New Orleans witnessed such an assortment of visitors, not all of them welcome. Trainloads poured into the Crescent City, each carriage bearing its quota of gunmen, confidence tricksters, pickpockets and gamblers. But there were plenty of decent, upright men to set the balance. Peter Jackson, described in the newspapers as 'black heavyweight champion', was one of the many well-known fighters seen around. He was supporting Corbett, hoping that, if Jim won, he would get next shot at the title. There, too, was the famous western lawman Bat Masterson, who had lost heavily in betting on Kilrain to beat Sullivan. Still convinced the champion was over-rated, he allegedly wagered every dime he had on Gentleman Jim.

The first event of the eagerly-awaited three-day fistic carnival, on 5 September, was watched by a crowd of 6,400 at the Olympic Club's new arena. Irish-born Jack McAuliffe, one of the few champions who went through an entire career without ever tasting defeat, knocked out Billy Myers in fifteen rounds to retain his world lightweight title. The following evening, George Dixon, the first black man to earn universal recognition as a world champion, disposed of Jack Skelly in the eighth round to keep his featherweight title. For the first – and last – time, the club allowed black spectators to see their 'Little Chocolate', but they were seated in a separate section from whites. The sight of Dixon handing out a savage beating to his over-matched victim did not go down well with the majority of the audience. 'A darky is all right in his place here,' wrote a local journalist, 'but the idea of sitting quietly by and seeing a coloured boy pummel a white lad grates on Southerners.' Although fears of crowd trouble did not materialise, the club bowed to pressure and forbade mixed matches from then on.

At last, on 7 September, came the 'clash of the Titans'. For Sullivan, the impressive, electrically-lit arena was a long way from his early days fighting in fields, dingy back rooms of saloons and on the deck of a barge in the Hudson River. Corbett, too, had battled Joe Choynski on a barge, but most of his bouts had been in the relative comfort of private clubs.

Reporters from almost every major newspaper in the country, as well as a fair representation from abroad, were in attendance. Western Union had fifty operators employed to handle the special dispatches from ringside. Poolrooms and saloons across the country were equipped with receiving sets, and off-duty railroad telegraphers were taken on to ensure customers got a round-by-round, minute-by-minute account of what happened.

Half an hour before the contestants entered the ring, a sudden cloudburst drenched New Orleans. John L., a deeply superstitious man, was unnerved. He believed it was a bad omen for the champion if it rained on the day of a fight. The heavy shower didn't concern the Corbett camp, but there was still plenty to worry about.

'My manager and three seconds looked like they were at a funeral,' observed the challenger. 'Bill Brady kept on wiping the sweat off his palms with a dirty handkerchief. Billy Delaney tried to settle his nerves by humming to himself and chewing on a cigar. I guess I was the only calm one in that dressing room.'

Gentleman Jim had decided he would arrive at the arena in style. He stepped from his carriage wearing a light summer suit, straw boater at a jaunty angle, and carrying a bamboo cane. The streets were crowded with people, but all he could hear was talk of 'Sullivan, Sullivan, Sullivan'. Brady, hoping he would not live to regret his rashness, banked $3,000 on his man at odds of 4/1 against. That was the entire proceeds of Corbett's recent tour.

Much of the credit for the challenger's cool demeanour was due to his workouts with Mike Donovan at the New York Athletic Club. 'Professor' Mike, a much-respected coach, had taught Corbett how best to defend against Sullivan's three basic blows: a chopping left to beat down his opponent's guard, a straight right, delivered with great force, and a right cross behind the ear. Jim proved such a good pupil that, by the end of their training spell, he was able to avoid every punch Donovan aimed at him. The trainer was so impressed that he put $1,000 on Jim to win.

In the pre-fight discussions, Corbett tried some typical games-manship to further irritate the testy champion. He refused to allow John L. to wear a heavy bandage around his waist, claiming that, after a few rounds, the sweat would cause it to harden. Then, on being told that Sullivan wanted the 'lucky' corner – the one that McAuliffe and Dixon had occupied for their wins – Corbett said he could have any corner he liked, but he (Corbett) would enter the ring last. The champion's side argued that this would be a break with tradition. A coin was tossed and Corbett got his way. On entering the open arena, however, he saw that Sullivan hadn't entered the ring. In that case, he said, he would stand at the back all night if he had to. Finally, a scowling John L. made his way down the aisle, to a tremendous ovation. The challenger's reception, by contrast, was subdued. To most of the crowd, it was a relief that he had showed up at all.

During the delay, fans had amused themselves debating the respective merits of the contestants and speculating on how long the fight would last. There was much talk, too, about Sullivan's 'little bit of diversion' in the hours approaching the battle. A reporter had alleged that John L. had sneaked 'Miss Mardi Gras' into his hotel room at 1.45 a.m. Such conduct, while unproved, would have been in keeping with the Bostonian's reputation of booking women, usually prostitutes, into his hotel rooms and registering them as his wife.

The benefits, or otherwise, of engaging in sex just before a fight have long been debated. Harry Greb, world middleweight champion from 1923 to '26, claimed that making love in his dressing room relieved tension. The opposing view is that it dissipates vital energy and induces an over-relaxed state. A fighter is supposed to be at his best when he is feeling mean and aggressive. Just before a sullen Sonny Liston, one of the ring's most notorious 'lover boys', stepped into the ring to challenge Floyd Patterson for the world heavyweight title in 1962, his handlers told him that torch singer Lena Horne had sent a message that she was waiting for him in her hotel suite. Liston showed such urgency to get the job over that Patterson was counted out in just over two minutes of the opening round.

At last the preliminaries were over and Sullivan and Corbett faced each other in the ring. Sullivan, wearing green tights and high shoes, scowled as referee 'Professor' John Duffy explained the rules. Jim, who wore drab-coloured trunks, with a belt in the colours of the American flag, tried his last bit of gamesmanship. 'What if he does this in the clinches?', he asked, putting his elbow under his rival's chin and pushing his head back firmly, 'Would that be a foul?' The referee assured him it would. 'All right,' said Corbett, 'that's all I wanted to know.'

'For the first time since entering the ring, I looked Sullivan square in the face and very aggressively too,' wrote Corbett in his auto-biography. 'He stopped his rising and falling on his toes and stood staring at me as if he were petrified, so surprised was he at my change of attitude, and I saw at once that I had him guessing. In a very cocksure manner, I jerked the towel from my shoulders, turned my back on him and ripped out, "Let her go!" '

The gong sounded at seven minutes past nine o'clock in the evening. An hour and twenty minutes later, a new heavyweight champion of the world was crowned. The once invincible John L. Sullivan had finally met his master. In the twenty-one rounds it lasted, there was never any doubt that the challenger's youth, speed of foot and hand, absolute self-confidence and the patience to wait until he was sure the Boston Strong Boy was through before applying the clinical finish, would be the deciding factors. In a nutshell, Sullivan was outclassed.

Corbett, initially a little concerned that the ring floor was made of turf – wooden boards would be normally used in an indoor arena – was soon satisfied that the ground was solid enough for him to nip around smartly on his toes. For the duration of the opening round, he contented himself with avoiding any attempts by the champion to land a blow. The crowd began to hiss at these tactics and Sullivan frowned and looked angry as the gong was struck. Jim repeated the pattern in the second round, but a fiercely determined champion caught him twice with head punches and seemed to shake him with a right uppercut. Corbett landed his first blow, to the body, but there was little power behind it.

As the crowd hooted at Jim's evasive methods, he momentarily turned his back on his opponent and, like a confident matador, gestured for quiet and shouted, 'Just wait a minute. You'll see a fight.'

For the sake of his self-respect, he decided that he must do something positive in the third round. He waited until John L. made a rush, then jabbed him hard in the face with his left hand. Blood spurted immediately and, for the first time, the mainly pro-Sullivan crowd was silenced. Corbett followed up his advantage by scoring with several more stinging hits. The champion looked very worried as he returned to his corner at the gong. He had reason to be. His nose was broken and he knew he was in for a tough time trying to pin his big punches on the nifty dude.

Jim was content to bide his time. It was a fight to the finish, so he could afford to let the older man wear himself out before moving in for the kill. The champion's swings became wilder and wilder. At one point, he stopped fighting and shouted, 'Come on and fight.' Corbett was in no mood to oblige. As Sullivan's puffing increased, his tormentor began to get bolder. At the start of the seventh round, Corbett sunk lefts and rights into the Bostonian's stomach, causing him to double over in agony. Still he did not press home his advantage, but backed off, feinting warily and looking for openings. More and more of his fast punches were hitting home.

By now, the audience sensed the unimaginable – defeat for the mighty John L. – was on the cards. His face covered in blood, Sullivan was looking more and more dispirited at his failure to catch his man. His arms felt like lead and he could do little to avoid the swift counterpunches that stung his face or sank into his bloated body. By the fourteenth round Corbett was landing straight shots to his battered nose without reply.

Only Sullivan's great pride kept him going. He kept ploughing forward, hoping his rival would stop running for just one split second so that he could land the big punch that would wipe out the shame of the boxing lesson he was being taught by the arrogant Corbett. Over and over he rushed in, only to find himself punching nothing but the ropes as the dancing master slipped out of harm's way.

John L. tried to make light of the beating he was absorbing. Now and again, after taking a punch, he would remark, 'That was a good one, Jim'. Growing more and more desperate, the champion repeatedly rushed at his tormentor, trying to bowl him over with sheer strength. Most times he ended up crashing into the ropes. The spectators, while feeling sorry for Sullivan, appreciated a display of scientific boxing such as they had never seen before.

Corbett drilled countless left jabs into his opponent's battered face and moved smoothly out of range of Sullivan's attempted counters. As Jim clinched with the champion and trapped his arms, there were cries of 'Foul' and jeers at his tactics. At the end of the round, Corbett raised his hands in the air and addressed the crowd: 'Gentlemen, before I get through, I'll punish this man so there'll be no question as to who is the champion.'

A brave Sullivan effort in the eighteenth round brought renewed hope for his fans as he landed a couple of right swings to the challenger's ear. But Corbett came back with two scorching rights to the jaw that sent him reeling. Jim followed up with a barrage of punches, and only John L.'s great heart kept him upright. It would have been no surprise, however, if he had stayed on his stool as the gong sounded for the following round.

But out he came, as belligerent as ever, forcing his tired legs to go forward and his fists raised for action. Corbett resumed his cat-and-mouse tactics, to the crowd's annoyance, tapping his rival to the face and getting away while the Bostonian swung and missed. Suddenly, Jim sunk home two hard rights to the heart, causing

Sullivan to reel away, badly hurt. Corbett tried to finish him off, but the gong ended the round.

Mike Donovan, in Corbett's corner, advised him to go for the kill, saying that John L. 'can't hit hard enough to dent a pound of butter'. The challenger mounted an all-out attack, raining punches on his helpless victim. Sullivan refused to go down, earning tremendous cheers for his great courage. Corbett, however, was determined to finish him off. The twenty-first round would prove to be the last.

The crowd winced as the old warrior took a succession of heavy blows to the head. He looked a sorry sight as blood flowed from his battered nose onto his chest. Gamely, he tried to defend himself against the onslaught, but Corbett would not be denied. A powerful right landed flush on the champion's jaw, sending him staggering into the ropes. His eyes glazed, mouth sagging open, brain numbed, he was ready for the taking. One perfectly-timed right ended the slaughter. Sullivan pitched forward onto his face. Feebly, he tried to rise, but it was no use. He rolled over onto his right side, deaf to referee Duffy's count of 'ten'.

The unbelievable had happened. John L. Sullivan had been beaten. And James John Corbett, of California, was the new – or, some say, the first – heavyweight champion of the world.

Though the largely pro-Sullivan crowd sportingly acknowledged Corbett's victory, there was great sympathy and concern for the deposed champion as his seconds helped him to his corner. After a few minutes, he recovered sufficiently to rise unsteadily to his feet. His seconds thought he was about to attack his conqueror and restrained him. But he stumbled into the ropes before finding a grip with his left hand on a ring post. Holding up his right hand, he waited until the cheers and applause died down before announcing, 'Gentlemen, all I have to say is that I came into the ring once too often, and if I had to get licked I'm glad it was by an American. I remain your warm and personal friend, John L. Sullivan.' The simple, but heartfelt, speech got a tremendous reception.

The new champion, who had to have police protection as the crowd fought to clap him on the back on the way back to his dressing room, was naturally elated at his performance. Yet, in the moment of his greatest triumph, he felt resentment towards his new supporters. He realised how fickle fight fans could be.

In *The Roar of the Crowd*, he said, 'I should have felt proud and dazed, but the only thing I could think of, right after the knockout, was Sullivan lying there on the floor. I was actually disgusted with the crowd and it left a lasting impression on me. It struck me as sad to see all those thousands who had given him such a wonderful ovation when he entered the ring turning it to me now that he was down and out. I realised that some day, too, they would turn from me when I should be in Sullivan's shoes lying there on the floor.'

How right he was.

CHAPTER 10

Packaging 'Gentleman Jim'

The news of Corbett's victory stunned America – and the rest of the world. It was scarcely credible that the mighty John L. Sullivan had been knocked off the heavyweight championship throne by the unregarded Gentleman Jim.

The result was flashed across the nation as quickly as the telegraph operators' fingers could move. In New York, where coloured lights had been set up on the dome of the Pulitzer Building (a red light would signify a good round for Sullivan, a white one for Corbett), dispatches on the outcome were read from theatre stages. Bigger crowds gathered in Washington around the newspaper bulletin boards than at any time during a presidential election. Similar excitement was experienced in cities throughout the United States. While Boston went into deep shock and despair at its hero's demise, San Francisco went wild, with crowds dancing in the streets.

Newspapers rushed special editions onto the streets. In New Orleans, the *Picayune* printed more than 10,000 extra copies and sent special trains along the Gulf coast so that readers could savour the details over their morning coffee. Overseas, the transatlantic cable relayed the news of the great event and sparked off widespread debate. In England, a young Sandhurst cadet named Winston Spencer Churchill expressed his delight at the result.

According to the *New York Times*, Sullivan was in a deeply distressed state in his dressing room after the fight, sobbing convulsively as his seconds tended to his wounds. Not even a night spent drinking champagne and whiskey could deaden the pain of losing his precious title. It was around five o'clock in the morning before he fell into sleep. When he was awakened at around noon, it was to realise that it had not been a bad dream: for the first time in a decade he would be no longer recognised as world heavyweight champion. Nor had the physical pain eased. When he tried to eat, he could not do so, as his mouth was too badly swollen. To the reporters who called to his hotel, he managed to mumble a tribute to his conqueror as 'the cleverest man I ever fought'.

Corbett, refusing his handlers' promptings to enjoy a night out on the town, fulfilled a promise to return to the Southern Athletic Club. A banner with his picture on it hung across the gymnasium where he had trained for the fight. Up to 2,000 members and guests cheered the new champion's short speech. As wine glasses were raised in a toast to his health, Jim responded – with a glass of milk. He later admitted his gesture was a sham. He actually hated milk, but believed he would set a good example to youngsters across the world when they read about it. At the same time, he was having a dig at Sullivan's intemperate lifestyle. The image of a high-living, hard-drinking, rough-and-ready heavyweight champion was consigned to history. For sure, boxing had entered a new era.

Sullivan's dejection over the loss of his precious championship was not eased by the realisation that he hadn't a penny of compensation for the terrible punishment he had suffered. It was his own fault. He was the one who had insisted on 'winner takes all'.

His supporters also took a financial beating. Billy West, the well-known minstrel, wagered $15,000 on John L., despite being advised otherwise by Bill Brady. Jim Cronin and Ed Butler, St Louis political bosses, between them dropped $60,000. New York gambler Al Smith, who lost $25,000, said he acted against his better judgement in betting on the Bostonian and vowed he would never again be swayed by sentiment. Steve Brodie, whose moment of fame was earned diving off the Brooklyn Bridge for a wager, went broke. He was so confident of a Sullivan victory that he bet all his money and pawned his jewellery to top it up. He had to borrow his train fare back to New York.

Somewhat more fortunate was Jack McAuliffe, the lightweight champion, who was one of John L.'s cornermen. He had wanted to stake all of his $10,200 purse for beating Billy Myers on his hero, and handed the money to his friend Dick Roche. To his great relief, he discovered that Roche had acted on the word of Billy Delaney,

Corbett's trainer, that Jim was a sure winner, and held onto McAuliffe's cash.

The early thoughts of the new champion, richer by $35,000 from his purse and the gain of Sullivan's sidestake, were for his parents. He telegraphed his father in San Francisco, promising that the $10,000 still owed on his home and livery stable would be paid off. Kate Corbett's only concern was that Jim had come through his ordeal in one piece. An elderly neighbour in Hayes Street who grabbed her in his arms and shouted, 'Kate, your boy is champion of the world', was met with, 'Yes, dear, I know, but are you sure that Jimmy is not hurt?'

In contrast to the attention he showed to his parents, Jim curtly refused to take his wife's telephone call from a New York hotel. 'Oh, I can't go now,' he told the messenger. 'Just give her my love and tell her I'm all right, feeling well and not a bit hurt.'

Bob Fitzsimmons got an ever colder reception when he knocked on the dressing room door after the fight, wishing to give his congratulations. Corbett shouted, 'Don't let him in. The big duffer wouldn't come near me before the fight, and I don't want to see him now.'

His prima donna attitude didn't go down well with some newspaper commentators. It was clear that his victory had quickly gone to his head, they observed. He bragged that the fight was a walkover and, apart from some soreness in his right hand from landing the knockout blow, he would not know he had been in a fight.

'People who want to study modest and generous impulses and refined manners will have to turn elsewhere,' suggested the Milwaukee *Evening Wisconsin*.

Jim tried to make up for his earlier snub by sending his wife a telegram the day after the fight: 'I will not forget you, darling. I love you with all my heart.'

Ollie said she was overwhelmed with the flood of cabled congratulations. 'My husband's success is all the more pleasing because so many said he was going to lose,' she said. 'I knew all along he would conquer Sullivan. I am sorry for Sullivan and thoroughly admire the honourable and manly way he acknowledged his defeat.'

Her elation was somewhat dampened when, shortly afterwards, she was sued by Henry Romeike, who had been making up a scrapbook of newspaper clippings of Jim's career. Ollie had signed a contract agreeing to pay $150 for the job. Jim thought this was far too much, so Ollie tried to get out of the deal. When Romeike heard he was being accused of being a swindler, and possibly a black-mailer, he hit back hard with a choice epithet of his own. As he didn't know Mrs Corbett's first name, he got his lawyer to address correspondnce to 'Mrs Jezebel Corbett'.

If Jim appeared to have grown thrifty, it was not without reason. He had known of so many ex-fighters ending up with nothing to show for their years in the ring but scars and misshapen noses. That wouldn't happen to him, he vowed.

The day after his title win, he set off for New York. He and Ollie had moved home to the metropolis, having paid $28,000 for a magnificent three-storey house at 146 West Eighty-Eighth Street. Over the next year, from his ring, stage and other earnings, he would invest $14,000 in a summer house at North Asbury Park, New Jersey, and pay off an outstanding $7,000 to complete the purchase of Thompson's roadhouse on Jerome Avenue, New York.

Corbett's elevated status as world champion meant he could take his pick of money-making opportunities. Nixon and Zimmerman offered him $2,000 for a week's engagement at the Academy of Music in Philadelphia. A theatrical company in Chicago topped that amount, and a Californian bid went as high as $5,000. Similar inducements came from New York, Baltimore, Pittsburgh and New Haven (Connecticut). Even Sullivan's home town, Boston, wanted to see at first hand the man who had beaten their idol. Jim could earn fifty per cent of the profits for allowing the use of his name on a saloon at the entrance to the World's Fair in Chicago. He could pick up an extra $2,000 for posing for a statue at the site.

No wonder he was in no hurry to fight again. He would not even think about defending his title for another year, he declared. An exhibition appearance, however, had been arranged for Madison Square Garden on 12 September. Long before the doors opened, a huge crowd clamoured for admission. Many had to be turned away. As well as thousands of ordinary fans, the gathering included business and professional men, together with a fair selection of the city's high society. It was an indication of how boxing had been uplifted on the social scale by Gentleman Jim's accession to the world championship.

Once the attendance had settled in, Bill Brady stepped up on the platform, only to find his words drowned by a huge outburst of cheering. The new champion's tall athletic figure, clad in white trunks and green stockings, had emerged from his dressing room without waiting for his introduction. As he stood in the centre of the ring and bowed, the spectators threw hats in the air, waved canes, stamped their feet and yelled their appreciation. Dainty handkerchiefs flitted down from women in the overhanging private boxes. The police had to intervene to prevent a rush by enthusiasts who wanted to shake Jim's hand. He told Nat Fleischer that this night was the most cherished of his ring remembrances.

Brady finally got a few moments' silence to announce that, at the same venue on 17 September, Jim would spar with John L. Sullivan in a benefit for the deposed champion. Loud cheers greeted such a fine show of compassion towards the hard-up Bostonian. The truth of the matter is that Corbett and his manager were more motivated by the benefit's value as a public relations exercise. They were all too aware that, whatever the sincerity of the widespread acclaim for Jim's magnificent win, it was overshadowed by the huge swell of sympathy for the man who had 'licked any son-of-a-bitch' who faced him until the dude came along. An apparent act of kindness towards a fellow professional wouldn't do Corbett's standing any harm at all.

Jim earned further marks for his address to the crowd: 'From my heart, I thank you for this kind reception, which I appreciate deeply. I sincerely hope that John L. Sullivan will succeed in all his future undertakings. I admire him very much and want to do everything in my power to assist him. For myself, I can only say that I will do my best to defend the title I have won, and to keep it in America.'

He proceeded to spar three rounds with his trainer, Billy Delaney. Spectators remarked, with wonder, that his face showed not a mark from the twenty-one rounds he had fought with Sullivan five days earlier. The only evident 'souvenir' was a light bandage he wore on his right hand. He did not use the sore hand at all, but his speedy left jab was well in evidence and his nifty footwork delighted the onlookers.

The Garden was again packed to capacity for Corbett's exhibition match with Sullivan. The ex-champion, the effects of his beating still showing on his face, was presented with a basket of flowers as he stepped into the ring. The two fighters stood side by side as the hall was filled with cheering for a full three minutes. No one doubted most of the applause was for John L. It was poignant that, for the first time, he was announced as a former world heavyweight champion. The old warrior raised his hand for quiet and, in his deep, rumbling voice, he stated that he had no excuses for his defeat and that he was glad his conqueror was an American. Corbett, too, made a short speech, but it was noted how weak his voice was compared to Sullivan's. The three rounds of sparring were harmless, with Jim's agility the most noteworthy feature. The crowd left the Garden well pleased with the presentation. Sullivan, too, was happy with his $6,000 share of the proceeds. It was badly needed. Not only had he failed a make a penny from his title fight defeat, but he had lost heavily by betting on himself.

It was now that Bill Brady came into his own. The ace hustler was anxious that Corbett should not waste a minute before cashing in on his new-found fame. Apart from arranging boxing exhibitions, deals were done with various companies. The champion, now a partner in the firm of Corbett and Brady, was one of the earliest endorsers of manufacturers' products. Cigarette firms produced collectors' cards with Jim's picture on them. A plaster cast was made of the right hand that had dethroned Sullivan. It was used as a model for a metal replica to be sold as a paperweight. Corbett made $1,000 on the arrangement.

But Brady's pet project was about to take off. James J. Corbett, boxer, was about to become James J. Corbett, full-scale actor. *Gentleman Jack*, the play Brady had commissioned from Charles T. Vincent, went quickly into rehearsal while Corbett's manager lined up locations for its presentation. Jim, who had picked up his first acting experience as a boy, appearing in minor and leading roles for his Sacred Heart College Amateur Dramatic Society, took to his new role like a natural thespian. Brady was so impressed with his ability to learn his lines quickly and with his natural stage presence that he said Jim could have had a successful stage career even if he hadn't made his name in the ring.

Later on, Corbett would give this self-assessment: 'I do not think I flatter myself when I believe I will make an actor. I never expect to be a Booth or a Silvini, but I think I can do light parts very creditably.' His attraction to the stage was natural, he said. 'We Irish are happiest showing off.'

The play had its premiere in Elizabeth, New Jersey, on 3 October, less than a month after Jim's enthronement as world heavyweight champion. Though generally well received by the public and the press critics, it was no dramatic masterpiece. Not even Brady was bold enough to claim it was anything more than a showcase for the new world champion. Without Corbett's name on the billboards, it would never have happened. It relied heavily on Corbett's personality and public persona to attract audiences.

Corbett's manager loved the Gentleman Jim tag. In calling the play *Gentleman Jack,* the slight variation was meant to tease audiences into believing they were seeing Corbett not as a stage performer, but as a real life hero. Brady made sure that Jim appeared in formal dress wear for most of the play's action.

Off stage, Corbett played up his stylish image for all it was worth. Sullivan's crude habit of winning favour by throwing a pocketful of silver on a bar and ordering drinks on the house was too low brow for the dude. He preferred to enter a crystal-chandeliered hotel dining room, or especially his favourite New York restaurant, Delmonico's, and order wine for the company. Even if it cost ten times Sullivan's average 'round', it was money well spent in cultivating his Gentleman Jim character. He was making $2,000 a week. Brady claimed that their hotel bills while on tour with the play averaged $1,000 a week. 'The money went out in bucketfuls, but it was coming in by tankfuls, so it didn't matter,' he said.

On its initial tour, *Gentleman Jack* was a knockout. Turnstiles clicked merrily as audiences flocked to see the man who whipped John L. Newspaper critics were magnanimous enough to highlight the strengths of his performance and play down his shortcomings. In Cincinnati, Ohio, the *Enquirer*'s critic was much taken with Corbett's 'graceful and easy manner' and said he looked more like someone accustomed to the footlights for several years than merely a few weeks. But the writer had some reservations. Jim's articulation could be improved and his voice was not strong enough for everyone to pick up what he said. The *Boston Evening Transcript*, while observing that he lacked the polish of a trained actor, said he was 'refreshingly free from rant' and played his part with conviction.

The plot of *Gentleman Jack* was neatly summarised by the *New York Herald* prior to its first Manhattan engagement in November:

> The play is in five scenes, the first showing the campus at Princeton, the second the private rooms of a banker, the third the Madison Square Garden Roof Garden, the fourth the pugilist's training quarters at Asbury Park, and the fifth the Olympic Club in New Orleans. Mr Corbett plays the part of a bank clerk, and he and the heavy villain are in love with the same girl. The villain robs the bank and places the blame on Jack, who loses his position. The villain then sends to England for Charlie Twitchell, the English pugilist, and Jack is badgered into a match. He is pressed for money to bind the agreement and, at the right moment, his sweetheart appears and furnishes him

with the necessary capital. The play ends with Twitchell's defeat and the heavy villain's eternal disgrace.

The character of Charlie Twitchell was an obvious caricature of the leading English heavyweight Charlie Mitchell, who had twice fought Sullivan and would later challenge Corbett for the title. Twitchell's introduction into the play and his subsequent defeat at the hands of the hero was a blatant appeal to the American chauvinism that was rampant during the 1890s, emphasised by Sullivan and Corbett when they spoke of the importance of 'keeping the championship in America'. Brady satisfied his own love of the spotlight, while saving on the cost of hiring an extra actor, by playing the principal actor's father-in-law.

The usually hard-to-please New York critics were agreeably surprised at Corbett the actor. The *Dramatic Mirror* said he had 'a strong and intelligent face, a sympathetic and clear voice, a figure that is athletic, and not suggestive of his original profession, an easy and dignified demeanour, and a naturalness and simplicity of gesture and deportment. He shows no signs of becoming an actor of any great power, but he has a charm that is separate from his celebrity in the prize ring'.

The Sun noted Corbett's easy manner, complimenting him on speaking his lines 'in clear, pleasant tones, and he was not un-mindful of the proper inflections'. Not quite so convinced was the *Herald*: 'Mr Corbett may be able as a fighter to knock out anything that comes in front of him, but as an actor he is rather handicapped. … Mr Corbett can act a little – a very little.'

Jim's rawness as a stage performer was revealed in his awkwardness when he was required to walk across the stage and turn back while speaking. Professor Alan Woods, of the Department of Theatre, Ohio State University, referred to this lack of finesse in an article he wrote for the North American Society for Sports History's journal in 1976:

> The sort of physical movement on the stage required here – a cross ending with a turn – is hardly complicated; if Corbett found it difficult, that implies (when coupled with his occasionally indistinct articulation) that the Champion was little more than an amateur on stage, carefully blocked by Brady with as little movement as possible. His inexperience probably resulted in under acting; most of the contemporary comments during Corbett's first tour (1892–93) refer to his naturalness, his easiness, or his freedom from melodramatic ranting, all of which

could be taken to mean that the boxer was a talented actor. In this context, however, they rather imply that Corbett's performance was minimal and that the new Champion was acceptable primarily because he was the Champion, not because of his acting ability.

At least Corbett played his role with considerable more subtlety and conviction than did John L. Sullivan in *Honest Hearts and Willing Hands*. The Boston Strong Boy delivered his lines in the same roaring voice as when bragging to bar-room customers how he could 'lick any son-of-a-bitch in the house'. Not that much more was expected of him. Sullivan's popularity, his brawn, and the reinforcement of his image as a patriotic, hard-drinking pugilist were enough to satisfy admirers who flocked to see him play the lead role in this and other dramas. Although, as Woods pointed out, John L. 'proved that theatregoers would pay in large numbers to see a champion boxer speak lines and woo heroines in addition to simply displaying his muscles, it remained for Corbett to combine the appeal of boxer, actor and matinee idol'.

Sullivan and Corbett were not the first ringmen to take to the stage. The possibility of fighters supplementing their earnings in the acting business was first realised in 1870 by Jem Mace, former bare-knuckle champion of England and claimant to the world title. Mace, who would spar with Corbett when Jim was in London with *Gentleman Jack*, played Charles the Wrestler in Shakespeare's *As You Like It*. Other prominent boxers who paraded their acting talents, such as they were, for audiences during the late 1890s included Jack McAuliffe and Bob Fitzsimmons.

Though *Gentleman Jack* netted a handsome $150,000 profit in its first season, its star risked losing public support through a sequence of incidents in 1893 that did little to enhance his 'gentlemanly' image. Maybe he missed the opportunity to get rid of his aggressive instincts by not having a fight throughout the year, but he stirred up quite a bit of animosity by playing the bully. Jim Daly, his regular sparring partner, walked out because of Corbett's rough treatment, which left him with two broken ribs. Despite repeated pleas from Daly, the champion refused to ease up when they had the gloves on.

More unwisely, he got into a public spat with the sports editor of an Omaha paper. Corbett objected to Sandy Griswold's contention that he was afraid to defend his title against Peter Jackson. He confronted the scribe and demanded an apology. Griswold said he was not obliged to explain his opinions and that he would not be intimidated by bullying tactics. A furious Corbett shouted, 'You're a liar if you say I won't fight Jackson. I can whip him any day. He won't fight me. Why do you stand up for an Australian nigger against an American?'

He offered to put up $1,000 there and then if the newspaperman would set up a match with Jackson. By now, a policeman had been called to the scene. He managed to calm down Corbett after advising him that his conduct was objectionable to some ladies who were nearby.

Gentleman Jim's moody nature was best summed up by a theatrical friend: 'One might spend weeks trying to find a more genial companion – when he likes you. When he doesn't, you are apt to appreciate the situation suddenly.'

If Bill Brady thought his man's appearance at the Chicago World's Fair would be a valuable public relations exercise, as well as raking in some handy cash, he was in for a rude awakening. Jim was booked to box a series of exhibitions at the fair, which ran from May to October. On two occasions, in rows over women, he was lucky to escape with his life.

'The female of the species raised more sand over Jim Corbett than I ever saw raised over any matinee idol,' said Brady. 'They got in our hair, they clogged our mail, they made themselves the worst nuisance possible ... but we were cashing in too, and don't forget it.'

One romantic adventure, with a woman called Hattie Clark, erupted into violence when her bookmaker boyfriend, Max Blumenthal, saw Corbett's photograph on her dressing table. A showdown with the champion resulted in a shot being fired by Blumenthal. It missed.

Corbett was not so lucky in another confrontation with a rival for a woman's affections. With lots of time on his hands between exhibition stints, Jim took to admiring the attractions at the World Fair – especially a pretty, red-headed colleen on the Irish stand. A member of the Sudanese delegation also fancied the girl and he feared Corbett was about to ruin his chances. His jealousy came to a head at the restaurant where the fair's personnel gathered after the gates closed for the day. Corbett and the girl were sitting together at a table when the irate Sudanese, ignoring her companion, demanded to know where he stood with his would-be lover. Corbett jumped to his feet and, after an exchange of angry words, a knife flashed and Jim was stabbed in the shoulder. Just as quickly, the champion floored his rival with a punch to the jaw. With different nationalities taking sides in the row, it looked like a full-scale riot might break out. Corbett and Brady decided the wisest move was to hightail it out of town.

While the various sideshows kept Gentleman Jim's name in the spotlight, if not always favourably, he couldn't lose sight of what had made him an attraction in the first place. If his theatrical bookings and boxing exhibitions were to maintain their lucrativeness, he had to pay attention to his main role – as heavyweight champion of the world. Demands were growing for him to defend his title. And there was no shortage of waiting challengers.

CHAPTER 11

Mitchell gets him 'too damn mad'

The field of leading contenders included the Australian, Frank 'Paddy' Slavin, Peter Maher, the Irish champion, and the two Englishman Charlie Mitchell and Bob Fitzsimmons. Oddly, there wasn't an American thought worthy of taking the opposite corner. Fitz, already in the bad books for hammering Corbett's friend, Jack 'Nonpareil' Dempsey, to capture the world middleweight title, had further annoyed Jim by calling to his dressing room after the Sullivan benefit and demanding first crack at the heavyweight prize.

'Corbett, I can lick you,' he declared, but was curtly told, 'Beat it, you freak'.

Peter Jackson, still smarting over the unsatisfactory outcome of his marathon duel with Corbett, also threw down the gauntlet, but reports of his heavy drinking and neglect of training did not suggest he was ready to renew acquaintances with his great rival. Nevertheless, Jim signed an agreement to face Jackson for $10,000 a side, but the match fell through.

The most vociferous of those in line for a crack at the title was Mitchell. A boisterous character, by all accounts, the Englishman had set out to insult Corbett at every turn. His first chance had come when Jim boxed an exhibition at Miner's Bowery Theatre in New York before he became champion. Mitchell openly challenged him to a fight there and then. Jim refused to be goaded into a street brawl and turned to walk away. Charlie, whose vocabulary of swear-words was considerable, directed such a vitriolic mouthful at Corbett that Jim had to be restrained from striking him. An enterprising

75

newspaperman who witnessed the incident was delighted with his 'exclusive'. He reported that Mitchell had challenged Corbett on the spot and that the American had 'turned yellow'. Mitchell's own colourful version of the encounter was that Corbett 'sneaked away after I called him a cur, then returned with a gang armed with swords and revolvers'. But the gang was no braver than Corbett and backed off rather than tackle him, boasted the Englishman.

The incident still rankled with Corbett when he became champion and he told Brady that he wanted Mitchell as his first challenger. The Englishman's backer, Squire Abingdon Baird, a wealthy theatrical entrepreneur whose productions regularly featured Lillie Langtry, the renowned 'Jersey Lily', made a formal offer of a winner-take-all contest, with a sidestake of $10,000. Corbett accepted and the two sides met at the offices of the *New York World*. Mitchell used the opportunity to unleash another verbal assault on the champion. An enraged Corbett was ready to have it out with his tormentor there and then, but wiser heads prevailed and the two were kept apart. Brady was so incensed by the challenger's bad manners that he wagered $2,000 to $1,000 that Mitchell wouldn't even show up for the fight.

Numerous attempts to stage the fight fell through, until the Duval Athletic Club in Jacksonville, Florida, made a successful bid. Its purse offer of $20,000 would be supplemented by a $5,000 side-stake by each man. The date was set for 25 January 1894. But, as the fighters completed training and the last nails were hammered into the specially-built arena, State Governor Henry L. Mitchell dropped a bombshell. He stated his disapproval of the contest and threatened to call out the militia, if necessary, to stop it. Brady, convinced Florida laws were flexible enough to allow the fight to go ahead, hired lawyers to clear the way. It was not until the night before the fight that the Supreme Court handed down a verdict in favour of the promoters, effectively blocking any action by the Governor. Unfortunately, the bad publicity and the late court decision caused many out-of-town fans to stay away. The arena, situated on the old Firefield race track, six miles outside Jacksonville, had a capacity of 10,000, but only about 2,000 paid in.

Corbett's concentration on the job had not been helped by a message he got from his brother Harry shortly before the fight. So confident was Jim of dismissing Mitchell easily that he had advised Harry, 'Bet your socks on it'. He soon learned, to his horror, that he had expressed his conviction too strongly. His brother would face financial ruin if the result went the wrong way. Harry, with backing from Jim, operated Corbett's Cafe, a saloon and betting parlour, at 30 Ellis Street, off Market Street, in San Francisco. He told his astonished brother that he had bet every dime he owned, plus a substantial sum he had borrowed, on Jim's success. In his dressing room, minutes before the fight, the champion was worrying, 'My God, Harry will go broke if I lose.'

Viewed from today, the Corbett vs Mitchell clash seems an odd pairing. Jim, six feet, one and a half inches tall and weighing thirteen stone, six pounds (184 pounds), might look puny beside the behemoths who bestride the heavyweight division a century later, but he was almost five inches taller and twenty-four pounds heavier than the challenger. It was truly a heavyweight against a middleweight.

Despite his physical disadvantages, Mitchell was a worthy opponent for any heavyweight of his era. He had proved it by giving John L. Sullivan a fright – twice. In their first meeting, under Marquis of Queensberry rules in New York in 1883, the Englishman, forty pounds lighter than the Boston Strong Boy, knocked down the champion for the first time in his career. He was made pay for his effrontery by getting clobbered in the third round. When they met again, five years later, it was under London Prize Ring rules, with Sullivan's bare-knuckle championship at stake. The fight took place in freezing rain on Baron Rothschild's estate at Chantilly, in France, and dragged on for three hours and ten minutes before being declared a draw. Mitchell survived the thirty-nine rounds it lasted by back-pedalling furiously and dropping to the turf whenever he was cornered. This was a common tactic in the era of bare-fist combat. Rounds, which had no time limit, ended when one man touched down. He then had the benefit of half a minute's rest before returning to 'scratch' (a line drawn in the centre of the ring).

Mitchell, born in Birmingham of Irish parents in 1861, had his first bare-knuckle fight at sixteen for £5 a side. Regarded as a plucky and clever boxer, he lost only once in his early ring outings – to a man who outweighed him by ninety-one pounds. He held Jack Burke, one of Corbett's victims, to a draw. The fight was interrupted by police after an hour and a quarter and both boxers ended up in jail for six weeks. After winning a middleweight competition in London, then adding a heavyweight prize, Mitchell left for America in 1883. He dispatched Mike Cleary in three rounds on his US debut and was acclaimed, outlandishly, by the *Police Gazette* as 'the greatest pugilist ever seen in this or any other country'. In between his two tussles with Sullivan, he fought Jack Burke another four times. Like their first match, all were declared draws. The most amazing contest of Mitchell's career was when he met Jem Mace in 1890 for the heavyweight championship of England. Charlie was twenty-nine years old. His opponent was fifty-eight. Mace, who had first won the championship in 1861, the year of Mitchell's birth, did well to last into the third round.

The widely-reported barracking of Corbett by Mitchell, together with the international flavour to the match, added greatly to public interest in the showdown. Up to two hours before the contest, efforts were still being made to stop it taking place. The officer in charge of the militia threatened to arrest the principals and disperse the crowd. Bill Brady, flourishing the court injunction allowing the fight to go ahead, persuaded the officer and his men to withdraw.

Jacksonville was abuzz with excitement as the hour of the big fight drew near. Saloons were packed with fight fans debating the respective merits of their favourites. Hotels cashed in by putting up their prices. Hack drivers also upped their charges to take patrons to the arena. Tickets for the bout sold for $25.

Corbett entered the ring as a two-to-one favourite. He was attended by his manager, plus Billy Delaney, John Donaldson, Jack 'Nonpareil' Dempsey and William McMillan, with Ted Foley as his timekeeper. Mitchell was accompanied by his father-in-law, 'Pony' Moore, and two prominent pugilists, Tom Allen and Steve O'Donnell. Bat Masterson was the Englishman's timekeeper. 'Snapper' Garrison, one of America's top jockeys, was the club's official timekeeper.

If Mitchell hadn't done enough to get under the champion's skin with his pre-fight jibes, he further antagonised him by keeping him waiting for ten minutes after Jim stepped between the ropes. When he finally arrived and walked to the centre of the ring to receive last-minute instructions from the referee, 'Honest' John Kelly, he still hadn't finished his diatribe. As Nat Fleischer described it, he 'called the Californian every foul epithet that his wide command of Cockney Billingsgate could suggest, reflecting on Jim's probable ancestry, raking him with language that would have made a hobo blush'.

Corbett kept his mouth shut while the challenger abused him, but inwardly he was fuming and raring to give the challenger the father-and-mother of a beating. 'No shaking hands,' he snapped at the referee.

As soon as the gong sounded, he sprang across the ring like a tiger and swung with both hands as Mitchell backed away. This was a new Corbett, one the fans had not seen before. Gone was the careful sizing-up of an opponent, the explorative left jabs, the fancy footwork. This was a Corbett venting his pent-up anger and all out to smash his antagonist to oblivion as quickly as possible. Mitchell's reaction to the champion's initial rush was to duck away, then grin and quip, 'Hello, Jim, started already?'

It wasn't just Corbett's temper, however, that drove him into an attacking mode. He believed that, with his considerable height and weight advantages, he had little to fear from the Englishman's counter-punches. Yet he was made to pay for his impetuousness when Mitchell met his next attack with a stinging left jab that split his lip. It was first blood to the challenger, and the first bets were paid out. Corbett, in his memoirs, surprisingly conceded that Charlie had the better of the opening round.

Resuming the offensive in the second round, Corbett rushed his rival to the ropes and knocked him down with a flurry of punches. Mitchell got to his feet at 'four', but went down again without being hit. He stayed on his knees until the count reached 'nine'. Later, Corbett claimed that a blow he sank into Mitchell's body in this round was the hardest punch he ever landed. 'I thought I had torn his ribs away from the cartilage,' he said.

Even while down, Charlie kept up his invective. The irate champion shouted to the referee, 'Count faster'. Losing his cool completely, he pushed the referee aside and struck the kneeling boxer on the side of the head. It was an obvious foul and one that could have cost Corbett his world title. As the gong sounded amid uproar, his seconds dived into the ring and directed him back to his corner. 'Honest' John Kelly dismissed the Mitchell corner's demand for the champion's disqualification. He figured that, as Charlie had also committed a foul by going down without taking a blow, it was now 'evens'. He did, however, lecture Corbett in his corner that he must control his temper.

Mitchell responded very slowly to the gong for the third round. He looked shaken and despondent. Corbett sprang at him and drove him into a corner. A heavy blow brought blood gushing from the Englishman's nose and a follow-up left to the jaw floored him. Charlie took his time in rising, to the further annoyance of the champion, who had to be restrained by the referee as he sought to get at Mitchell. As soon as the challenger was on his feet, Corbett smashed him down again. In those days, there was no requirement for a fighter to go to a neutral corner when he scored a knockdown. It was perfectly legitimate for him to stand beside the referee as he counted, then strike his rival immediately his gloves were off the floor. But Jim didn't even want to wait that long. He wanted to finish off his hated rival. As the referee struggled to push him away, Corbett's cornermen jumped into the ring to give the official a hand. This action might have incurred the champion's dismissal, but the referee decided they were acting in his own interest and let them get away with it. Once more, the brave challenger staggered to his feet, completely at Corbett's mercy. Jim measured him for probably the hardest punch he threw in his entire career, a terrific right that crashed against his jaw. Mitchell toppled forward onto his face, out to the world. Without even waiting for the count to be completed, Corbett strolled to his corner and asked his seconds to remove his gloves.

The victor, now cool and collected, bowed in response to the cheers of the crowd and embraced his manager and seconds. 'Honest' John Kelly, who had been holding the $20,000 purse money, showed Corbett the roll of banknotes and told him he could have it as soon as he wished. Together with the $5,000 sidestake, it was nice pickings for what had not been a difficult night's work. Brady's only grumble was that he had to pay $2,000 to Mitchell for turning up, in fulfilment of their wager.

Mitchell, when he recovered, was gracious in his comments on the winner. 'Corbett is the cleverest man I ever saw,' he said, 'and his style was a complete surprise to me. America has reason to be proud of the greatest fighter who ever stood in a ring. If he keeps his health, he will never be beaten.'

Asked about his tactics to get the champion mad, he smiled rue-fully and quipped, 'The trouble is I got him too damn mad.'

The morning after the fight, the principals were arrested and charged with taking part in an illegal prize fight. Bonds were signed to secure their freedom. It was three months before the case came to court and it was all over inside ten minutes. Jim knew he was home and dry when one of the jury members gave him a big wink. All concerned were found not guilty.

Despite their mutual animosity, Corbett and Mitchell got together a month after their title fight to box a four-round exhibition at Madison Square Garden. It was a charity occasion in aid of the *New York World*'s Free Bread Fund. Hard times had hit the country and up to 125,000 people were out of work in New York City alone. Admission to the arena was just one dollar and it was packed to 'breathing capacity'. As well as the Corbett-Mitchell sparring match, there were performances by Attilla, the German strong man, wrestling bouts, and a contest between a giant black man and a boxing kangaroo. William Muldoon, the famous wrestler and trainer of champion boxers, including John L. Sullivan, remarked that the animal put on a better boxing display than many fighters he had watched.

CHAPTER 12

Backing a loser in Britain

If there had been any lingering bitterness towards Corbett for taking over John L. Sullivan's mantle as world heavyweight champion, it was well dissipated by now.

His acceptance as a worthy successor to the Boston Strong Boy was underlined by his easy dismissal of Mitchell. The tumultuous reception he received all along the east coast, where John L. had been king, on the trip from Jacksonville to New York was conclusive proof that all had been forgiven. At every railway station, huge crowds gathered to cheer Jim to the echo. When the train reached Pennsylvania station in Jersey City, an estimated 5,000 demanded that he leave his carriage and take part in celebrations. He was asked to make a speech, but merely responded by doffing his hat. Bill Brady asked that they be excused as Jim was due to appear in an exhibition match at Madison Square Garden that evening.

Some 7,500 fans paid two dollars a head to pack the Garden and the cheers rang out for fully five minutes after the champion made his appearance. Throwing off his Ulster (a long, loose overcoat of a rough cloth that originated in Belfast), Corbett made a short speech of thanks, which sparked off another prolonged outburst of applause. After his three rounds of sparring with Dan Creedon, he had to battle his way to the dressing room through a wildly enthusiastic throng of back-slappers and well-wishers. The evening raised $10,000 for charity.

Bill Brady, eager to capitalise on the champion's increased popularity, organised a second tour with *Gentleman Jack*. The play was booked all over the United States and drew capacity houses in all the big cities. Its appeal was enhanced by Corbett's improvement as an actor and his manager's 'beefing up' of the big scene. In the original version, the last act, in which the hero defeated 'Charlie Twitchell', champion of England, was quite brief. By 1894, however, the scene was expanded. The 'Twitchell' sub-plot was ditched in favour of a showdown between 'Gentleman Jack' and 'Bat Houston, the Texas Bruiser'. Brady had recognised that it was the Corbett-Sullivan fight which was most in people's minds, not Jim's clash with Mitchell. Thus, the last act was a recreation of the New Orleans contest, not the Mitchell bout, though this was more recent. The elaborate scene included a twenty-four foot ring in the centre of the stage, a referee, timekeeper, seconds and bottle holders. Most impressive of all was the use of several hundred 'spectators' on three sides of the ring. These 'fans' were not paid actors. Not even the play's financial bonanza would justify such an outlay. At every stop on the tour, Brady was able to convince enough locals how privileged they were to get such a close-up view of the world heavy-weight champion. They willingly lent their services, cheering and waving their arms on cue, free of charge. The new realism went down a treat with the audiences.

If the Americans had taken Corbett to their hearts, thought Brady, maybe it was time to see what the rest of the world thought of him. Gentleman Jim, as *Gentleman Jack*, was bound for Europe. Brady went on ahead to arrange the bookings. Corbett and the rest of the cast set sail from New York on the *Feurst Bismarck* on 12 April 1894.

Jim persuaded his parents to make the trip with him, as he knew how dearly they longed to visit Ireland. They had not seen the land of their birth since they left some forty years earlier. Jim took great delight in having the means to give them such a treat. He told his father to treat him as a 'pal' rather than a son and introduced him to some lively poker sessions on board the ship. The cagey old man would not risk any more than a dollar a game. If the stakes went higher, he would lay down his hand. On arrival in London, Jim organised a terrific surprise for his father. He had invited Pat's younger brother, the Rev. James Corbett, after whom Jim was named, to London. The brothers met in the hotel dining room, threw their arms around each other and wept with joy. All that Pat had remembered of his brother was that he had red hair. The future priest had been ten years old when Pat emigrated to America.

For Kate, Jim's mother, there was also a happy reunion, with a woman she had befriended on the boat to America all those years ago. The family had so often heard about 'Miss Wilkinson' and it was beyond Kate's dreams that they would meet again some day. It turned out that her friend, now Mrs James Cotamore, was living in London, where her husband was the scenic artist at Henry Irving's Lyceum Theatre. She got to hear the Corbetts were in town and made her way to the hotel. Both women were short and stout and Jim recalled people in the dining room 'giggling at the sight of these two little roly-poly old ladies embracing each other and crying from joy'.

Unfortunately, *Gentleman Jack* was not the hit Brady and company had envisaged. While quite well patronised in London, it was a flop outside the capital. The reason it did not make a bigger impact is clear. Corbett's name was well known – his ring triumphs had been well reported – but he was little more than a curiosity to the British public. Crowds gathered wherever he put in an appearance, but only when they could gawk at him for free. When it came to handing over money at the box office, they would have wanted to see James J. Corbett, the established boxing master, not Corbett, the novice actor.

For the first two weeks of its London run – it opened at the Drury Lane Theatre on 21 April – ticket sales were high. They fell off considerably throughout the third and final week. As in America, it was the spectacular final act that won applause and diverted attention from the drama's general mediocrity. *The Times'* anonymous critic noted that Corbett was 'natural and unpretentious on the stage, and not without some refinement of manner ... his acting was quite good enough for the rest of the company, though that is perhaps not extravagant praise'. As for the piece itself, the reviewer ridiculed its descent, by the end of the third act, into a kind of variety show, with two of the leading artistes, Florrie West and Robert Gaylor, performing 'turns' at the Madison Square Roof Garden. By then, the story, such as it was, had been forgotten. Corbett's display of bag-punching pleased the audience, observed the writer, but this and the final fight scene 'might find a more congenial atmosphere at a music hall than on the boards of the historic theatre in Drury Lane'.

Other papers were more scathing. The *Illustrated Sporting and Dramatic News* described the play as 'utter rubbish'. Its only redeeming feature was Corbett's 'astounding' dexterity at sparring and punching the ball. The reviewer's main advice to patrons was to arrive shortly before ten o'clock, just in time for the last two acts, having the good fortune to miss what went before. The *Sporting Times* dismissed it as 'altogether unworthy of comment or discussion as a stage play'. The *Licensed Victuallers' Mirror* said it would not bother itself describing 'the so-called play, which is plotless', but it was agreeably surprised at 'Jem' Corbett: 'They came expecting to find a puffed-up braggart, and saw a fine, handsome man, of modest demeanour, and really, compared to the rest of the cast, not such a bad actor at all.'

Kindest of the critics was Clement Scott of the *Daily Telegraph*. While passing over the play, 'for it was not a play at all', he conceded that the people got what they wanted – the chance to see, in person, the man who had defeated Sullivan and Mitchell. The fight scene, with its tier upon tier of cheering spectators on stage, was 'nothing less than marvellous'. The great secret of its success was that the actions of the 'fans' were so natural. Brady had once again done his bit, sending hundreds of free tickets to pubs and sporting clubs, promising the bearer free admission and the opportunity to share the stage with the world champion. The staged battle was realistic enough to keep the unpaid extras engrossed. Brady, acting as referee, directed the crowd with pre-arranged hand signals, making sure they would cheer and boo at the appropriate moments. Scott was totally captivated by the final scene:

> The address calling for fair play, the description of the combatants, the weighing of the gloves, the warning of the men, the sound of the gong to start the rounds, were all as lifelike as possible, and the excitement may be guessed when Corbett went at it hammer and tongs – Corbett with his greyhound movements and his tremendous reach – until the fatal moment, when Bat Houston of Texas was floored, and Corbett pronounced champion of the world as the curtain fell. No horse-race or fire or shipwreck on the stage was ever so accurate and realistic, and in a measure so effective, as this prize-fight.

Brady was so delighted with the *Telegraph* review that he paid for it to be re-printed in the *New York Dramatic Mirror*, carefully under-lining the best bits. Like any publicity agent worth his salt, he neglected to pass on the less favourable notices to the American public. The bad reviews, however, took their toll. The London run finished with a net loss of £1,500.

Years later, when Corbett had turned stage raconteur, he would tell the story of how a trick played on the Drury Lane theatregoers backfired. Someone, probably Brady, thought it would be a good idea to plant a 'challenger' in the audience. Robert Gaylor, who was not due on stage until later, was given the extra role. At the appropriate moment he jumped to his feet and loudly challenged Corbett to a fight. Unfortunately, his acting was so convincing that a group of burly spectators grabbed him from his seat, tore his clothes and gave him a rough going-over. Other members of the cast had to dive to his rescue, while it was announced from the stage that the 'challenge' was not meant to be taken seriously. A badly-shaken Gaylor refused to repeat the performance.

Two regular members of the audience during the London run wouldn't hear a bad word said about the play, or its leading star. They were Corbett's parents. Several times Jim booked them for other West End presentations, but the tickets would go to waste. All they wanted was to see their beloved son, night after night.

After its London engagement, *Gentleman Jack* moved on to week-long bookings in the provinces. It did quite well in Liverpool and Edinburgh, but audiences were poor in Sheffield, Newcastle-on-Tyne, Birmingham, Manchester, Leeds and Glasgow. When Jim stepped outside his hotel in Liverpool, police had to be called to make way for him through the crowd. Typically, the immense public interest in the man did not translate into healthy bookings at the city's Royal Court Theatre. The local *Daily Post* lambasted the play as 'almost entirely without merit', though 'Mr Corbett comes through the histrionic ordeal with flying colours'.

In Birmingham Corbett blotted his copybook with the local population by getting involved in a street altercation. It was American Independence Day and Jim was out walking with a woman member of the theatrical company. She wore an American flag in her coat. A passer-by made an insulting remark and Jim struck him. What might have been accepted as an act of chivalry if someone else had done the deed was condemned as the act of a bully. The unwritten code was that world heavyweight boxing champions didn't hit anybody outside the ring.

He further antagonised a group of influential townspeople by refusing to accept an invitation to a rat pit. Boxing might be considered barbaric, but the idea of watching a snarling terrier tearing a hundred rats to pieces was even less his idea of 'sport'. *Gentleman Jack*, after eight performances in Charlie Mitchell's hometown, only took in £300.

It was the same disappointing story elsewhere. Everyone wanted to see him, but too few were prepared to shell out cash for the privilege. He walked on stage at the Tyne Theatre, Newcastle-on-Tyne, to rapturous applause and proved himself 'a player of many good qualities', said the *Daily Journal*. The drama itself, noted the paper, was 'rubbish'. Less vicious was the rival *Daily Chronicle*, which labelled it an 'amusing' piece, 'though not to be judged by the ordinary standard of dramas'. The play was obviously contrived as a showpiece for its star, who, the paper observed, was tall and handsome and 'not in the least resembling the typical bullet-headed bruiser'. The *Edinburgh Evening News* didn't pull any punches, lashing the drama as 'a large tax on public patience'.

Corbett, back in London for a poorly-supported stint in Islington, took a break from the boards to spar a couple of rounds with Jem Mace, the last champion of England under the old London Prize Ring rules. Mace was known as the 'father of the modern school of British scientific boxing' and he was anxious to compare his skills with the American master. Though now sixty-three, Jem was lively enough to enjoy the session. 'Young man,' he told Corbett, 'you are the most scientific boxer I have ever seen.' Jim graciously accepted the compliment. Coming from one so revered as Mace, it really meant something. The old-timer presented Jim with a gold-headed cane and told him, 'I expect you'll keep the championship until this stick wears out'.

Though they finished up with a £5,000 loss on the British visit, Corbett and Brady were consoled with the generous reception they had received in most places. The champion's neat appearance and good manners put him a league ahead of some of the uncouth brawlers England had produced. Charlie Mitchell, for one, hadn't won many fans for the way he threw himself about, his foul language, and his nasty habit of bashing policemen on the head with his cane. He overstepped the mark when one 'bobby', in trying to arrest him, had his skull fractured when the stick came crashing down. That little bit of 'fun' cost the Birmingham boxer fourteen months in jail.

If Corbett's British sojourn had proved a costly experience, a trip to France more than made up the deficit. A series of exhibition bouts at the famous Folies Bergère in Paris reaped $10,000 over eight days. Jim's displays of boxing skills against Jim Daly delighted Parisians, though boxing in this form was unfamiliar to them. The popular French contact sport was *la savate*, in which feet as well as fists were used. It would be quite some years before France would become one of the leading European boxing nations and would produce fine champions like Charles Ledoux, Eugene Criqui and Georges Carpentier. Arrangements were made for Corbett to go three rounds with the national *la savate* champion, Charlemont, but the Frenchman pulled out at the last minute. Bill Brady gave a different version of events. According to the showman's memoirs, the mixed match did take place and Corbett, after having his face bloodied by a kick from Charlemont, laid his aggressor out cold with a right to the jaw. It made a good story, but Brady once again allowed his imagination to stray into fantasy.

Corbett and his manager were overwhelmed by the generous reception they got from the French. The newspapers carried lots of details of the champion's appearances, one headline extolling him as 'the world's greatest fighter'. He was honoured to accept an invitation to dine with President Carnot, who, that same year, would be assassinated by an Italian anarchist at Lyon.

As word of his French success spread throughout the continent, Jim was offered engagements in Berlin, Barcelona, St Petersburg, Rome and Brussels. The most flattering invitation was to spar an exhibition with Leopold II, King of the Belgians, a keen sportsman and competent amateur boxer. Unfortunately, Corbett had to decline all the offers, as he had theatrical dates to fulfil back in the United States.

CHAPTER 13

Don't hit him until you're in focus!

Before heading home Jim undertook the last leg of his European tour – to Ireland. His parents had already visited the 'Old Country' and had returned to America by the time he arrived, but his wife had now joined him.

Jim had invited Ollie over with great reluctance. They had not been getting along for quite some time and it was evident their marriage was heading for the rocks. Corbett only had his wife with him to appease his parents. The pretence of the happy couple was staged for the benefit of the deeply religious Corbett family in Ireland. Any hint of a marital rift would have led to embarrassing questions and unwanted counselling on their Catholic duties. Photographs taken in County Mayo show a grim-faced Jim, while Ollie, at least, managed a weak smile as she 'watched the birdie'.

Not helping the champion's mood was the fact that, unlike other places on other occasions, he was unable to avail himself of any extramarital activity. The *Tuam Herald*, commenting a year later on Corbett's 'success as a lady killer', recalled an interesting encounter with an English actress while he was in Ireland. The woman, apparently, was infatuated with him, to such an extent that she organised an introduction and presented him with no less than six photographs of herself. Each was signed 'To my own darling Jim'. To the chagrin of the newspaper's readers, no doubt, it was more intent on castigating Corbett for 'boycotting' Tuam in favour of Ballinrobe than it was in following up the story of the prizefighter and the actress.

Although Tuam had a special affection for the Corbett clan – Jim's father and three of his uncles, Francis, John and Edward, had gone to school and grown up there – the town didn't cherish happy memories of a visit by Gentleman Jim's younger brother Jack a few years earlier. The boisterous young man, who found the town 'too tame', got into several fights and 'kicked up great ructions' at the Gurranes Races. It was with great relief that his Uncle Francis saw him off from Queenstown (now Cobh) for the trip home to America. (Jack later became a morphine addict and died, aged thirty-six, in Seattle, Washington, in December 1901.)

Some 10,000 people enthusiastically greeted Gentleman Jim on his arrival at Westland Row railway station in Dublin on 9 July 1894, but, if his manager is to be believed, they didn't show their support where it mattered most – at the box office. According to Brady, the opening performance of *Gentleman Jack* at the Queen's Theatre took in only £20. This claim is not borne out by the report in the *Freeman's Journal*, which said the house was packed to capacity. It was notable how many females were present, remarked the paper. Good attendances continued throughout the week-long run, even though ticket prices were double the normal rate. One thing that delighted Jim was the realisation that the Irish showed no animosity towards him for ending the career of the idolised John L. Sullivan. They seemed to accept that one fighting Irishman was as good as another.

Years later, Corbett told Nat Fleischer of how a ruse to divert attention from himself backfired, with amusing results. Aware that a band parade had been organised and that a committee of leading Dublin citizens was waiting to formally greet him, but unsure how he would be received by the general public, he sent his sparring partner, Con McVey, on ahead to 'test the water'. The crowd, unsure of what Jim looked like, took McVey to be the champion. They grabbed him, shoved him into a waiting carriage, unhitched the horses and drew the vehicle all the way to the Metropole Hotel in O'Connell Street. McVey, a burly six-footer, tried to explain he wasn't Corbett, but his protests couldn't be heard above the roar of the crowd. Accepting the situation, he sat back, lit a cigar and bowed gracefully to the adoring crowd as the carriage rolled along. Corbett, in the meantime, laughed his head off as he took a following cab, along with his wife. He did apologise to the welcoming committee over the mix-up and smoothed things out with the crowd by making a speech from the hotel balcony. All he had to do was remind them that his mother was from Dublin and his father from Galway (in fact, he was from Mayo but close to the county boundary with Galway) for the tumultuous cheers to assure him all was forgiven.

On the final night of the play's Dublin presentation, Corbett and Brady accepted an invitation to visit the Abbey Street offices of the *Freeman's Journal*. On entering the paper's composing room, they were greeted with a 'knockdown', the printing trade's long-established custom of welcoming VIPs by knocking together pieces of metal to create an almighty din. The American visitors were much impressed and expressed appreciation of their unique reception. As for the printers, they could always brag about the time they 'knocked down' the world heavyweight champion!

After Dublin, it was on to Belfast. Again a large crowd was waiting for Corbett's arrival at the Great Northern Railway station and another band of supporters was on hand to cheer him as he checked into the Grand Central Hotel. A packed house at the Theatre Royal patiently tolerated the play's first three acts, then broke into sustained applause at the champion's dextrous exhibition of ball-punching. 'It was well worth seeing on its own account', said the *Belfast News-Letter*. The play itself scarcely called for detailed criticism, observed the reviewer, but 'Mr Corbett's acting was distinctly good – modest and capable – and created a very favourable impression.'

There were further bookings of the play in Londonderry, Waterford, Limerick and Cork, but it was in Ballinrobe, his father's home town, that Jim's appearance created most excitement. The proceeds of the single presentation of *Gentleman Jack* were donated to his uncle, the Rev. James Corbett, parish priest at the nearby village of Partry. Father Jim had been delighted to accept a magnificent set of vestments from the champion's mother during her visit a short time before. Now, thanks to her son, he would be able to pay off the long-standing debt on the church building.

Special trains were run from Claremorris and Westport for the performance at Ballinrobe town hall on 23 July. The venue, with tickets priced from five shillings to two shillings, was packed to the rafters. Hundreds more, refused entry, had to content themselves with catching a glimpse of the champion as he arrived and left. The event raised enough money to build a three-foot high wall around the church grounds. A plaque attached to the wall acknowledged the champion's generosity. Father Corbett didn't think so kindly of his illustrious nephew two years later, when he heard he had been divorced. The irate priest ordered that the plaque be removed and cast into exterior darkness!

There are variations of the story of how exactly Father Jim vented his anger. On a trip to Ireland in recent years, Richard T. Corbett, of New Jersey, a distant relative of the boxer, interviewed Martin Gibbons, who was baptised by the priest in 1906. The old man's recollection was that the church gates were taken down. Certainly there is no sign of gates – or a plaque – at Partry church today. One story that can be discounted was that a stained glass window donated by the world champion was removed. Bearing the inscription 'Presented by James J. Corbett, USA', it is still intact, along with several similar windows donated by the priest himself.

The Rev. James Corbett was quite a remarkable character. A founder member of the Land League in County Mayo, he campaigned aggressively for justice for tenant farmers, who had few rights in relation to the land they farmed. The movement grew into a national organisation, leading to violent struggles between landlords and tenants before most of the wrongs were put right.

Born at Ballycusheen, in the parish of Kilmaine, where his father farmed forty acres on the Dalgan estate, James was only fourteen when he made his first stormy protest against oppressive landlordism. The Protestant Bishop of Tuam, Lord Plunkett, owned land which housed a Catholic school, run by the Christian Brothers. When the bishop wanted the building for another use and evicted the Brothers, young Corbett and a half-dozen of his schoolmates attacked the school, smashing all its windows and doors. Later, they watched gleefully as locals finished the job by burning it to the ground.

After he joined the priesthood, James was given a remote posting to the Aran Islands, which lie at the mouth of Galway Bay on the west coast of Ireland, where it was thought he couldn't get up to any mischief. It wasn't long before James found cause to take action against the hated absentee landlords. The granting of land was a common method of rewarding those who had helped the United Kingdom government. The islands had been given to two English women, who rarely visited their property, but left it in the care of a local baker. This agent was condemned as a 'souper', a term which grew out of the Great Famine, when Catholics were enticed to change their religion in return for soup and other desperately needed nourishment. The rebel priest encouraged the islanders not to buy the agent's bread. The authorities hit back by banning the import of any bread from the mainland. The dispute raged on for four months, until the priest finally got his way. The embargo was lifted. Father Corbett next turned his attention to a racket whereby islanders who collected seaweed were forced to sell it to the agent's factory at a much cheaper price than they could get on the open market. Again he was successful in getting justice, just as he was when he stopped the practice of 'duty work'. This required road workers on the landlords' estate to go without pay for several days each month. Father Jim made sure they got paid for every hour they toiled. When permission was refused for a school on Innishmaan, one of the three Aran islands, he went ahead and built it anyway.

Having earned the eternal gratitude of the islanders, he was transferred to the parish of Balla, in County Mayo. Here, and in subsequent postings, he continued to publicly denounce landlords who evicted tenants. His peak as an agrarian agitator was reached in Claremorris, where he became president of the local branch of the Land League.

Finally installed as parish priest at Partry, Father Corbett served as secretary to a commission which investigated the 'apparition' of the Virgin Mary at Knock in 1879. As a result of the commission's report, Knock became a major centre of pilgrimage for Catholics from all over the world. He also played a major role in a probe into the murder of five members of a family who occupied boycotted land in a remote part of County Galway, a case known as the Maamtrasna Massacre. The clergyman's strong influence with the local people and his fluency with the Irish language, which was more widely spoken than English in the area, helped secure the arrest and conviction of the killers.

Father Jim was seventy-four when he died on New Year's Day 1919. His grave, immediately next to the front door of Partry parish church, is marked by a large headstone 'erected by his devoted parishioners'.

On 26 July 1894 Gentleman Jim and his party sailed for home on the White Star liner *Majestic*. His arrival in New York was the signal for another great demonstration by admirers who thronged the pier. Bill Brady had gone ahead a week earlier to publicise the champion's return and to fill eager newspapermen's notepads with tales, many of them invented, of their adventures in Europe.

One story, that Corbett's generous gesture towards his uncle's church had earned him high commendation in the British House of Commons, appears to have no basis in fact. In both of Brady's autobiographies, he credited the remarks to John Redmond, the Parnellite Member for Waterford. Nat Fleischer, who knew Corbett well, said it was a different Irish MP, John Dillon, who made the laudatory speech. Both Members' statements on other matters are faithfully reported in *Hansard*, the official record of proceedings at Westminster, but Corbett is not mentioned. Redmond, or Dillon, might have sung the champion's praises elsewhere, but the House would have had more important things to debate than the doings of a boxing champion on tour in Ireland.

The most outrageous of Brady's gimmicks was the huge poster he had commissioned showing Corbett shaking hands with the British Prime Minister, William Gladstone, while gazed upon admiringly by Queen Victoria, the German Kaiser, the King of Italy, the Czar of Russia and other European royal personages and heads of state. Underneath the painting, which measured twenty-four feet across, were the words, 'James J. Corbett, Champion of the World, on his return from his triumphal tour of Europe'. It was prominently displayed wherever *Gentleman Jack* played on its resumed American run. The hoax was admitted by Corbett in *The Roar of the Crowd*: 'I never met a single one of these people.'

When all the bluster had run its course, it was down to the real business of what Corbett was all about. His fame was due to his status as heavyweight champion of the world, so when was he going to defend his title? During his three months' sojourn in Europe, a queue of contenders had formed. The main challenges came from his old rival Peter Jackson, hard-hitting Irishman Peter Maher, Kid McCoy, a tricky middleweight with heavyweight ambitions, and Bob Fitzsimmons, the reigning world middleweight champion. Fitz was the most persistent. He had been calling for a meeting with Corbett ever since being refused entry to the champion's dressing room after the Sullivan fight.

Of much more immediate interest to Corbett was the proposition put to him by the inventor Thomas Edison. Edison's machine, the kinetoscope, was causing much excitement by showing the first moving pictures. A fight, captured on film, would be ideal material as a public attraction. Corbett jumped at the idea. Having already made his mark in history as the first world heavyweight champion under Marquis of Queensberry rules, he was now going to take part in the first film of a fight. The egocentric pugilist would be able to see himself as others saw him, the supreme ring artist of the age in action in front of his own eyes.

No-one could be sure if the venture would work. The introduction of motion pictures, feared Edison, was a novelty that would soon wear off. His kinetoscope studio, built at his plant near Llewellyn Park, New Jersey, looked like something knocked together in an afternoon by a couple of kids let loose with a hammer and nails. Dubbed the Black Maria, the crude structure was covered with tar paper on the outside and painted black on the inside, so that actors stood out against the background. Swinging from a pivot post, the studio was manoeuvred to follow the sun, which shone through a large opening in the roof. Within a year of its invention, patrons were enjoying their first glimpses of moving pictures at Kinetoscope Parlors all over the United States.

To view the images, patrons had to drop a coin into a slot at the top of a cabinet, inside which a length of film revolved on spools. An electric light shone on the film, which was projected onto the end of the cabinet. Customers saw, through a peephole, a fifty-foot 'moving picture' that lasted less than a minute. The subjects of the initial films were simple – a baby being bathed, a dog munching a bone, dances and vaudeville turns – anything that showed movement. Who could resist a movie entitled *Fred Ott's Sneeze*? Ott, an Edison lab assistant, was noted for his uncontrollable sneezing, and his unfortunate affliction was put to good use by his boss.

Though Corbett and Peter Courtney made history as the first boxers to engage in a filmed fight, they were not the first ringmen to appear in a motion picture. A couple of obscure fighters, Mike Leonard and Jack Cushing, boxed a six-round exhibition for the camera on 15 June 1894, three months before the heavyweight bout. Each round lasted one minute, as that was all the camera could manage before re-loading. The ring was twelve feet square, so that all the action could be captured by the stationary camera. Leonard, slightly the better known of the pair, was paid $150 and Cushing got $50. The venture was not a commercial success, however. Each round was shown in a different 'peepshow' machine so, at ten cents per round, it cost sixty cents to see the whole exhibition bout. This was too costly for most customers, who opted to watch just one or two rounds.

It was clear to Edison's company that, to make the thing profitable, a real fight would have to be filmed. John L. Sullivan was first offered the job, but his demand for $25,000 was totally unrealistic.

Corbett showed a better business head than his old adversary by accepting a guarantee of $4,700 for the winner and $250 for the loser. No-one doubted who would have his hand raised. Courtney, though claiming to be the heavyweight champion of New Jersey, was a truck driver described by Brady as 'tenth rate'. Corbett, he said, 'could flatten him in ten seconds fast asleep, but with careful rehearsal he could be made to look like a fighter'.

As well as his purse for the fight, Jim signed a royalty agreement earning him $150 per week (later reduced to $50) from each Kinetoscope Parlor that featured the film. The countrywide showings went on for several years, even after film projection had caught on, and netted Corbett a grand total of over $20,000.

Corbett and Courtney squared off in the Edison Laboratory on 7 September. The New Jersey fighter wore calf-length tights, while Corbett favoured very brief trunks to facilitate his mobility. Though it was a straight contest, the fighters had to follow Edison's shouted instructions so that Corbett – the star of the show – would be shown to best advantage. In what would become the best Hollywood tradition, Corbett was repeatedly told, 'Keep your face to the camera, Jim', 'Hold up that right hand punch till you get him in the middle of the ring' and 'We don't want your back, Jim. Force him around so that you are facing the camera'.

The makers wanted a dramatic finish, so the champion was instructed to take it easy until the sixth round, when he should score a knockout. The first round, in which Corbett exhibited his speedy footwork and snappy left jab, lasted one and a half minutes. The cameraman found he could manage more film, so the subsequent rounds were stretched to two minutes. Rest periods were also of two minutes' duration, as it took that long to re-load the camera. Jim, as prone to exaggeration as his manager, claimed the enforced breaks each lasted up to half an hour. At any rate, the respites were welcomed by the boxers as the heat inside the primitive studio was stifling. A constantly grinning Corbett treated his opponent like a plaything, easing up whenever Courtney looking like keeling over. In the sixth round, on schedule, Jim cut loose and hammered the New Jersey champion against the ropes. A well-timed right to the jaw sent Courtney crashing for the count of 'ten'.

No sooner had the victor reached the railway station to head back to New York than he was accosted by the local sheriff, who had been tipped off that an illegal prize-fight had taken place. Not sure who it was he was supposed to arrest, the lawman asked Corbett for his identity. 'Why, don't you recognise me?' retorted Jim, putting on an affronted look, 'I'm Maurice Barrymore, the actor.' The sheriff, unwilling to show himself up by not knowing such a renowned performer, decided there were other crimes worth his urgent attention and left Corbett to board the train.

The showing of the Corbett-Courtney fight in Kinetoscope Parlors, though profitable, was not a complete success for a particular reason. Each of the peepshow machines could show only one of the six rounds. So most patrons, to save expense, opted to view the last round, containing the knockout, and ignored the rest. Nevertheless, the novelty whetted the public's appetite for more boxing showings as the movie industry grew in rapid strides from its humble beginnings. By 1895, Thomas Armat had developed the film projector, enabling cinemagoers to watch on large screens the exciting adventures – real and imaginary – of their heroes and heroines. Within two more years, Enoch Rector would expose 11,000 feet of film in recording Corbett against Bob Fitzsimmons, the first world championship fight ever filmed and the longest motion picture made until then of a single event.

For many years it was believed that no copy of the Corbett-Courtney film had survived. However, thanks to the vigilance of Jim Jacobs, a former US handball champion whose passionate hobby was collecting rare fight films, an amazing discovery was made in 1960. As Jacobs was heading for his sixth national four-wall title at the San Francisco Olympic Club, Corbett's old haunt, an old man sidled up to him after the third round match. 'Mr Jacobs,' he whispered, 'I hear you've been looking for a print of the Corbett-Courtney fight. Well, I've been saving one for the past fifty years.' A delighted Jacobs bought the nitrate film, painstakingly re-photographed it on modern, sprocketed stock and added it to his great collection at Turn of the Century Fights, Inc., the company he co-partnered with Bill Cayton.

Corbett's effortless disposal of Courtney did not satisfy fight fans' demands for a genuine test of the champion's ability. He would have to take on one of his main challengers if he was not to lose support – and see his earning power as a stage star fall away. According to his manager, Corbett had developed a real fear of losing his title. The newspapers noted that he repeatedly turned down challenges from Fitzsimmons, who, although a middleweight, was considered the most dangerous contender.

Brady hit on a ruse to stave off the threat to his man by promoting Steve O'Donnell, Jim's main sparring partner, as the man to beat

Fitzsimmons. He told Fitz he could have a shot at Corbett if he first defeated O'Donnell. While O'Donnell, an Australian based in America, was a useful boxer, he was no world beater.

In order to boost his protégé's prestige, Brady matched him with veteran Jake Kilrain, who had been outclassed by Corbett some years earlier. It looked an easy job, but Kilrain upset the applecart by holding O'Donnell to a draw. Though the Australian beat Kilrain in a re-match two months later, it took him twenty-one rounds to do so. Brady's stalling tactics had to be abandoned. Corbett entered into an agreement to defend his title against Fitzsimmons in New York. The champion did not attend the signing ceremony at the *New York Herald* building, but when Fitzsimmons berated Corbett for his absence, Brady somewhat rashly threatened to throw him out the window. Jim was furious when he heard about the challenger's insulting remarks. This would be a grudge fight, to be sure. Though the contract was signed on 11 October 1894, numerous problems got in the way of staging the fight. It was two and a half years after they put pen to paper before the bitter rivals faced each other in the ring.

CHAPTER 14

The lady in the box

The champion's 'Gentleman Jim' tag seemed a total misnomer in mid-1895, when intimate details of Corbett's tangled love life hit the newspaper columns. His marriage, on stormy waters for some time, finally crashed on the rocks. The man Ollie had eulogised as an 'even-tempered, gentle, considerate' husband had been exposed as a cheat and an adulterer. He left her to live openly with his lover Vera Stanwood, a young widow with a distinctly shady past. When on tour with his theatrical company, he insisted on Vera being referred to as his 'wife' and they booked into hotels as 'Mr and Mrs Corbett'. Within a fortnight of his divorce from Ollie he married Vera.

To the spurned Ollie, her husband had been 'a strange mixture'. Ever since he joined a minstrel troupe, shortly after the Peter Jackson fight, she had seen little of him. 'He never liked me to travel with him,' she told the *San Francisco Examiner*. 'He insisted on his freedom. Yet he never begrudged me anything. I had all the money I wanted. He has always been very generous'. She knew women were fascinated by him, and the way they pursued him was 'almost beyond credence'. However, her suggestion that Jim was 'too gallant to fly from them' might seem to be stretching tolerance too far.

Olive Lake, born in Amsterdam, New York, and raised in Santa Cruz, California, had planned on becoming a teacher until she met Jim and everything changed. 'He was a big, handsome boy and we met at an entertainment in Santa Cruz,' she recalled. 'We used to go to hops and had lovely times. Jim was one of the best dancers I ever knew. Before the summer was over, we became engaged.'

They had been going out together for quite a while before Jim, then working as a book-keeper for $100 a month, revealed that he was a boxer at the Olympic Club in San Francisco. Ollie's father didn't think much of Jim's pugilistic ambitions and refused to allow the planned wedding. So the couple ran away to Salt Lake City and got married.

When Jim got the job as instructor at the Olympic Club, Ollie was pleased for him. She disliked boxing, however, and refused to attend his fights. She would stay at home, trembling with fear, until her husband returned. Every time, he would promise to give it up, but always went back on his word. Boxing was his great obsession. He would not let go until he had achieved his ambition to be heavy-weight champion of the world.

As his success in the ring and on stage took him more often away from home, Ollie grew tired of living alone in San Francisco. She insisted on joining him in the East, where he was now almost permanently based. They had a row, but Jim relented. The move didn't make much difference to their relationship. They still saw very little of each other. Even when he went to New Orleans for his title challenge to Sullivan, he made his wife stay in New York. He travelled to Europe without her, but sent for her during the trip. Still they hardly spent any time together. It was obvious to their close acquaintances that the marriage had gone cold.

Ollie's intolerance of her husband's long absences, together with the constant reports of his dalliances with other women, led to a legal separation in March 1895. Under its terms, Mrs Corbett kept their home, along with a guarantee of $100 a week for life. Jim had bought the magnificent three-storey house at 146 West Eighty-Eighth Street, New York, with its fine carved oak stairway and tastefully decorated rooms, as a birthday present for Ollie. The house was always filled with guests whenever Jim was in town. The only indication that the owner was a boxer was a photograph on the dining room mantelpiece of Jim in ring costume. Visitors were most impressed with the second floor Turkish room, where a coloured glass chandelier shed a quaint light when the gas was lit. A large settee, covered with silk cushions, was the champion's favourite resting place. He would sit there enjoying his after-dinner Turkish cigarette. In a corner was a piano, used mainly by Ollie, but on which Jim would play 'a chopstick waltz, with great feeling and effect'. Mrs Corbett also sang and played the banjo. At these impromptu parties, Ollie's father would sing and the maid and cook would join in. That was before it all turned sour between Ollie and Jim.

Four months after the separation, she sued for divorce. The hearing, which opened in the Broadway office of divorce referee Edward Jacobs on 15 July, aroused huge interest across the nation and abroad. Newspaper editors hoping for some juicy copy were not disappointed. There was a scare for the waiting press at the start, when lawyers representing both parties asked that the testimonies be taken in private. The referee's refusal was greeted with an audible sigh of relief. The only frustration for the newshounds was that Corbett did not attend the hearing. He left matters in the hands of his lawyer, David A. Sullivan.

Ollie, described as 'a tall blonde', looked attractive in a straw hat with white veil, high-collared blue and white blouse, blue skirt, tan shoes and light yellow gloves. Smiling constantly, she toyed with a gold lorgnette as she gave her testimony in a low voice. Before her marriage, she said, her name was Olive Lake and if the divorce was granted she wanted to be known by her maiden name. Corbett's lawyer asked Ollie just one question: had her husband paid her separation allowance six months in advance? He had, she said.

Next to give testimony was Ollie's friend, Marie King, who said she had been an actress with the *Gentleman Jack* company for two years. Her stage name was Blanche Howard. She knew Mr and Mrs Corbett intimately.

'What was Mr Corbett's behaviour the first year?' asked Abe Hummel, representing Ollie.

'It was very good,' said Miss King.

'And the second year?'

'It was very bad.'

Asked about a woman named Vera, Miss King said the first time she had seen her was in January of that year. Vera was with the company a great deal after that, though she was not an actress. She would arrive at the theatre with Jim and leave with him. She was his companion at all times. Vera was with Corbett in Parkersburg, West Virginia, Cincinnati, Charleston and Indianapolis during April, testified Miss King. She had seen Vera in Corbett's dressing room and at his hotel. They had entered the same stateroom on a train and locked the door behind them. At hotels they were registered as 'Mr and Mrs Corbett'.

'What was the nature of their conduct towards each other?' asked Hummel.

'Very affectionate,' said Miss King.

'Did Mr Corbett make any effort to conceal his relationship with this young woman?'

'Not in the slightest.'

Before the second day of the hearing, reporters learned that there were other women named in Ollie's complaint. However, her lawyer felt that the evidence brought out concerning Vera Stanwood would be sufficient on its own to secure the divorce.

Resuming her evidence, Marie King said she was on a train to Zanesville, Ohio, when she saw Corbett with his arms around Vera, while she rested her head on his shoulder. It was a very loving attitude, she noted. The case was then adjourned to 26 July.

The *New York Times* took a jocular line when introducing the resumed hearing: 'The curtain rose today on the third act of Referee Jacobs' merry comedy, in four acts and epilogue, entitled "Is Marriage a Failure?", the joint work of Mrs Ollie Corbett and James J., her husband. The final act is set down for tomorrow, and the epilogue will follow when the court acts upon the report of the referee.'

It was serious business, however, when Jay H. Wilson took the stand. Wilson, an actor with A.H. Palmer's Trilby Company, testified that Corbett and Vera had registered as 'man and wife' at hotels in Cincinnati and Madison, Wisconsin. Jim had, on several occasions, spoken of Vera as 'my girl'.

Lawyer Hummel asked the witness if he had seen Vera go to Corbett's dressing room while he was dressing.

'Yes,' replied Wilson, 'while he was changing his costume.'

'He had to disrobe down to his skin?'

'Yes.'

Referee Jacobs, interrupting, asked: 'What was Vera doing at the time in Corbett's dressing room?'

'She was with him,' said Wilson.

On another occasion, he continued, he had gone to the Cincinnati Hotel to see Corbett. A bell boy, sent to the room, returned to say that Vera had come to the door and said Mr Corbett could not be disturbed. Vera was known to the manager and clerks as the wife of James J. Corbett.

'That is the plaintiff's case, may it please your honour,' concluded Hummel. It had been shown, he said, that Corbett and Vera (her surname was never mentioned throughout the hearing) had been living a life of illicit relations. Their guilt had been established. If that were not so, Mr Corbett could come to the hearing the following day from New Jersey and contradict the allegations made by the witnesses. Sullivan, Corbett's counsel, did not wish to cross-examine. He moved for a dismissal of the complaint on the grounds that the allegations had not been proved.

Referee Jacobs, in his report filed to the Superior Court, found that Corbett was guilty and that Ollie was entitled to an absolute divorce. 'Taking into consideration the facts referred to,' he stated, 'that defendant repeatedly introduced Vera as his wife, that she was present with him when he was dressing and undressing in the dressing-room of the theatre, their occupation of the same stateroom in a sleeping car, rooming together in a hotel in Cincinnati, the conclusion is irresistible that the defendant did commit acts of adultery with the person named.' As to the question of alimony, Corbett would be bound by the terms of the separation agreement, that he should pay Ollie $100 a week for the rest of her life. Mrs Corbett would be allowed to resume her maiden name.

On 2 August, in the Superior Court, Judge Gildersleeve signed the decree granting Ollie an absolute divorce. Under its terms she could resume her maiden name of Olive Lake and was free to marry again. Should she do so, however, the alimony of $5,200 a year paid by Corbett would cease. It was also stipulated that, if Corbett's financial circumstances should ever worsen, he could apply to the court to have the alimony reduced in accordance with his circumstances. His freedom to re-marry was dependent on the ceremony taking place outside New York state.

Jim, reported to be very angry with Ollie for exposing him in court, moved quickly to show she was out of his life for ever. Just thirteen days after the divorce, he married Vera Stanwood. The ceremony, at midday on 15 August, took place at Corbett's property in Asbury Park, New Jersey, where the couple had lived together for the past two months. Jim's decision to get married so quickly took everyone by surprise, including Vera. She knew nothing of Jim's plans until he told her, 'We will be married this morning'. Not even Corbett's manager, Bill Brady, was told about it. The six hastily summoned witnesses included Joe Corbett, the champion's brother, and Alice Brown, his long-serving black cook. No-one else was present except for two newspaper correspondents. Jim had invited them so he wouldn't have to make any public announcement.

There had been a delay while Justice John J. Borden awaited delivery of a marriage certificate – he had brought a birth certificate by mistake. Corbett was in good spirits, chatting away with his guests while he played with his two Scotch terriers. He wore a black broadcloth suit, with a black satin scarf adorning his shirt-front. Vera, in contrast with Jim's sombre attire, wore a lavender silk dress with lace trimmings. It was cut in pompadour style and edged with delicate blue ribbon at the neck. On her fingers were three rings set with diamonds and rubies. She was just as light-hearted as Corbett. After the long delay, the marriage ceremony itself took just two minutes.

Jim's snap decision to get hitched meant that no arrangements had been made for a honeymoon. The couple decided to catch the 1.10 pm train from Asbury Park for a tour that would take in Buffalo, Niagara Falls, Saratoga and the Thousand Islands. By the time they reached the station, however, word had got out about the wedding and up to a thousand people were there to give them a send-off. Jim, upset to hear the train would not leave for another two hours, angrily called a cab and told the driver, 'Go anywhere, as long as you shake off this crowd.'

They were eventually sneaked on board the train via the stationmaster's gate. Vera, exhausted after her ordeal, slumped into her seat and sighed, 'Oh, dear, I almost wish I was home.' She brightened up when a large bouquet of flowers from a friend was delivered to the carriage. The honeymoon lasted ten days. Corbett was booked to play in Bobby Gaylor's new comedy *In a Big City* at Fall River, Massachusetts, on 19 August. After that, he was due to get down to serious training for his contracted fight with Bob Fitzsimmons. More obstacles were cropping up at every turn, however, and it looked like the contest might never come off.

Corbett often referred to his marriage to Vera as the most fortunate event of his life. Nat Fleischer called the union ' a thoroughly happy one for both parties'. They were together for thirty-eight years until Jim's death. But the seemingly idyllic partnership had plenty of rocky periods, especially during their early years together. There were frequent rows, usually over Corbett's inability, or unwilling-ness, to resist other women. An exasperated Vera sued for divorce five years after their wedding, but she dropped the action when her contrite husband promised to behave himself from then on. He did, except for the occasional foray, and the couple eventually settled down to a life of quiet domesticity at their home in Bayside, New York.

Vera Stanwood, also known as Stanhope, Stanley or Holden, was actually Jessie Taylor. That was the name given on the certificate of her marriage to Corbett. Jim dedicated his autobiography, *The Roar of the Crowd*, to 'Vera Taylor Corbett, for all the happiness and success she has brought me'. Not surprisingly, he did not disclose how much Vera told him about her disreputable past life when they met – or if he cared. The newspapers at the time of his divorce from Ollie certainly were not reticent in their comments on his new woman's notoriety.

Vera, or Jessie, was born in Omaha, Nebraska, where her father was a railroad switchman. With little formal education, she took a job as a waitress at a local cafe. An attractive blonde, 'she acquired a list of admirers long enough to turn her giddy head', said one newspaper. She married one, a hack driver called Alonzo George, and they had a baby. The boy died when he was two years old. Vera's husband became an alcoholic and treated her so badly that she left him. George died not long afterwards. The young widow, apparently, fell into a loose lifestyle. As the Milwaukee *Evening Wisconsin* put it, she 'graduated from the married state into a life of shame'. She became 'notorious' in Omaha, according to the *San Francisco Chronicle*, before drifting to Chicago. Another San Francisco paper, *The Call*, suggested that 'extravagance and love of dress were her ruin'. Describing her as 'a tall blonde with exceedingly pretty features and complexion', it was not as complimentary about her character: 'She is refined and, on the surface, impresses one favourably, but her morals are weak'.

None of the reports threw any further light on Vera's reputation, but the implication is that she had a promiscuous love life, and perhaps even drifted into prostitution. She certainly had no qualms about moving in with Corbett while he was still a married man. Clearly, her show of contempt for the rules of society appealed to Jim. As a fighter, he too was a risk-taker.

Corbett was glad that his profession had taught him how to duck – for Vera had a violent temper. During their quarrels, he had to be ready to take evasive action from any readily available missile. Once, before she married Jim, Vera was enjoying a wine-drinking session with a friend, Grace Lee. The pair got well intoxicated. Vera, seeing Corbett's lithograph on the wall, stretched up and kissed it. Her pal rebuked her and proceeded to vilify her lover. During the ensuing row, Vera pulled a small implement from her manicure bag and stabbed the other woman several times. Corbett, on being told of the incident, wrote to Vera praising her for taking to the sword in his defence.

The pair had first met in 1894, while Corbett was appearing in *Gentleman Jack* in Kansas City. Vera, in town visiting a male friend, admired the champion's picture on an advertising poster and asked her escort to book tickets for that afternoon's matinee. She made sure her box seat was situated where the play's star couldn't fail to notice her. In fact, so smitten was he that he could barely keep his concentration on his performance. Vera found out Jim was staying at the Midland Hotel, so she decided that was where she should dine. Her escort, who knew the champion, introduced him to 'the lady in the box'.

From then on they were inseparable. Gentleman Jim was said to be 'completely in her power'. He lavished presents upon her, including a gold watch, a diamond hairpin and a diamond ring.

Although Vera would cause a sensation, a few years later, by denouncing Corbett as 'a human brute' who cheated on her, tortured her and threatened to kill her, she stuck with her man. Even on the occasions he left her, she took him back every time. Whatever his faults, she knew, more than anyone, how kind and generous he could be. Few could have believed, however, that such a volatile pair would go on to enjoy a rock-solid, life-long partnership. Vera was probably the only one who ever fully understood Gentleman Jim.

CHAPTER 15

A brawl with Sailor Tom

When Corbett's popularity took a dip for allegedly avoiding Bob Fitzsimmons, he saw a ready opportunity to win back support. He agreed to spar with John L. Sullivan at a benefit for his old adversary at Madison Square Garden on 27 June 1895. The Bostonian, down on his luck, was still the nation's sentimental favourite. What better way for Gentleman Jim to re-ingratiate himself with the fans than by helping out the man whose fighting career he had finished.

Corbett and the grey-haired, portly ex-champion went through the motions for three rounds and the show, which also featured exhibitions by Fitzsimmons, Jim Hall and other prominent ringmen, raised $15,000 for Sullivan. The hearty welcome given to Corbett on that occasion was not, however, echoed by the sportswriters over the subsequent period. They kept up a barrage of criticism, telling him he should either defend his title or give it up. Fitzsimmons jumped on the bandwagon, using every opportunity to declare that the champion was afraid of him. It looked like the pressure had paid off when Corbett and Fitzsimmons agreed to an offer from the Dallas Club of Texas to stage the fight. There would be a $41,000 purse, plus a $10,000 side bet. Once again, through no fault of either fighter or their handlers, the proposal fell through.

The champion had already set up his training camp at San Antonio racetrack, while Fitzsimmons was located in Dallas, when word came through that Governor Charles A. Culberson would not allow the fight to take place in Texas. The promoter, Dan Stuart, argued that there was no law in the state banning boxing. So the

107

governor called a special session of the legislature to pass its prohibi-
tion. The *New York World*, in an editorial, lashed the hysteria over a
prize-fight in a state where murders, lynchings and other criminal
lawlessness were so commonplace as to scarcely raise an eyebrow.

The battle to stage the contest moved to Arkansas, where the
citizens of Hot Springs were convinced a well-hyped promotion
would be a great boost for the town. However, from Little Rock, the
state capital, came a declaration by Governor James P. Clark that he
would not allow the staging of an event that was 'brutal and morally
wrong'. The matter threatened to reach farcical proportions when
the sheriff of Hot Springs defied the governor by giving his blessing
to the bout. The lawman, a formidable character named Reb
Houpt, who had shot dead sixteen men, said he would organise
vigilantes to surround the town and keep the state militia out. The
governor countered by calling the boxers and their managers to a
meeting and bluntly telling them they would be shipped out of the
state in wooden boxes if they attempted to go ahead. One look at
the revolvers casually laid on the table was enough to convince all
concerned it would be better to forget about the plan.

By now Corbett was fed up with the boxing business and all its
uncertainties. He wanted to concentrate on a new play written for
him by Charles T. Vincent. *A Naval Cadet* was due to open in Lynn,
near Boston, Massachusetts, on 25 November. Bill Brady considered
it a better effort than Vincent had managed with *Gentleman Jack* and
he brought in a top-rank director and actor, McKee Rankin, to play
the villain and improve the star's acting ability. The drama was to
reap handsome rewards over the next three years.

Nevertheless, it was something of a sensation when Corbett
announced that he was giving up his world heavyweight championship and handing it over to Peter Maher, the Irishman who had just
demolished Steve O'Donnell in sixty-three seconds. Of course, he
had no authority to pass on the title to anyone. Besides, Maher, a
terrific hitter but not the most punch resistant, had been knocked
out in twelve rounds by Fitzsimmons three years earlier. Even
Maher didn't consider himself worthy to be called world champion.
His true worth was exposed when he was flattened in the opening
round in a re-match with Fitzsimmons. Clearly, 'Ruby Robert', as
the balding, red-haired Englishman was known, was the only one
who could legitimately claim to be Corbett's successor. But he made
no attempt to do so. The only way to prove he was best was by
beating the man who had beaten Sullivan.

Whenever he appeared in *A Naval Cadet*, Corbett was frequently interrupted by shouts from the audience of 'Why don't you fight Fitzsimmons?' When the play finished its initial run, its star went back into light training and no more nonsense was heard about his 'retirement'.

An attractive offer to box in San Francisco, where he had not fought since the marathon duel with Peter Jackson five years earlier, was taken up. Jim was guaranteed the first $10,000 taken at the box office, plus fifty per cent of all receipts above that sum. The contest was scheduled for the Mechanics' Pavilion, an arena capable of holding 8,000 spectators, on 24 June 1896. Corbett's opponent was Tom Sharkey, a tough brawler but lacking in skills. The fight was limited to four rounds, at the champion's insistence. After nearly two years out of the ring and the soft living that went with his theatrical engagements, he simply was not fit enough for a long contest.

Though San Francisco was the city of his birth, Corbett had lost plenty of local support by choosing to re-locate to the east coast after winning the world championship. Sharkey had a good following in California, where he had scored some impressive wins, the most notable success being over Corbett's old rival Joe Choynski. Nevertheless, the raw Irishman was not considered much of a threat to a master craftsman such as Corbett. Sharkey, born in Dundalk, County Louth, was known as 'Sailor Tom' because he had started boxing while serving with the US Navy. He was immensely strong and determined, but his crude style looked ready-made for Corbett to show off his clever footwork and precise punching. Things did not quite follow the script, however. It turned out that Corbett seriously underestimated his opponent.

Sharkey was one of the toughest and bravest heavyweights in history. Though he stood only five feet, eleven inches and weighed no more than thirteen stone (182 pounds), he packed great power into his squat frame. His massive chest, decorated with tattoos of a sailing ship and a large star, was topped by broad shoulders, a bull-like neck and a solid, square jaw that took the hardest punches from the world's best heavyweights without much effect. Though he never won a world title, he twice took heavyweight champion James J. Jeffries the full distance, the first time over twenty rounds in a non-title bout, then in an 1899 championship bout that lasted twenty-five rounds. Conceding thirty-five pounds to 'Big Jeff' in the title scrap, Sharkey refused to go down under severe punishment and dealt out plenty of his own. Many observers thought he deserved to be crowned champion. In his eleven-year career, 'Sailor Tom' was knocked out only twice, by Bob Fitzsimmons and Gus Ruhlin.

Corbett was favoured to win inside the scheduled four rounds. This was surprising, as he was not renowned as a knockout specialist, while Sharkey had a reputation for great durability. The capacity audience at the Mechanics' Pavilion was disappointed with what turned into an untidy maul, with both men guilty of excessive clinching. The champion, in poor condition after his long lay-off, found it difficult to handle the Irishman's rough style, while Sharkey's main tactic was to get in close and hold with one hand while slugging away with the other.

For the first two rounds, while he was still fresh, Corbett was able to pick off the onrushing Irishman with stinging counter-punches that left Sailor Tom looking like Popeye, with one eye closed. His face was also badly bruised. But Sharkey found his tin of spinach. Tireless and refusing to be discouraged, he surged into the attack. Roughing up Corbett in the clinches, he wrestled him to the canvas in the third round. Though Jim sprang up quickly, he seemed shaken by the fall. Badly tired, he was again thrown to the floor in the fourth round and seemed unable to cope with Sharkey's enormous strength. The champion continually tried to set himself for a damaging punch, but his efforts were frustrated by the Irishman's bull-like rushes. The crowd was yelling encouragement to the underdog, for they could see that Corbett was getting the worst of it. The fact that most of Sharkey's work was illegal was beside the point.

The round was almost over when the chief of police, believing the fight had turned into a brawl which could incite a section of the crowd, jumped into the ring and called a halt. The referee declared it a draw, much to the disgust of the spectators, who felt Sharkey had deserved to win. Sailor Tom was so incensed that he tried to rush to Corbett's corner and finish what he had started. Only his quick-acting seconds, aided by a couple of burly policeman, stopped him. Corbett, blaming his poor condition for his below-par performance, thought he was the one who was robbed. Sharkey had not hit him once in the four rounds, he insisted.

The news relayed across America that Corbett had come close to defeat obliged the champion to accept a challenge from Sharkey to a re-match, this time with the title at stake. Jim felt that, properly trained, he would have little trouble with the unskilled Irishman. It also gave him the opportunity to put the more dangerous Fitzsimmons fight on the long finger. The parties met to sign articles of agreement for a 'fight to a finish' to take place in the United States or Mexico within six months. Side-stakes of $10,000 were called for, and an initial deposit of $2,500 was put up by both sides.

The arrangement infuriated Fitzsimmons and his manager Martin Julian, who said their claim to first crack at the champion was being ignored. On the night of an exhibition match between Sharkey and John L. Sullivan at Madison Square Garden, Fitzsimmons was introduced from the ring. The lanky, near-bald Englishman, now turned thirty-four, repeated his long-standing challenge to Corbett and received thunderous applause. Fitz might have weighed less than twelve stone (168 pounds) but he was thought to be the only man who could seriously threaten Gentleman Jim.

Rather unfairly depicted as a 'physical freak' by some writers, the only odd thing about Fitzsimmons was how skinny his legs were in comparison to his muscular upper body. He had developed a powerful chest and arms working as a blacksmith during his youth in New Zealand. Certainly, his scarcity of hair made him look much older than he was, and his skin was generously embellished with freckles, but he hardly qualified as the mistake of nature that some over-imaginative scribes labelled him. Unquestionably one of boxing's all-time greats, Fitz is, understandably, claimed by several nations. He was born in Cornwall, England, on 26 May 1863, moved to New Zealand with his family as a child, learned to box in Australia, and was an American citizen when he won the world heavyweight title. A crafty boxer, with tremendous hitting power in both fists, he was the first man to win world championships in three weight divisions. He took the middleweight title from Jack 'Nonpareil' Dempsey in 1891, administering a savage beating to the brave Irishman before knocking him out in the thirteenth round. Despite conceding lots of weight, he was good enough to beat the cream of the heavyweight crop. He shocked Corbett by taking his heavyweight title, but lost it in his first defence to James J. Jeffries, who outweighed him by a massive fifty-five pounds. A new weight division to bridge the gap between middleweight and heavyweight was introduced in 1903 and the amazing Fitzsimmons, at the age of forty, outsmarted Irishman George Gardner over twenty rounds to become light-heavyweight champion. He lost the title two years later to Philadelphia Jack O'Brien, but continued boxing for another nine years. His last two fights, in 1914, were 'no decision' bouts over six rounds, when he was fifty. Three years later, he died in Chicago from lobar pneumonia.

Corbett, aged 17, as an amateur boxer and
(*below*) as a bank clerk. (*Both photos courtesy
Academy of Motion Picture Arts and Sciences.*)

(*Top left*) Jake Kilrain, one of Corbett's early victims. (*Courtesy Bill Schutte.*)
(*Top right*) Joe Choynski fought Corbett five times, but couldn't beat him.
(*Bottom left*) Peter Jackson, denied a title shot because he was black. (*Courtesy Bill Schutte.*)
(*Bottom right*) Corbett and Peter Jackson in their epic 61-round battle, which was declared 'no contest'.

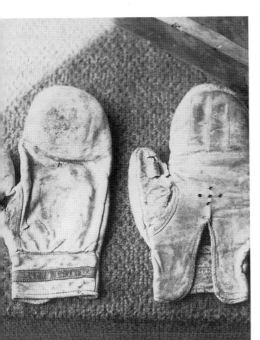

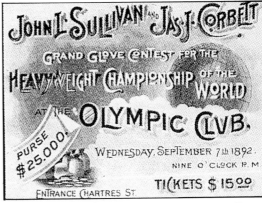

(*Top left*) John L. Sullivan, the Boston Strong Boy.

(*Top right*) Cover of Frank Leslie's *Illustrated Weekly*, showing the contestants and venue for the New Orleans Fistic Carnival of 1892.

(*Left*) Corbett's gloves from the Sullivan fight sold for $41,250 in 1992. (*Courtesy Don Scott.*)

(*Above*) Ticket for the Sullivan *v.* Corbett fight.

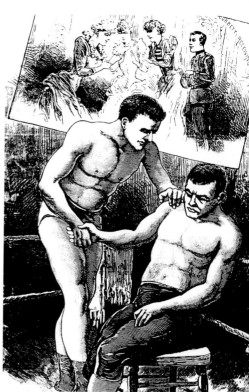

(*Top left*) Corbett and Sullivan exchange greetings 24 years after their fight, but they never became friends. (*Courtesy Don Scott.*)

(*Top right*) A consoling word for the beaten Sullivan, while (*inset*) Corbett's wife Ollie receives the news of his triumph.

(*Below*) Corbett (*right*) and Sullivan shake hands before their bout, the first for the world heavyweight title under Marquis of Queensberry Rules. (*Courtesy Jack Fiske.*)

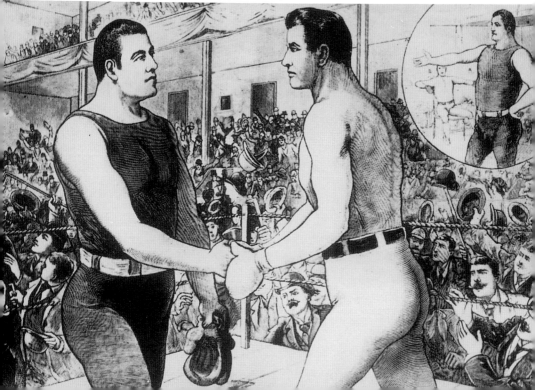

Corbett in classic fighting pose as world heavyweight champion.

(*Left*) Milwaukee advertisement for Corbett's stage appearance in *Gentleman Jack*.

(*Above*) William A. Brady, Jim's manager and master showman.

(*Below*) The poster allegedly showing Corbett meeting leading statesmen and royalty on his European tour in 1894 was a fake. (*Courtesy Library of Congress.*)

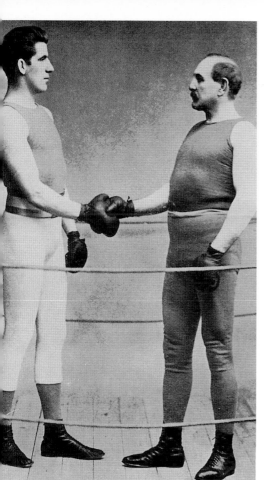

Corbett and former English bare-knuckle champion Jem Mace sparred in 1894, when Mace was 63.

Gentleman Jim during his London visit.

A grim-faced Corbett with his first wife, Ollie, in County Mayo in 1894. They were divorced two years later. (*Courtesy Tricia Forde.*)

Vera Stanwood (Jessie Taylor), who married Corbett two weeks after his divorce. (*Courtesy Bill Schutte.*)

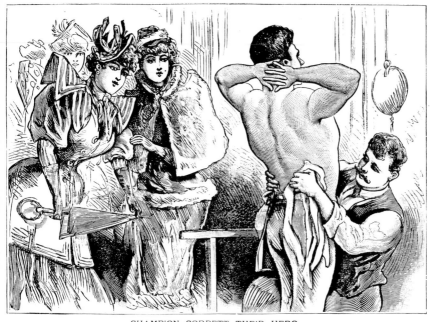

CHAMPION CORBETT THEIR HERO.

PRETTY WOMEN ADMIRE THE BIG PUGILIST, WHILE HE TRAINS FOR HIS CONTEST WITH MITCHELL.

(*Below*) The San Francisco *Examiner* front page showing Fitzsimmons landing his 'solar plexus' punch to win the title.

This Issue of
THE EXAMINER
Is Copyrighted
By W. R. Hearst, 1897.

The Examiner.

VOL. LXIV.   SAN FRANCISCO, THURSDAY MORNING, MARCH 18, 1897.   NO. 77.

DURING THE WEEK ENDING MARCH 11th "THE EXAMINER" PUBLISHED
— 1,723 —
MORE ADVERTISEMENTS THAN WERE PUBLISHED BY ANY OTHER SAN FRANCISCO NEWSPAPER DURING THE SAME PERIOD.

THE PRIZE-RING HAS A NEW CHAMPION.

INGALLS DESCRIBES THE FIGHT.

How the Battle Impressed the Noted Ex-Senator.

To Him the Contest Seemed Like a Duel on the Stage.

LACKING IN SINCERITY.

Corbett Could Hit the Cornishman Easily but Had No Force.

Fitzsimmons Depicted as Awkward, Clownish and Silly in His Demeanor.

CHARACTER OF THE AUDIENCE.

Spectators Gathered From the Ranks of the Decorous, Average American Citizens

How the Contest Came That Gives the New Champion Glory, Fame and Fortune

BY JOHN J. INGALLS

CARSON (Nev.), March 17.—The delegation to the convention began to gather at the coliseum soon after breakfast. The weather was of incomparable loveliness, the Sierras were marble, the sky turquoise and the wind

amphitheatre, like a huge bowl, with tiers of benches ascending from the platform in the center to the upper rim, filled gradually, till by noon it contained an audience of 7,000 or 8,000 well-dressed, orderly, decorous, average American citizens—miners, merchants, farmers, cowboys, ranchmen, lawyers, with some toughs and crooks that,

"FITZ" TELLS HOW HE WON.

Corbett's Conqueror Discusses His Greatest Victory.

The Knockout Blow the Same That He Gave Sharkey.

BOTH LEFT-HAND JABS.

He Says He Was Determined to Win the Championship or Die.

Victory Made Sweeter Because of Bitter Personal Feeling.

MANY OLD SCORES WIPED OUT.

Bob Says He Was Offered $750,000 in Good Coin to Throw the Fight.

The Cornishman Says He Will Never Enter the Prize Ring Again, Regardless of Jim's Challenge.

BY ROBERT FITZSIMMONS.

CARSON (Nev.), March 17.—I have fought and won the last prize-fight I will ever engage in. It has given me the additional joy of promise that a middle-weight could dispose of a heavy-weight and so

against me by the man I whipped.

For five years, although I have had the opposition of the press and the sporting fraternity and various authorities, it has been my ambition to meet James J. Corbett in a fight, Marquis of Queensberry rules. Unmindful of the rtrain I had to challenge him and loudly assert my readi-

R. Edgren on "Examiner"

FITZ LANDS HEAVILY NEAR CORBETT'S HEART AND ENDS THE GREAT BATTLE.

Sketched at the ringside, and the drawing made aboard "The Examiner" lightning special.

Corbett floors Fitzsimmons in the sixth round. He claimed the challenger got the benefit of a long count.

Clutching his stomach in agony from Fitzsimmons's blow, Corbett is counted out in the 14th round.

Corbett (*right*) with another great champion, France's Georges Carpentier. Centre is Barney Bernato. (*Courtesy Academy of Motion Picture Arts and Sciences.*)

Jim and Vera in their Locomobile car outside their home in Bayside, Long Island, New York. (*Courtesy Bayside Historical Society.*)

P. J. CORBETT MURDERS WIFE AND KILLS HIMSELF.

DONE IN FIT OF INSANITY.

Four Pistol Shots Startle the Family.

Children Awake to Find Both Their Parents Dead.

Violent Death Had Come to Mrs. Corbett in Sleep.

Evidence That the Father of the Prize-Fighter Had Been Failing Mentally for Two Years Past.

After forty years of peace and happiness with his wife Catherine, Patrick J. Corbett, father of the prize-fighter, killed her yesterday morning and then committed suicide at his home, 620 Hayes street. There were no witnesses to the double crime, which was enacted shortly after 5 o'clock, and those of the family who were aroused by the fatal shots found the bodies on the bed in the room where the couple slept. Both were dead. Two gaping wounds in the cheek and temple of the wife and one through the mouth of the husband showed the fatal course of the three bullets.

Temporary insanity, it would appear, drove Corbett to the fearful deed. His conduct for the last few weeks as described by his relatives and acquaintances bears out the theory that his mental balance had for some time been uncertain. Beyond a serious illness of two years ago, which left him dull and without appetite, the causes of his aberration are not known. Statements that he drank heavily and suffered from the effects of his excesses are denied by his family and intimate friends.

Yesterday morning Corbett's son-in-law, Charles King, and his daughter, Mrs. King, who slept in a room near by,

(*Above*) The San Francisco Chronicle report of Jim's parents' tragic deaths.

(*Right*) Pat and Kate Corbett on their wedding day.

Sailor Tom Sharkey (*left*) held Corbett to a draw and won the re-match on a disqualification.

Corbett's last fight (*right*), the re-match with James J. Jeffries in 1903. The fighters pose beforehand, watched by referee Eddie Graney.

The fight between Corbett and Kid McCoy (seen below sparring for the movie camera) was widely held to be fixed, although both boxers strenuously denied it. (*Courtesy Bill Schutte.*)

Mae West (*left*) befriended many boxers, including Corbett. (*Courtesy British Film Institute.*)

Corbett as an interlocutor (*right*) in the 1929 movie *Happy Days*, his first 'talkie'. (*Courtesy Academy of Motion Picture Arts and Sciences.*)

Gentleman Jim in a friendly spar with Charlie Chaplin (*below*).

Errol Flynn (*left*) in a scene from the 1942 biopic *Gentleman Jim*. (*Courtesy British Film Institute.*)

Corbett giving Gene Tunney some pointers (*right*) before their sparring match in 1925, when Jim was 59.

Corbett's bronze coffin is carried from St Malachy's Catholic Church, Manhattan, on a rainy day in 1933. (*Courtesy Bill Schutte.*)

CHAPTER 16

Putting Fitz's nose out of joint

Corbett, aware that his popularity would nose-dive unless he took on his legitimate challenger, agreed to meet Fitzsimmons for discussions at New York's Hotel Bartholdi, on the corner of Twenty-Third Street and Broadway, on 13 September 1896. The two fighters did not try to hide their bitterness towards each other.

Jim, resting his elbows on the table as he glared at Fitzsimmons, opened the discussion. 'I read of your challenge from the Garden ring,' he said. 'Don't you think it is a rather cowardly piece of work in view of the fact that I am matched to fight Sharkey?'

'No, I don't,' retorted Ruby Robert.

The Englishman's manager interrupted to point out that Fitzsimmons had posted $5,000 as a challenge before Corbett signed to meet Sharkey. This irritated the champion. 'Keep out of this,' he snapped. 'If you don't, I'll leave the room and there will be no match. If you allow just Fitzsimmons and me to do the talking we will come to an understanding without any trouble.'

After further talk, Fitzsimmons told Corbett that he had posted the $5,000 with Dave Holland, a respected sportsman, to bind the match between them. He asked the champion if he intended to cover it.

'You said you would fight me for fun,' chided Jim.

'I did and I'm prepared to live up to it. I repeat, I will fight you for fun,' said Fitzsimmons, to the consternation of his manager.

'All right,' replied Corbett. 'Let us have the articles of agreement drawn up.'

Such loud objections were made by the friends of both men that it looked like the meeting would break up in stalemate. Corbett, however, held up his hand for silence and announced, 'Nobody wants to fight for fun. I will fight for $10,000 a side and we will sign the articles now.'

Pen and paper were produced and it was agreed that the contest would take place sixty days after Corbett's fight with Sharkey. If the Sharkey match fell through, the champion would fight Fitz before 1 March 1897. Jim suggested Tom O'Rourke as referee, which caused some surprise, as it was known the two had not been on good terms for over a year. Fitzsimmons wanted George Siler to officiate and Corbett eventually gave in. Jim got his way in the selection of the temporary stake-holder. Al Smith was appointed to collect a $5,000 cheque from each, the amount to be forfeited in the case of non-appearance on the finally agreed date of the contest.

A surprise insertion in the contract was Fitzsimmons' insistence that he would not accept the *Police Gazette* Championship Diamond Belt if he won. He was following the example set by John L. Sullivan, who had infuriated the donor, Richard Kyle Fox, by refusing to accept the handsome trophy after he had beaten Paddy Ryan for the bare-knuckle heavyweight title in 1882. No one insulted Fox, perhaps the most influential sports figure in the country, and got away with it lightly.

Fox, born in Belfast, had emigrated from Ireland in his twenties, without a penny in his pocket but with plenty of ideas. He got a job with a New York newspaper, saved hard, borrowed some more and, within two years, bought the *Police Gazette*, a financially troubled scandal sheet. Aware of the growing interest in sport among the leisure-craving public, he introduced a special sports section to the paper, giving particular prominence to boxing. He gave full coverage, including lavish artwork, to fights. Circulation of the paper shot up. Fox, not content with merely reporting on sports, got involved in promoting events. The fact that he invited ridicule by staging such bizarre attractions as oyster-opening, one-legged dancing and steeple-climbing competitions didn't worry him. If there was a demand, Fox met it. By the time he was in his mid-thirties, the impoverished immigrant was a millionaire.

One fateful evening in 1881, at Harry Hill's Dance Hall and Boxing Emporium on New York's East Side, Fox saw Sullivan, then making a name for himself as a serious contender for the heavyweight title, enjoying a drink with some friends. He asked a waiter to tell the Boston fighter he would like a word with him. John L., in his best bellowing voice, replied, 'You go tell Fox that if he's got anything to say to me he can come over to my table and say it.' The newspaper proprietor was so incensed at the snub, and Sullivan's subsequent refusal to accept the *Police Gazette* belt when he became champion, that he used his columns to attack the Boston Strong Boy over several years. Sullivan's townsfolk, backing their hero's stand, raised $8,000 to make up a magnificent belt of their own. Measuring eight feet long and twelve inches wide, it had a base of flat gold and contained 397 diamonds, 250 of which made up the champion's name. Sullivan, on accepting the trophy, declared, 'Compared to this, the *Police Gazette* belt is nothing more than a dog collar.' Later, as his finances declined, he would pick out the diamonds one by one and sell them. He eventually got rid of what was left of the belt for $175.

Corbett, in the meantime, had no misgivings about accepting the *Police Gazette* belt, which, if not quite a dog collar, was certainly a more modest prize than the one the Bostonians had bestowed on Sullivan. Fox's belt, a gaudy affair riddled with 200 ounces of silver and gold, with a ring in the centre encircled with diamonds, was valued at $2,500. Jim took the trophy with him on his theatrical tours, allowing it to be put on display in towns where he performed. In 1893, in Indianapolis, it was stolen from a shop window and was never seen again. Unfazed, Fox had a replacement belt made up.

On signing the agreement to defend his title against Fitzsimmons, Corbett ignored his earlier deal for a re-match with Tom Sharkey. The affronted Irishman was instead offered a match with Fitzsimmons, who was anxious to get in some useful practice before fighting for the championship. The Sharkey vs Fitzsimmons bout was arranged for 2 December 1896, at the same Mechanic's Pavilion in San Francisco where Sailor Tom had had his four-round brawl with Corbett six months previously. Fitz's manager, Martin Julian, violently objected to the famed lawman and gunslinger Wyatt Earp being appointed as referee, to no avail. The fight ended in farce, with Fitzsimmons, all set to finish off the tottering Sharkey, being disqualified for an alleged low blow in the eighth round. Earp, who had been a deputy marshall in such boisterous Wild West towns as Dodge City and Tombstone and was alleged to have shot dead ten men, was rumoured to be a good friend of Sharkey's. Public sympathy was with Ruby Robert over such a blatant injustice. So dominant had he been over Sharkey, who had given Corbett so much trouble, that many were convinced he had the beating of the champion. In a return meeting with Sharkey four years later, Fitz won by a knockout in the second round.

Corbett, despite his conviction that he was a much superior fighter to Fitzsimmons, realised he would have to get into top physical shape to retain his title. Since becoming champion, he had fought only three times, the third-round knockout of Charlie Mitchell, the effortless disposal of Peter Courtney for the movie cameras, and the unsatisfactory four-round draw with Sharkey. He knew that while he had been growing soft and sluggish on the stage, Fitzsimmons had kept busy with a series of impressive victories. It would do Corbett's cause no harm at all if he could introduce a little psychology to upset the challenger before he got too cocky. The first opportunity arose while both men were in Philadelphia. Fitz tried to book into Green's Hotel, where Corbett was already installed.

As Fitzsimmons was checking in, he was spotted by Corbett's brother Joe, who called the champion out of the dining room. Putting on his boldest front, Jim strode over to Fitz, slapped him on the back and told him in a scathing tone, 'Hey, you can't register by just making your mark.' Turning to his brother, he said, 'Joe, take the pen and sign Mr Fitzsimmons' name. He doesn't know how to.'

Not surprisingly the Englishman flared up at the calculated insult and let fly with a tirade of colourful language. Gentleman Jim cut him short by gripping his nose between two fingers and giving it a torturous tweak. At that, all hell broke loose. Hotel guests excitedly rushed into the lobby, sure they were going to see a fight between the world's top two heavyweights for free. Corbett's companions held onto him while his brother grappled with Fitzsimmons. The Englishman broke free, picked up a decanter and hurled it at Joe, but missed.

'Then what must Fitz do,' Jim would recall, 'but step into the dining room, seize a castor from the table and hurl it, pepper, salt, vinegar, oil and cayenne and tabasco, as red as his hair, at Joe – Joe who had simply held him, when it was I who had twisted his nose. Joe ducked and the salad dressing splattered the wall.'

The hotel manager eventually managed to calm things down. Fitzsimmons, wisely, decided he would find somewhere else to stay.

The incident incensed Martin Julian, Fitzsimmons' manager. He gave a *Houston Post* reporter his version of what happened: 'That was a bum proceeding. Corbett and his heelers found Fitz alone and they took advantage of it. ... The insult was offered by Corbett and

Fitzsimmons was held, with his hands behind his back, by two or three while Corbett attempted to spit in his face. And then that half-brother who was with him caught Fitz around the neck, giving him the "strong arm". It did Corbett no good. His title of "Gentleman Jim" was proved to be unearned.'

Corbett claimed that Fitzsimmons was 'beastly drunk' on the occasion, and it was Fitz who had been going around threatening to twist the champion's nose when they next met. All he had done was beaten him to it, he explained.

The unseemly affair, while it whetted the public's attitude for the inevitable showdown between the bitter rivals, did little to head off criticism that the Californian was playing the bully a bit too often. Another incident, when he physically attacked a stage manager, emphasised the point even more. It was bad enough getting into an altercation with a fellow boxer, but striking a man of five feet, five inches, with no chance of hitting back, was unforgivable.

The incident occurred in January 1897 at a Detroit theatre where Corbett was appearing in *A Naval Cadet*. Already in a bad mood because the scenery was late arriving in town and was not in place for the opening act, he blew his top completely after the third act. The effectiveness of a love scene depended on the blowing of a steam whistle. Because the normal whistle was not yet available, the house whistle was used. It failed to sound properly and Corbett missed his cue. At the drop of the curtain, he rushed off stage and grabbed the stage manager, Orlando Battaglia, by the shoulders. He called him all the foul names he could think off, then struck him twice and knocked him to the floor. Battaglia took his attacker to court. Corbett pleaded guilty and paid his fine, but refused to pay the stage manager his salary.

Gentleman Jim's fiery temper had got him into trouble, exactly a year earlier, at the National Theatre in Philadelphia. He was caught smoking in his dressing room by a fireman appointed by the local authority to see that the 'no smoking' law was enforced. Fire Officer William J. Murphy had seen smoke coming from the half-open door of the star's dressing room. When he challenged Corbett, the door was slammed in his face. Murphy demanded access and was confronted by a furious Corbett, who grasped him by the throat and hit him with both hands. Bravely, the fireman struck back, drawing blood from the champion's mouth. Corbett threw him to the floor and kicked him in the back. As Murphy tried to get away down a flight of stairs, he was followed by his attacker. Corbett was grabbed by the legs and was sent sliding to the bottom of the steps. By the time they were separated by stage hands, both men showed the scars of their encounter. Their faces were cut and swollen. Corbett's back was badly bruised, while Murphy's back showed the marks of the champion's boot. The *Evening Bulletin*, commenting on the affair, said the fireman 'displayed as much spirit and gameness as any scientific boxer could be expected to show'.

Bill Brady had his work cut out trying to play down the unwelcome publicity emanating from the public brawls. What his man needed was a platform to show off his fistic capabilities where it mattered – in the ring. It was with delight, and not a little relief, that he learned Dan Stuart had won the right to stage the eagerly awaited title defence against Fitzsimmons.

The purse was $15,000, winner-take-all, with sidestakes of $5,000. The promoter also promised Corbett and Fitzsimmons a third of the fee paid by the Kinetoscope Exhibition Company, who planned to make the first motion picture of a world championship bout. (This part of the agreement was to end up in a dispute between Stuart and Brady.)

The indefatigable Stuart, foiled at every turn in his earlier attempts to get the fighters together in the ring, at last found a friendly state governor. Nevada was almost bankrupt, its days as a rich mining centre long past, and there were only some 60,000 people still living in the territory. Although boxing was illegal there, a bill was hastily drawn up to clear the way. Three Nevada cities clamoured to stage the potentially lucrative event. Out of Reno, Virginia City and Carson City, Stuart opted for the last, which was named after Kit Carson, the famous scout and frontiersman.

Opposition to the battle was strong, especially from Protestant groups and moralistic legislators. Congressman William F. Aldrich, acting on the prompting of the National Reform League, submitted a bill to ban the transmission of any picture or description of the fight, or any record of betting, to newspapers. Clergy gave numerous well-publicised sermons attacking the event. Typical of the fire-and-brimstone denunciations was that rendered by the Rev. Levi Gilbert, of the First Methodist Church of Cleveland: 'This state (Nevada), this deserted mining camp, revives brutality by an exhibition that must make its Indians and Chinamen wonder at Christianity. Corbett is called a gentleman, yet acted like an infuriated animal in his last fight. He is dissipated as is John L. Sullivan, who clubs his wife, and both of these are shining lights of the theatre, and

Christian people are lampooned for non-attendance. Such exhibitions promote criminality by feeding the bestial in man. They debauch the public ideal. Such men sell their bodies for merchandise as surely as the harlots of the street. They show pluck, yes, but no better than the bulldog or the terrier.'

All the protests came to nought and St Patrick's Day, 17 March 1897 was the date chosen for the fight. Work commenced on building the arena, which was situated in the middle of a racetrack, about a third of a mile from the city's main street. The reason for holding the event outdoors was to allow the movie cameramen maximum daylight. The twelve-sided structure, surrounded by a fence twenty-six feet high, had six entrances, four for reserved seats and two for general admission. Some 500,000 feet of timber was used to provide the seating accommodation, with plank seats arranged in tiers, each ten inches higher than the row in front. In the centre of the arena, the twenty-four-foot ring was on a platform four feet high. The cost of timber and erection was put at $10,000.

Special wide-angle cameras were made to take in the whole of the twenty-four foot ring. Two side-by-side cameras were used, one to take over from the other as it ran out of film and had to be re-loaded. As the cameras were rooted in a stationary position, they were unable to follow the fighters as they moved from one side of the ring to the other. Eleven thousand feet of film was used, a record at that time for a single event.

Corbett did his preliminary training in San Francisco before transferring to Shaw's Springs, near the fight site. The challenger chose New York, where he ran every morning in Central Park, accompanied by his great dane Yarrum. A month prior to the contest Fitzsimmons re-located to Cook's Ranch, on the outskirts of Carson City, where he was joined a week later by his wife Rose and their two young sons.

While Jim's victory over John L. Sullivan had received unprecedented newspaper coverage for a sporting event, it paled into insignificance alongside the attention paid by editors to the Corbett vs Fitzsimmons fight. The champion signed a contract with the *New York World* giving the paper exclusive rights to his comments prior to the big day. Fitzsimmons was hired by the Hearst press in a similar capacity. These literary gems, given birth on the clattering typewriters of skilled writers, were syndicated all over the United States and throughout the world, with handsome profits for all concerned.

No doubt many unsophisticated readers wondered how the star pugilists found time to knock off these verbose human interest yarns while faithfully attending to their training. The employment of ghost writers to record the words of sports personalities has long been an accepted practice, but it had its first innings in connection with the Carson City contest. Even the referee for the fight, George Siler, doubled up as a correspondent for the *Chicago Tribune*. His account of the battle was hailed by Nat Fleischer as 'one of the best things of its kind ever written'. Later reprinted in a book, *The Battle of the Century*, Fleischer proudly kept it in his boxing library at the offices of *The Ring*.

Inevitably, the huge amount of publicity attracted a wide variety of visitors to Carson City. The day before the fight, troublesome roughnecks, hoboes and small-time con men were rounded up and put in jail to keep them out of the way of the respectable folk who arrived on special trains from all the major cities. But gamblers and whores plied their trades briskly and without interference. Among Fitzsimmons' supporters were a group of copper and tin miners who, like their hero, had emigrated from Cornwall. They wagered on their man at the best odds they could find, which were four to five, the challenger being considered a slight underdog. He had started at six to ten.

A reason for the drop in the odds could have been the reports of friction in the Corbett camp. Bill Brady had brought in Charlie White, who had formerly acted as trainer to Fitzsimmons, to pass on his knowledge of the challenger's style and temperament. White's advice clashed with the instructions of Billy Delaney, Jim's regular trainer, and the champion spent a lot of his time trying to appease both men. Another distraction was the feud between Corbett's pet mongrel Ned and a handsome collie presented to him by his brother Frank. The two dogs were at each other's throats whenever they got the chance. At night Ned was confined to the hall of the training quarters, while the newcomer, Laddie, was given preferential treatment, being allowed to sleep in the champion's room. One stormy evening, Jim was shocked on returning from town to stumble over something on his doorstep that looked like a bundle of snow. It was the mongrel, almost frozen to death. That did it. The collie got his marching orders, while Ned regained his status as his master's pet.

Corbett was anything but a happy camper, however. He grew more irritable as the big day neared, taking offence at the slightest criticism of his training methods and becoming more reluctant to accept advice from those around him. The only decent workouts he got was with a big, strong Californian named Jim Jeffries, who had been recommended by De Witt Van Court, boxing instructor at the Los Angeles Athletic Club, as someone who would be good for the champion to practise 'roughing it'. Corbett didn't spare his sparring partner in their brisk workouts, but later claims that Jeffries vowed to avenge the punishment he took are unfounded. The raw youngster was extremely grateful for the trouble Corbett went to in teaching him some of the basic skills of boxing. The advice and the lively sparring sessions would stand Jeffries in good stead when, years later, he twice faced his mentor in world title fights.

About a week before Corbett and Fitzsimmons met in the ring, they had another of their nasty face-to-face encounters. Jim, accompanied by Billy Delaney, Charlie White, Billy McCarthy and Jeffries, was out walking when he saw the challenger jogging towards him, alongside his dog, with his retinue trailing behind. As the two groups met and exchanged greetings, Fitzsimmons offered Corbett a handshake.

Gentleman Jim kept his hand in his pocket, telling his rival, 'I'll shake hands after I've licked you.'

'Then we'll never shake,' replied the Englishman.

'You don't really think you can beat me?' scoffed Corbett.

'What do you think I'm out training for?' retorted Fitzsimmons.

'I'll see you on the seventeenth over there,' said the champion, indicating the arena. Turning his gaze to Bob's dog, he said, 'You'd better bring him along too. You'll need him.'

Fitzsimmons turned on his heel and resumed his training run. He saved his feelings for his newspaper column: 'I will fight a square fight, an honourable fight, but there shall be no mercy, no quarter, no tenderness. I will fight him to the bitter end and conclude this issue and wipe out his insults.'

The verbal fisticuffs continued in the newspaper columns right up to fight time. On the champion's boxing ability, Fitz noted that 'he doesn't know how to infight, and he won't until I teach him something.' Corbett retorted, 'I am going to make this foreigner take his medicine or crawl.'

Though Carson City was blanketed in snow and slush for most of the week coming up to the event, St Patrick's Day dawned promisingly. The sun shone and there was a slight breeze as patrons made their way to the arena for the fight, scheduled to start at ten o'clock in the morning. To the west snowcapped mountains of the Sierra

Nevada provided a perfect backdrop for the cameras focused on the ring. The turnout, however, was disappointing. Only about four thousand paid into the arena, which was built to accommodate four times that number. Existing photographs show lots of bare boards where customers should have been seated. The poor attendance was due to two major factors, the remoteness of the venue from the big cities and, after so many failed attempts to stage the fight, uncertainty that it would come off on this occasion. Few wanted to travel a great distance to find some last-minute hitch meant a wasted journey. At least the promoter had the consolation that it was the dearer seats which sold best.

Dan Stuart engaged Bat Masterson, the famous Western marshall, and a bunch of his deputies to watch out for undesirables and would-be gatecrashers. All firearms and knives were taken away from patrons at the entrances. The owners were given receipts so they could collect the weapons afterwards.

As the fans began arriving, it was noticeable that there were some women among them. The promoter had set aside an enclosed box for them, six feet from the ringside, and out of earshot of any coarse talk among the menfolk. It was the first time women had been openly welcomed to attend a fight, although the innovation did not please John L. Sullivan. 'It is natural that ladies should admire fighters, but they should not watch fights,' he said.

Sullivan, and others in the audience, was further shocked when Rose Fitzsimmons brazenly took a seat near her husband's corner and acted as one of his seconds. Legend has it that she played a crucial role in Bob's victory, not least with her timely advice on the punch that brought about Corbett's dramatic downfall. 'Hit him in the slats, Bob' might not have been the actual words of wisdom she used, though this was the phrase favoured by the more imaginative reporters. But never was the belief that behind every great man is a woman better borne out than that day in Carson City.

CHAPTER 17

The solar plexus punch

At noon, two hours behind schedule, the contestants ducked between the ropes for the eagerly-awaited 'Battle of the Century'. Corbett, his thick black hair greased and parted in the centre, looked immaculate in his specially designed ankle-length dressing gown. Cool and confident, he smiled as he chatted to ringsiders. The balding challenger, wearing a Japanese-style robe, appeared to be more apprehensive. Grim-faced, he chewed vigorously as the master of ceremonies introduced an array of fistic celebrities, past and present, then announced the three timekeepers: Jimmy Colville from Boston for Corbett, Lou Houseman from Chicago for Fitzsimmons, and William Muldoon, ex-wrestler and strongman, for the promoter.

The weights were given as thirteen stone, one pound (183 pounds) for the champion and eleven stone, thirteen pounds (167 pounds) for the challenger. Fitzsimmons' trainer, Dan Hickey, claimed Bob was only eleven stone, three pounds (157 pounds) when he stepped on a different scales two hours before the fight. Nat Fleischer, in his Corbett biography *Gentleman Jim*, surprisingly accepted the lower figure, but admitted he had not witnessed that weigh-in. It is highly unlikely Fitzsimmons entered a fight for the heavyweight title weighing a mere three pounds over the present light-middleweight (or junior middleweight) limit. In his previous contest, against Tom Sharkey, he had tipped the scales at eleven stone, eleven pounds (165 pounds). That was just two pounds less than his official weight for the Corbett fight. At any rate, the

Cornishman was a genuine middleweight tackling a heavyweight, if not a very big heavyweight by modern standards. In height, there was not much between them. Corbett, at six feet, one inch, was just one and a quarter inches taller.

The challenger wore tight-fitting shorts, akin to a modern swimming costume, but Corbett donned the same skimpy briefs, exposing most of his buttocks, as he had in the Courtney bout. It was not uncommon for fighters of the period to appear in such scanty wear. Some, indeed, wore little more than jockstraps. Boxers who used fast footwork, like Corbett, liked the utmost freedom of movement they provided. In the era of bare-knuckle boxing, and even into the early days of gloved combat, calf-length tights had been the normal attire.

Referee George Siler called both men to the centre of the ring and invited them to shake hands. Corbett extended his hand and Fitzsimmons, acting instinctively, nearly took it, but Martin Julian yelled, 'No, Bob, he wouldn't shake hands with you on the road, so let him go without now.' The champion shrugged his shoulders, turned around and walked back to his seconds. Corbett had won the toss of a coin for choice of corners, so his opponent was forced to come out for each round facing the sun.

In Corbett's corner were Charlie White, Jim Jeffries, Con McVey, Joe Corbett, Billy Woods and Bill Hampton. With Fitzsimmons were Martin Julian, Billy Ernest, Ernest Roeber, Dan Hickey and Jack Stenzler.

At the opening bell, both men moved forward cautiously. Jim knew he was up against a crafty foe who was never more dangerous than when hurt, while Fitzsimmons was aware of the huge task he faced in trying to overcome the most scientific boxer the world had seen up to then. A left lead was avoided by Corbett, who, worked into a corner, slipped neatly out of danger, to the cheers of the crowd. He made Bob miss several more times, forcing his aggressive rival to laugh at his own wild efforts. The champion used his jab to good effect and landed several hard punches to the head and body, taking little in return. It was clearly Corbett's round.

Well settled and looking very confident, Jim caught the Englishman with smart blows from both hands in the next two rounds and had no trouble avoiding Bob's counter attempts. Already Rose Fitzsimmons was getting anxious. In the interval between the third and fourth rounds, she told her husband, 'Hit him in the body, Bob.' She knew he stood little chance of matching the champion in skill. He had to force the fighting and wear down Corbett with swinging blows to the ribs. Easier said than done, thought Fitz to himself.

By the end of the fifth round Fitzsimmons' bloody features bore testimony to the accuracy of the champion's punches. The sobriquet 'Ruby Robert' had taken on a literal meaning. His wife, growing more agitated, was causing some annoyance to spectators seated near the challenger's corner as she jumped up and down from her seat. The *Chicago Tribune* reported, 'As the battle went on, she became more and more demonstrative, sometimes breaking out with exclamations which bordered on the profane.'

Bob, bleeding from the nose and from a split bottom lip, assured her from his corner stool, 'Don't be scared of a little blood. I can take the best he can give me.'

'I know you can,' said Rose, 'but keep going for the body. That's his weakness.'

Corbett's supporters were euphoric over his dazzling display of speedy footwork and accurate punching. In the sixth round it looked like he was about to finish the fight. He rained blows on his rival's head – jabs, hooks and uppercuts – to send Fitzsimmons reeling. A hard left hook caught the challenger on the jaw and buckled his knees. To stop himself hitting the floor, the Englishman grabbed Corbett's legs, but the champion wrenched himself free and Bob went down. As he rested on one knee, Corbett yelled to the referee, 'You're counting too slow.' Siler ordered him to 'Step back', although there was nothing in the rules at that time to prevent a fighter standing over his fallen rival and hitting him as soon as he rose to his feet. (The stipulation that the aggressor must retire to a neutral corner was not introduced until some thirty years later because of Jack Dempsey's habit of hovering over downed opponents. Failure to observe the new rule cost the 'Manassa Mauler' dearly in his bid to regain the title from Gene Tunney, who got the benefit of a fourteen-second rest while the referee tried to persuade Dempsey to go to a neutral corner before taking up the count. That 1927 bout earned its place in ring history as 'the Battle of the Long Count', but Corbett moaned that the injustice was first suffered by him.)

Fitzsimmons rested upon his right knee until the referee reached 'nine', then got up to not only weather the Californian's follow-up attack, but fight back so courageously that the crowd broke into sustained applause. From that eventful sixth round, two significant points emerged. Fitzsimmons had taken the champion's best punches and was still in there fighting. Corbett had had his opponent at his mercy and had failed to finish him off.

For the moment, however, the champion was very much in command. His unerring left jab had his rival's face in such a bloody mess that the gore was spattered on Rose Fitzsimmons' face. In the heat of the action, Jim said he could hear her 'yelling at me things that were not at all flattering to my skill as a fighter or my conduct as a gentleman'. As Leo N. Miletich amusingly suggested in his book *Dan Stuart's Fistic Carnival*, 'At that point, Corbett probably would have backed Sullivan on his bias against female spectators.'

By the seventh round Fitzsimmons, despite his battered appearance, appeared to be getting stronger, while the champion was puffing hard. Bob tossed several right-handers which failed to land, but he was not concerned. He had achieved his objective of causing Corbett to raise his guard, leaving his midriff unprotected. A stiff left to the stomach clearly hurt the Californian. At the end of the round, Fitzsimmons said to his manager, 'I found the right spot that time.'

Jim was noticeably slower in the next couple of rounds, and the challenger stepped up his attacks. Thanks to his wonderful skill, Corbett still managed to outbox his rival, but his punches lacked the snap of the earlier action. He looked so tired that, by the end of the tenth round, the betting had shortened to 'evens'.

While Corbett was still landing more punches, it was clear that the challenger carried the real power. He was getting his punches home more frequently and gradually wearing down his opponent. Growing more confident all the time, Bob looked over the champion's shoulder in the clinches and winked at his seconds. It was Corbett who held on at every opportunity and, while the only blood on his face came from Fitzsimmons, he looked a worried man. Rose, realising that the tide had turned, cried out, 'You've got him, Bob. Can't you see he's gone? Go right in and finish him. He can't beat you now. He's exhausted.'

A heavy left to the body in the twelfth round almost doubled Corbett in two, but he was not finished yet. In the next round, he answered another hard right to the ribs with a left to the chin that jolted the challenger's head back. A left to the nose brought another gush of blood, but Fitzsimmons did not seem unduly concerned.

In *The Roar of the Crowd*, Corbett insisted the Englishman, with his wild swings, was 'worse than an amateur. To see him flailing away so blindly at me convinced me that he was bewildered and panicky over the fact that he couldn't time me at all and I was outsmarting him'. Corbett believed he was so superior that 'one good punch would finish him'. He was right about the single deciding punch – but wrong about who would deliver it.

The dramatic climax was graphically described in the *New York Times*:

> After the first minute of the fourteenth round had been spent in a few harmless clinches and counters, Fitzsimmons made a 'fake' lead with his right for the jaw. It was a simple ruse, but it caught the Californian napping. Instead of keeping his body inclined forward and throwing down his head to allow the blow, which was of the lightest kind, to slip by, Corbett contemptuously bent his head and chest backward and thus protruded his abdomen. Fitzsimmons' small eyes flashed and, like lightning, he saw and availed himself of his advantage. Drawing back his left, he brought it up with terrible force, the forearm rigid and at right angles to the upper arm. With the full force of his wonderful driving muscles brought into play, the Australian fairly ripped the blow into Corbett's stomach at a point just under the heart. Corbett was lifted clean off his feet and, as he pitched forward, Fitzsimmons shot his right up and around, catching Corbett on the jaw and accelerating his downward fall.

The spectators, many of whom had missed the body punch, so quickly had Fitzsimmons struck, jumped to their feet in one mass movement as the referee began to count. Corbett's cornermen, along with some his supporters, yelled 'Foul', claiming that Bob's head punch had landed when the champion was down. The referee, ruling that the blow to the midriff was the one that caused the knockdown and that the follow-up right was incidental, ignored their pleas. Corbett, gasping for breath, tried to prop himself up on his right arm and managed to straighten his left leg. He reached for the bottom rope, missed and fell on his face. 'I was conscious of everything that went on, the silence of the crowd, the agony on the faces of my seconds, the waiting Fitzsimmons, but my body was like that of a man stricken with paralysis,' he would recall. He was still struggling to rise when Siler reached 'ten'. Rose Fitzsimmons cried out, 'Oh, Bob, Bob, you've done it.' Indeed he had. Her bloodied, but broadly smiling, husband was the new heavyweight champion of the world.

Corbett, once he was back on his feet, reacted with fury. He rushed across to Fitzsimmons' corner and attempted to strike him. 'You'll have to fight me again,' he screamed at the new champion.

'If you don't, then I'll go at you in the street the next time I see you.'

'If you do, I'll kill you,' said Fitzsimmons calmly.

The half-demented Corbett was pulled away by his handlers. Later, he calmed down and apologised to his conqueror for his outburst, admitting he was beaten 'fair and square'. By the next day, however, he was claiming that it was a 'lucky punch' that beat him. 'I believe in the main I fought as well as ever I fought in my life, but luck was against me,' he said. 'The blow which won the fight for Fitz was in a large measure an accidental one.' He also blamed the high altitude at which the fight was held – six to seven thousand feet above sea level – for his failure to get his breath back more quickly during the crucial ten seconds. They were feeble excuses from a man who couldn't accept what had happened – the title was no longer his.

The new champion was more gracious, but then he could afford to be. 'He outboxed me completely those first seven rounds,' he said. 'His speed was incredible. I never believed any man could hit me as often as Corbett did.'

The knockout blow has earned its place in boxing folklore as the 'solar plexus punch'. A San Francisco physician, John W. Gardner, was the man who coined the clinical term for the debilitating strike. Bob Davis, who was reporting on the fight for the *New York Journal*, heard him discussing the punch with a medical colleague and jotted down the description. The solar plexus is a network of radiating nerves at the pit of the stomach. A heavy punch to that area affects muscular movement and breathing. Davis, aware that the 'new' punch made good copy, cabled his story and other newsmen picked up the angle. In fact, the 'solar plexus punch' was nothing more than a solid dig in the 'breadbasket'. Way back in 1730, English champion Jack Broughton had discovered its effectiveness, tagging it the 'projectile'. Other bare-fist bruisers called the vulnerable target area 'the mark'.

Fitzsimmons laughed off compliments on his 'invention'. 'It was just a bloomin' good belly clout,' he said.

Referee Siler, in his account of the fight for the *Chicago Tribune*, was of the opinion that Corbett had over-trained and had 'left his fight on the road'. Nat Fleischer agreed. He recalled that Jim, 'always a highly-strung person', had been in a bad state of nerves when he started his preparation at Carson City. He had already reached peak condition for the earlier date in Arkansas and was upset by the cancellation. The more worried he became, the harder he worked. His handlers could not persuade him to slacken off. 'For half a dozen rounds, he could go at a lightning clip,' wrote Fleischer. 'After that he had but scant reserves to draw upon. In ring slang, he had "shot his bolt". The bitter result was defeat by the pugilist he despised.'

Though Corbett could have no genuine grumbles about his loss, his manager tried to convince all and sundry that Jim had been 'robbed' when he knocked Fitzsimmons down in the sixth round. Brady said he could prove that Bob got away with a 'long count'. When the film of the fight was shown at the Academy of Music in New York, if his account can be believed, he asked the projectionist to stop the screening at the precise moment Fitzsimmons touched down. Holding a stopwatch and asking the audience to check with their timepieces, he counted thirteen seconds before the Englishman was on his feet. What the crafty showman failed to disclose was that the projectionist, a Corbett fan, had agreed to slow down the hand-cranked machine to suit Brady's argument. So what people were seeing was a slow-motion picture of what actually happened. One member of the audience, however, was wise to the trick. William Muldoon, official timekeeper for the fight, jumped to his feet and roared, 'Brady, you're a liar.' Accepting the weakness of his case, Brady slipped quietly out through the stage door.

Foiled in his audacious bid to have the fight result altered, Brady switched his attention to getting a better share of the motion picture profits. He had been upset to discover that Dan Stuart had formed a corporation with himself as president and his brother as treasurer. This gave Stuart control of the film's world-wide distribution. It took in three-quarters of a million dollars, but Brady complained that, by the time Stuart got through juggling the books, there was little left for anyone else.

Without doubt the filming of the Corbett vs. Fitzsimmons fight was one of the milestones in motion-picture history. Putting the whole thing together was a masterpiece of imagination, enterprise and technical expertise. Two miles of film was used, taking 165,000 separate pictures. The screening, lasting nearly an hour, showed all the preliminaries to the contest and each of the fourteen rounds in their entirety. Only the intervals between rounds were cut down to save time.

The 'Battle of the Century' thrilled large audiences throughout America and abroad. For the first time, a motion picture was shown in high-class theatres, such as Chicago's Grand Opera House and the Boston Theater. It packed houses in Britain, Australia, China, Japan, India, South Africa and Cairo. The vast majority of viewers had never seen a boxing match before and expected a wild slugging match with blood flowing in all directions. There was some disappointment at the frequency of clinches, but the skill and bravery of the fighters often caused the theatre audiences to break into applause. Shot from a distance, the film failed to capture the knockout blow in clear detail, but Corbett's agonised expression as he struggled to rise was plain enough.

In London customers who paid a guinea to five shillings at the Westminster Aquarium 'showed by their remarks that they fully appreciated both the marvellous fidelity of the reproduction and the skilful tactics of the combatants'.

For quite some time after his defeat, Corbett was inconsolable. Not only had he lost his precious title, but he had made no money out of the fight, apart from his share of the film profits (the purse was on a winner-take-all basis and he also forfeited his $5,000 side-stake). On top of that, he had suffered the humiliation of being beaten by a middleweight, a foreigner and, worst of all, an Englishman.

Like most children of Irish parents who left their homeland around the time of the Great Famine, Jim had learned harrowing tales of the terrible toll of successive potato crop failures, and how the Westminster government had given too little, too late to alleviate the suffering. The bitterness of the Irish-Americans towards all things British lay deep. John L. Sullivan once upset his fellow guests at a high-class dinner by refusing to drink a toast to Queen Victoria. It was widely believed by the Irish that the Queen had donated a miserly 'fiver' to the famine cause. (In fact, she gave £2,000). Sullivan, asked to raise his glass, roared, 'I'll drink no toast to the damned Famine Queen.' It was no co-incidence that Corbett's least favourite ring opponents were two Englishmen, Fitzsimmons and Charlie Mitchell.

When Fitzsimmons spurned Brady's offer to put up $20,000 for a return match, Jim's depression deepened. Not even an increased bid of $35,000 would tempt the new champion. Corbett, feeling totally frustrated, sunk so low that he contemplated suicide.

Fitz was in no hurry to fight again. He followed his predecessor's example by trying his hand at acting. The fact that Corbett had made between $75,000 and $100,000 on the stage during his five-year title reign convinced Fitzsimmons that he, too, could cash in on his elevated status. He toured in *The Honest Blacksmith*, a two-act drama specially written for him, which should not have stretched his thespian capabilities. Bob failed to adapt as well as Gentleman Jim had to the stage, however, and frequently forgot he was play-acting. More than one cast member quit after being on the receiving end of an over-enthusiastic Fitzsimmons slap. He got plenty of laughs, but usually in the wrong places.

Corbett, after so much bad publicity following his public brawls and his unsportsmanlike reaction to his title loss, at last merited favourable mention in the papers when he was proclaimed a hero for his part in saving lives in a rail disaster. Jim, who had been appearing at Troy in *A Naval Cadet*, was due to travel with his company on the ill-fated train from nearby Albany to New York. As their baggage exceeded the weight limit, the group missed the journey. They sorted out the problem and caught the next train. Their journey was interrupted when they found part of the preceding train had plunged into the Hudson river. Corbett, borrowing an axe, used his strength to smash through a carriage roof and help rescue victims.

Having abandoned any hope of getting a re-match with Fitzsimmons, Jim returned to one of his early loves, baseball, and played with the Paterson, New Jersey, club in the Atlantic League. Jim and his manager were on a percentage of the gates and it proved a hugely profitable venture. Brady, who often slipped the opposing pitcher 'a little something' to make Corbett look good, said they raked in between $500 and $1,200 every afternoon. Although Jim signed a contract to play with Milwaukee, the club wanted to drop their crowd-pulling, but novice, first baseman for an important game against Minneapolis. Corbett stood his ground, however, and proved his worth with the best game of his life. 'Milwaukee began to understand what a bargain they had got,' wrote Brady. 'Corbett stepped up to the plate at an extremely crucial moment – no fixing the pitcher this time – and slashed a double into the left field as cool and neat as Ty Cobb in his best days.'

If 1897 had not been a year Jim remembered fondly, the following year was to bring him further great anguish. He would be accused of taking part in a 'fixed' fight and, worst of all, he would lose both his parents in a shocking, violent incident.

CHAPTER 18

Gunshots in Hayes Street

Just before five o'clock on the morning of 16 August, 1898, a loud noise awakened the occupants of 520 Hayes Street, in San Francisco. Charles King, who was married to Mamie, one of Pat and Kate Corbett's daughters, thought it was something to do with the downstairs boiler, but he jumped out of bed when three more bangs followed in quick succession. They sounded like gunshots.

On running into his parents-in-laws' bedroom, King lit the gaslight and saw, through a cloud of smoke, the terrible cause of the explosions. Lying in bed with blood pouring from her head was Kate Corbett. Slumped on top of the bedclothes, on his back, was the partly clothed body of her husband. His mouth was open and filled with blood. On the floor beside the bed lay a revolver, still smoking from the shots. It was evident that Pat had shot his wife, then turned the gun on himself.

King, who had been followed into the room by his wife and her unmarried sisters, Esther and Katie, checked for signs of life. He got no response and immediately telephoned Dr Robert O'Connell, who resided two blocks away, and Father Cullen, from the Sacred Heart Catholic Church. The doctor said that death for both must have been instantaneous.

The news of the crime spread quickly through the city and by 9 am a large crowd had gathered outside the house and stable yard, where Pat had run his livery business. Urgent dispatches were sent to the other members of the family telling them of the dreadful deed.

Jim was training with his sparring partner Steve O'Donnell at the barn adjoining his home in Asbury Park, New Jersey, when the telegram from his brother Harry arrived. At first he refused to believe it, but when the news was confirmed by newspaper dispatches, he 'broke down and wept like a child'. He cabled back to Harry, 'Can you keep them (the bodies) until we get home? I cannot believe they are gone until I see them. I am about half crazy.'

He left that evening for San Francisco. His brother Tom, who had been staying with him, went ahead on an earlier train. Another brother, Joe, was more difficult to locate, as he was on vacation in San Jose.

Before leaving on the trans-nation journey, Jim told reporters that his father must have been insane to do what he did. There was no other way to account for it. Jim had received letters from the family telling him his father's mind had become unbalanced. His parents were the best in the world, he said, and family relations had always been pleasant. They had always taken a great interest in his affairs and had wanted him to retire from the ring after the Fitzsimmons defeat. A forthcoming fight with Kid McCoy was now uncertain, said Corbett, but if necessary he would forfeit the $2,500 he had already put up. He would not continue boxing at all but for the fact that he was the family's chief support.

Bill Brady's reaction to the shooting, when he was told the news in Chicago, was remarkably cold and insensitive. The manager's main concern was that the McCoy fight would go ahead. 'The money is up and he will be ready,' he said. 'Of course this will have a bad effect on Jim for a time, but he will be ready and fit when the gong sounds on the night of the fight. Corbett is six days away from his people, so it will do him no good to leave off training and go home. There are several brothers and sisters there who can look after everything that is necessary.'

Kid McCoy, a fighter not renowned for his compassion towards opponents, was a model of decorum on this occasion. On hearing the news of the tragedy, he immediately wired condolences to Jim and said that, if the fight had to be called off, he would not claim the forfeit.

Temporary insanity was thought to have driven Pat Corbett to murder his wife and then commit suicide. Family members and acquaintances confirmed he had been acting strangely for some time. Various reasons were suggested for his state of mind. It was said that he suffered from the effects of heavy drinking. Another rumour was that he had lost everything he had in betting on his son to beat Fitzsimmons and that the banks were about to foreclose on a mortgage. It was also reported that he had suffered heavy financial losses after becoming bondsman for a receiver who failed in his trust. All these stories were emphatically denied.

'My father never waged a penny on me or any other pugilist,' said Jim. 'Six years ago I paid the mortgage on the home of my parents, with part of the proceeds from my fight with Sullivan. They never wanted for anything.'

What no-one tried to deny was that Pat had been suffering from hallucinations. He had accused his wife of fancying other men. His jealousy stemmed from his belief that he had seen her winking at prospective lovers. Kate, almost sixty years old, grey-haired and weighing over twenty stone (280 pounds), at first laughed off the accusations, but she grew increasingly concerned about her husband's irrational thinking and behaviour.

The couple had been on vacation at Bartlett Springs, near Clear Lake, up to two days before the shootings. Pat had sunk into a bout of depression and his wife decided they should return home. On the night before the tragedy he seemed to be in good spirits, reading the paper and chatting to his wife, his three daughters and his son-in-law, Charles King, before going to bed around 9.30 pm. Around 4 am, King and his wife were disturbed when their four-month-old baby started crying. It was the ever-vigilant Kate who came into the room and comforted her grandson. It was the last good deed she ever did. An hour later she was dead, along with her husband.

'I think he was crazy,' King told a *San Francisco Chronicle* reporter the next day. 'He had been acting queerly for weeks, and had not been well for two years since suffering an attack of acute gastritis. He ate sparingly and was sullen and cross. We all knew and spoke of these peculiarities, but put them down to old age. He owned this building and other property and was well-to-do. He had no creditors. He only drank in moderation.'

Other members of the family agreed that he must have been out of his senses to commit the terrible deed. Though reluctant to talk about it, they did confirm there was another instance of insanity in the family. Pat's sister, Margaret Griffin, had been confined to the Napa Insane Asylum for six years. She suffered from periodic madness, the same affliction suffered by her brother, and had sometimes been seized with the desire to commit violent acts.

Pat was not known to own a pistol and the condition of the weapon used in the shooting showed that it had been bought only recently. His actions during the afternoon of the tragedy left no doubt that he premeditated suicide, if not murder. Initially, it emerged, he had intended to use a lethal dose of poison. He was refused a request at one drug store for a quantity of arsenic because the assistant was suspicious as to its purpose. Corbett then went to another pharmacist, J.A. Bright, whom he knew well. He was supplied with a half-ounce of the poison after saying he wanted it to kill rats in the stable.

'I have known him for twenty years and he always seemed level-headed and rational,' Bright said later. 'I think he was temporarily insane and intended to poison the whole family. When the clerk told him a certain patent prescription would be the best remedy for ridding himself of the pests, he said he had tried it without success.'

For whatever reason, Corbett changed his mind about the poison and bought a gun. On the morning before the tragedy he told Pete Smith, a clerk at Clabrough, Golcher and Company, that he wanted a revolver to protect himself from burglars who infested the neighbourhood. He had been held up a short time before, he claimed. Smith showed him a hammerless revolver, explained its action, and, at Corbett's request, loaded it for him. Pat said he wanted the weapon only for an emergency and did not need any spare cartridges.

Several people told of meeting Corbett that day and noticing his odd behaviour. He told a policeman friend that he had been feeling very ill since his return from Bartlett Springs and that he did not think he 'was long for this world'. When the two met again a few hours later, Pat's mood had totally changed. During a half-hour conversation, he laughed easily and made no mention of his illness. The policeman noted that Corbett had polished his boots and put on a clean white shirt since they had met earlier.

Dr O'Connell, who would later be called to the scene of the tragedy, said he had met Corbett in the street and Pat offered him $1.50. The doctor said he was not owed any money, but Pat insisted he take it. 'He said he thought a great deal of me and wished to make me a present,' he said.

No-one noticed anything strange about him, however, when he signed his name on the Hayes Valley voting register that afternoon. Corbett had not missed this duty for thirty years, said the clerk, Jim Silvey. Pat's name was the last to go on the register of Precinct Six of the Thirty-Seventh District that day, and Silvey told him he had performed the same service for the father of John L. Sullivan in Boston many years before. The two men spent some time discussing the merits of the two famous fighters and the probable result of Jim's upcoming fight with Kid McCoy. Pat was of the unwavering opinion that his boy could whip any man in the ring, including Fitzsimmons. On returning to his livery stable, Corbett remarked to an employee that it was the last time he would ever register on the voting list.

Pat, aged sixty-two, and his wife, three years younger, were due to celebrate their fortieth wedding anniversary three months after the tragedy. Kate, noted the *San Francisco Call*, was 'the soul of human sympathy and good humour'. She was particularly active in church work and, whenever there was a fair, she was generous with her time and money. Local children loved her. They were always sure of candy or ice cream when they played around the Corbett house.

At the inquest, a witness, H.B. McIlroy, said he saw Corbett the evening before the tragedy and he seemed 'pleasant in manner and not intoxicated'. Dr O'Connell stated that Pat had spoken to him of his 'desire to die a sudden death'.

Dr Gallagher, the autopsy surgeon at the coroner's office, said he found three bullet wounds on the two bodies, though the revolver contained four empty cartridges. Mrs Corbett had been shot in the right temple and through the right cheek. Her husband was shot through the mouth. Mrs Corbett evidently had been shot while she slept, as her features were composed and the body was in a natural position in bed. It appeared that her husband had shot himself while standing by the bed and fell over. Deputy Coroner John O'Brien, who had been at Bartlett Springs some days earlier, noticed that Corbett seemed to brood over imaginary things and to be under a strain. The inquest jury returned a verdict 'that P.J. Corbett killed himself while temporarily insane, and that Mrs Corbett had come to her death at the hands of her husband'.

The funeral took place on 18 August. After a short service conducted at the couple's home by Father J. Flood, parish priest of the Sacred Heart Church, the bodies were taken in two hearses to be placed in a vault at Holy Cross Cemetery. There they lay, side by side and exposed to the views of mourners, until the arrival of their sons, Jim and Tom, from the east. A requiem mass concluded the funeral rites.

Jim tried to put away the gruesome memories of the family tragedy by immersing himself in a new enterprise. On the advice of a friend, George Consodine, owner of the famous Metropole Hotel in New York, Jim opened a high-class saloon at Broadway and

Thirty-Fourth Street, which later became the site of Saks' store. With the owner's name emblazoned in an electric sign above the entrance, Corbett's place attracted lots of prominent sport and show business people. It was just across the street from the old Manhattan Theatre and many an actor enjoyed dropping in for a drink and a chat with the host. 'I have met all sorts of people, from presidents to pickpockets,' said Jim, 'but the actors have always been my greatest friends.'

The trouble was that Corbett was not nearly as gregarious a character as John L. Sullivan, who loved the tavern atmosphere and happily joined in prolonged drinking sessions with back-slapping admirers. Jim, said Nat Fleischer, was 'temperate, rather select at choosing acquaintances, and speedily grew tired of being in contact with the members of the hand-shaking brigade who came to gape at him'. Bill Brady, who had a quarter-share interest in the place, also saw that Corbett 'wasn't the type to stand around all day and night, shaking the hands of bar-flies who had come there just to meet him and brag about it afterwards'. When he saw that the business would not prosper, the ex-champion's manager gave up his part of the business. Corbett, in return, forfeited his quarter-share in Brady's new stage production *Way Down East*. It was Jim who lost out on the deal. He sold the saloon at a loss, while the play, including the sale of movie rights, made well over $1 million. (The play was made into a successful film by the great director D.W. Griffith in 1920.)

It was the end of the line for the partnership of Corbett and Brady, but both acknowledged how successful they had been together and the parting was amicable. Though both seemed to have bade farewell to boxing, they would meet up again in the not-too-distant future, when Corbett would attempt to regain his world heavyweight title. This time, however, Brady would be in the opposite corner, advising the rugged big fellow who had been Jim's sparring partner for the Fitzsimmons fight, James J. Jeffries.

Towards the end of 1898 Corbett began to get the urge to fight again. And why not? He was still only thirty-two and looked the picture of health. Unlike many fighters when they leave the ring aside, he never developed excess fat. He was still the same lean, athletic figure of his prime years, though his nimble footwork and lightning reflexes might not be quite what they were. On 22 November Corbett stepped into the ring for the first time in twenty months. He didn't look for an easy comeback opponent. Tom

137

Sharkey, who had given him such a rough time in their four-round draw two years earlier, was again in the opposite corner.

Sailor Tom was delighted with a second chance to prove he had the style to upset Corbett. He still claimed he had been cheated of victory in the first encounter. Since then, he had improved his rating by going twenty rounds with the much-bigger Jim Jeffries and knocking out another top heavyweight contender, Gus Ruhlin, in the first round. The Irishman would never claim to be a fancy boxer, but he firmly believed he had the natural strength and endurance to overcome Corbett's cultivated approach. Once again, however, the bout would end in bitter controversy, with accusations of fake and conspiracy flying.

The capacity attendance at the Lenox Club in New York City included a large delegation from the Atlantic fleet docked in the harbour. Every seaman who had shore leave headed for the venue to put their money on Sharkey. They would have cleaned up nicely if the referee, 'Honest' John Kelly, had not declared at the end of the fight that all bets were off.

Sharkey, true to form, opened the ring proceedings with a rush. Corbett jabbed him off, but the Irishman stormed in again and surprised Jim with a hard left to the nose. The former champion responded with a rat-tat-tat of rapid jabs and, by the end of the round, one of Sharkey's eyes was already badly swollen. Corbett, realising he was not as speedy as he once was, chose to duck or pull away from blows rather than use nifty footwork. This tactic came unstuck in the second round, when he misjudged a Sharkey right swing and caught it on the chin. He fell on his face.

'All I could see was the stage revolving,' wrote Corbett in *The Roar of the Crowd*. 'In a few seconds I was up, dazed, but realised where I was. Knowing that the best thing to do when a fellow begins swinging these haymakers, which was all that Sharkey did, is not to get in range of them, but to bore in close, so that the blows just whistle around your neck and head, I called on all my reserve and dove in. To the amazement of the crowd, I began slugging him clean across the ring and had the best of the round. But just the same, I came to my corner a bit hazy and the seconds had to work hard to freshen me up.'

Jim's head cleared in the interval but, in trying to side-step a Sharkey rush in the third round, he twisted his ankle. The injury restricted his mobility and he believed this caused him to be accused afterwards of 'not trying'. Nevertheless, his better boxing had him well ahead after six rounds. Sailor Tom, though he never relented in his efforts to pin a decisive punch on the elusive ex-champion, was badly cut and bruised around the face from the attentions of Jim's precise punches.

A desperate Sharkey went for the kill in the seventh round and, for the first time, hurt his opponent with a solid right to the stomach. The blow took a lot of the wind out of Corbett, though he continued his mastery at long range. Two heavy swings landed high on Corbett's head in the eighth round and dazed him slightly, but he rallied and stopped the Irishman in his tracks with a stiff left counter.

From that point on, the bout developed into a brawl, with protests being shouted from both men's corners about alleged fouls. Sharkey's superior strength was much in evidence at close quarters as he threw his opponent around and tried to dig to the body, much to Corbett's annoyance. Jim later insisted there had been a prior agreement that neither man would hit in the clinches. Such a pact would have been more beneficial to Corbett, but the rough-hewn sailor paid scant regard to such niceties.

Jim, fed up with his opponent's rough tactics and feeling increasing pain from his ankle injury, admitted in his memoirs that he was hoping for Sharkey's disqualification as a way out of his difficulties. The fight did end on a foul, but it was Jim who got his marching orders from the referee.

Corbett started the ninth round by digging a left hook low into the Irishman's midriff and followed up with another in the same forbidden territory. This caused some surprise, as Jim was renowned as a fair fighter. Besides, he was such an accurate puncher that no one could imagine him accidentally hitting below the belt twice in succession, especially against a much shorter man. Sharkey didn't wait to argue, but waded in to resume his assault on the ex-champion's body. It was at this stage that the incident occurred that was to cause such a lasting outcry.

Con McVey, Jim's chief second, was so incensed at Sharkey's wild slugging and his continued disobedience of the 'no hitting in the clinches' pact that he jumped into the ring, demanding that the Irishman be ruled out. His action was, of course, against the rules, as no-one apart from the fighters and the referee is allowed in the ring during a contest. Referee Kelly immediately called a halt to the fight. He told the announcer, Charlie Harvey, to inform the crowd that Corbett had been disqualified and that all bets were off. Jim protested vigorously, but he could have no real complaint. His cornerman, either intentionally or because he had momentarily lost his head, had given the fight to Sharkey. Corbett turned on McVey, calling him names and striking him several times. He had to be hauled off by his other cornermen.

Allegations of a 'fix' were led by Bill McNaughton, the prominent western sports writer. His story, which appeared on the front pages of all the Hearst newspapers, claimed that a gambling clique, which stood to gain heavily from a Sharkey win, was foiled by the referee's 'all bets off' ruling. He insisted that Corbett knew nothing of the conspiracy. The implication, therefore, was that McVey was 'in' on the deal. Bob Fitzsimmons, in Chicago when he heard the result, laughed and said, 'What did I tell you? I knew all along it would be a fake fight.'

The aftermath of the fiasco was a meeting presided over by Senator Tim Sullivan, author and sponsor of the Horton Law which permitted boxing in New York, to investigate the charges of fraud. All of the principals who gathered at the offices of the *Police Gazette* for the hearing swore they were innocent of any pre-arranged result.

Corbett said that, as he was way ahead on points in the ninth round, there was no reason why he should have wanted to lose. The statement infuriated the hot-headed Sharkey.

'Why, you were whipped and you didn't have a Chinaman's chance of winning,' he yelled. 'That's why McVey came to your rescue. You needed him badly.'

Corbett reacted angrily to the charge and, for a moment, it looked like the fighters were going to resume their battle. Tim Sullivan intervened and managed to calm them down.

'Honest' John Kelly got Corbett off the hook by stating that, in his opinion, the former champion had no part in any conspiracy. 'Up to the time of the unfortunate ending,' he said, 'I thought both men were fighting hard and strictly on their merits. Nobody asked me to declare all bets off. That action was taken on my own judgement, and I still think I was right. I wanted to protect the bettors, because I fancied somebody might have got to McVey and induced him to get into the ring to help some gamblers. I don't believe he wanted to aid Corbett, for Jim didn't need any such help. Corbett is innocent. He only suffered through McVey's action, for which he wasn't responsible.'

Corbett, in his statement, reiterated his claim that he fought on the level. He also exonerated his chief second of any blame for what happened. 'I have been roundly abused in the newspapers,' he said, 'and been called a faker and conspirator because I have stood by McVey, my steadfast friend, who has given me faithful service for years as a sparring partner and second. I simply can't believe that Con would throw me down. I'll stick to that belief until I have better evidence than the talk of scandal-mongers. McVey might make a mistake in judgement, but he is incapable of treachery. He was not there to make sure I would be disqualified. I sincerely believe Con was acting for the best. He told me he couldn't bear to see me beaten, but that was an error on his part. I can't see where I was getting any the worst of the fight. On the contrary, I believe I had the better of things when it was stopped.'

Unexpected support for Corbett came from Tom O'Rourke, Sharkey's manager. He said he was certain Jim would not do anything crooked, but couldn't understand why McVey jumped into the ring. His only regret was that he thought Sharkey was in the lead and would have won decisively but for the 'fool action' by McVey. The referee acted wrongly in declaring all bets off, he said. That was what caused all the speculation about a 'fix'.

Charlie White, a well-known sportsman and referee, said he had acted as Corbett's 'chief of staff' and was seated near Jim's corner. 'If I had the least idea that Con McVey was going to pull such a boner,' he said, 'I would have stopped him, even if I had to brain him with a water bottle.'

Senator Sullivan was convinced of Corbett's sincerity, as were most of the journalists present at the meeting, but the taint of scandal hanging over the affair never really went away. Twenty-seven years after the bout, Jim wrote in *The Roar of the Crowd* that he was still hearing stories about the alleged 'fix'. In his earlier work, *My Life and My Fights*, he said he hardly ever had a fight without being approached beforehand with a bribe offer. 'During his preparation for a big fight,' he wrote, 'a boxer has to be as cunning as a fox. He is surrounded by spies. In the guise of friendship, people make overtures to him. Take my championship struggle with Fitzsimmons. I was a big favourite over Fitz and, had I undertaken to lose, I could have made a ton of money.'

Down through the years, there have been recurring allegations of big fight results being arranged in advance. Whenever a big favourite is upset, the know-alls appear out of the woodwork with their tired conclusions that gamblers had paid him to lose. In the vast majority of cases the so-called evidence does not stand up to close scrutiny. The main knock to such claims is that it simply doesn't pay for a champion to lose his title, or a leading contender his high ranking, for a once-off payment. The bribe would go nowhere near compensating him for the loss of future earnings when he took a drop in the ratings. There *are* big fight 'fixes', certainly, but they are much rarer than the sensation mongers would have us believe.

In Corbett's case it is inconceivable that such a proud man, anxious to re-establish himself as a viable world title challenger, would have agreed to lose to Sharkey. He was well aware of his unique place in boxing history and he was not going to ruin his hard-earned reputation as a ring great for a minor share in a betting coup.

The Sharkey debacle wasn't the last time Jim would be accused of taking part in a pre-arranged fight. He would have even greater difficulty getting rid of the mud that stuck after his clash with Kid McCoy, even if this time he was the one who had his hand raised by the referee.

CHAPTER 19

Loser – but a hero

On 9 June, 1899, the world heavyweight championship returned to America. Bob Fitzsimmons, in his first defence, was battered to defeat in eleven rounds by the much bigger and stronger James J. Jeffries.

The result rekindled Corbett's boxing ambitions. He had lost interest in the game through Fitzsimmons' refusal to give him a chance to regain the title. Now there was a completely new, and more promising, situation. He couldn't forget how easily he had handled the lumbering Jeffries in their sparring sessions. Obviously the Fighting Boilermaker had improved greatly, but he would never be anything near the gifted craftsman that was his former boss. Corbett knew he could dazzle Jeffries with science, but wondered if he had the stamina, at thirty-three, to outlast the powerful new champion, nine years younger, in what was sure to be a long, gruelling contest. The nagging belief that he could become the first man to regain the world heavyweight crown grew into an obsession. He would regret it for the rest of his life if he didn't give it a try.

It helped that Jeffries was managed by Bill Brady. Corbett, though no longer a business associate, was still on friendly terms with his former manager. Jim's approach was timely. Brady's efforts to make Jeffries into an actor, in a woeful vehicle called *Eighty Minutes in New York*, had failed miserably. A simple country boy at heart, Big Jeff hated being paraded before the public. 'I was embarrassed being put on exhibition like a prize pig,' he said. 'I couldn't give people a show like Sullivan and Corbett did.' The one thing he could do well was fight. But there was a lack of good opposition about.

Corbett's initial suggestion of a challenge to Jeffries was not taken seriously by Brady, who considered him finished as a fighter. This view was shared by Jim's former trainer, Billy Delaney, who had now joined up with Jeffries. Corbett kept up the pressure, however, playing on his old friendship with Brady and telling him that, due to his unsuccessful saloon venture, he needed the money, even if it was the loser's end of the purse. He finally convinced his ex-manager of the merits of his proposal. Brady, aware that Gentleman Jim was still a glamorous figure, could see the match as a big money-spinner. The deal was done. Corbett and Jeffries signed to fight at the Seaside Athletic Club, Coney Island, New York, on 11 May 1900. The contest was scheduled for twenty-five rounds.

Brady was convinced Jeffries would be too young, too big and too powerful for the ex-champion. He didn't realise that Corbett had tricked him into thinking he was washed up. In fact, Jim had kept in shape in secret workouts at Wood's gym on Twenty-Eighth Street, just off Fifth Avenue. Once the contract was signed for the fight, he went into intensive training at Lakewood, New Jersey. He left no stone unturned in getting into the best shape of his life. His daily schedule included walking, swimming, rowing and horse-riding. In the gym, he spent half an hour working out with dumb-bells, pulley-weights and doing callisthenics. Fifteen minutes each were given to working on an eighty-five pound bag and a lighter bag. Wrestling was also part of his routine. This 'suppled up' his neck muscles, though he had to be careful not to risk a wrench or strain. He went to bed early and kept to a well-planned diet. A staunch advocate of the 'apple-a-day' theory, he regarded the fruit as a 'splendid tonic'.

A vital part of his training was working on a strategy to deal with Jeffries' great bulk. 'I knew how much it jars and tires a man to hit a heavier opponent,' he said. 'To hit such a man hard and frequently takes more out of one than to receive an almost equal number of blows. I studied the thing out and found that, while the hitting of blows against an unyielding, massive surface jars the whole body, the principal strain comes on the thighs. The thighs, then, had to be strengthened.' Through specific exercises and steady pounding of the heavy bag, he found his thighs had increased in girth by one inch in a month.

A couple of weeks before the fight, Corbett brought in Gus Ruhlin, the Akron Giant, for rigorous sparring sessions. He got Ruhlin to box out of a crouch, *à la* Jeffries, and worked on ways to combat it. Gus had boxed Jeffries to a twenty-round draw, so he knew the champion's style pretty well. In order to prepare Jim for the scheduled championship distance, Corbett and Ruhlin twice sparred over twenty-five rounds, with no punches pulled. All the training was done behind closed doors. Everything was geared towards not revealing – especially to the Jeffries camp – how perfectly geared Jim was to win back his old title.

The champion, in contrast, found it difficult to get down to the hard grind at Allenhurst, a beach community just north of Asbury Park. Jeffries liked his glass of champagne, staying up late and messing about with his prankster pals. He regarded training as unnecessary drudgery, believing that his natural strength would always win out. It didn't help when, a month before facing Corbett, he demolished over-matched Jack Finnegan in fifty-five seconds, the shortest world heavyweight title fight on record. It gave the Fighting Boilermaker a dangerous dose of over-confidence. Corbett might hang around a little longer, but what was the hurry? Twenty-five rounds was an awfully long time to keep away from a Jeffries' knockout special.

Though a domiciled Californian, James Jackson Jeffries was born in Carroll, Ohio, on 15 April 1875. When he was seven, his family moved to a farm just outside Los Angeles. A fine athlete in his youth, he excelled at boxing, wrestling and track events. While working as a boilermaker, and later in a meat packing company, he boxed at the East Side Athletic Club. In his first professional fight, at the age of nineteen, he beat Hank Griffin in fourteen rounds. Making rapid progress, he drew with experienced heavyweights Gus Ruhlin and Joe Choynski, and knocked out a faded Peter Jackson in three rounds. Tough Tom Sharkey lasted the twenty-round distance.

When Jeffries came under the managership of Brady, he was taught his peculiar, but effective, crouching style by the former world welterweight and middleweight champion, Tommy Ryan. Bent low, with his left arm extended and his face protected by his right forearm, Jeff threw a terrific left hook. His right, too, was a devastating weapon. Jimmy McLarnin, twice world welterweight champion during the 1930s, said of Jeffries: 'As far as I'm concerned, he was the greatest fighter of all time. He had unbelievable strength and a lot more skill than people gave him credit for. He could take an opponent's head off with a left jab.'

In his challenge for Bob Fitzsimmons' heavyweight title, Jeffries, nicknamed the Californian Grizzly as well as the Fighting Boilermaker, was much too powerful for the champion, who was three inches shorter and a massive fifty-five pounds lighter. He floored Fitzsimmons three times before finishing him off in the eleventh round with a left hook and a right uppercut.

After defending the title seven times, Jeffries would retire as undefeated champion in 1904. Sadly, he was lured back to the ring six years later in a fanatical drive to depose the widely despised black champion Jack Johnson. Unable to get himself back into his old fighting shape, the thirty-five-year-old Jeffries took a savage beating and was stopped in the fifteenth round. It was the only time he lost in his twenty-one fights. In retirement, Jeffries owned a bar and a farm where he bred prize cattle. He also performed in vaudeville and appeared in movies. He died, aged seventy-seven, on 3 March 1953.

In the days leading up to Jeffries' title defence against Corbett, reports inevitably leaked out about the former champion's superb fitness. Knowledgeable fight fans, however, were not convinced Jim stood much of a chance of dethroning the unbeaten 'Boilermaker'. They could get even money by betting he would last fifteen rounds, and two-to-one if he lost inside twenty-five. Corbett supporters, who were in the minority, thought that if he could go fifteen rounds, then why not twenty-five?

A couple of days before the battle, Corbett sent his friend, now his manager, George Consodine, to talk to the referee, Charlie White. 'Tell him I want a fair, stand-up fight,' he instructed him. 'Other referees let Fitzsimmons and Sharkey maul me around in the clinches. I don't want that to happen again.'

Bill Brady, remembering how he taught Jim all the tricks about gaining an advantage, told a reporter: 'Let Corbett stop trying to teach the referee his business. Jeffries never sought an edge and never will.'

Gentleman Jim had the last word: 'I see they have nerves. Well, I promise to shake them up a bit more. Jeffries is going to find out that he'll have to fight my fight.'

The day of the contest was hot and muggy. Jeffries, a little worried about his condition, hoped his vitality would not be sapped. Although the odds were three-to-one in his favour, he wondered if he could get Corbett to stand still long enough to pin him with his heavy punches. He recalled only too well how difficult a target the then champion had been when they sparred together.

The public turn-out for the fight was a major disappointment. Most fans, aware of how Corbett had struggled in his last fight against the aggressive, but smaller, Tom Sharkey, figured he would not last too long against the hulking Jeffries. The Seaside Athletic Club was no more than half full. Brady reckoned the proceeds hardly reached $35,000, of which Corbett took 'far less than $10,000'. Unfounded rumours that the fight was 'fixed' helped put potential customers off, said the showman.

Those who stayed away missed a masterly boxing exhibition by Gentleman Jim, who bamboozled his opponent with science until he succumbed to a desperate Jeffries attack in the twenty-third round. Although he lost, Corbett earned undying acclaim for his great skill, bravery and effort. Many experts regard it as his best performance. Had it been a modern title fight, restricted to twelve rounds, or even a twenty-rounder, Jim would have regained the world heavyweight title on an undisputed points decision. Regrettably, no film was made of the classic encounter.

When he threw off his bathrobe, Corbett's thorough preparation was evident to all. He looked every inch the perfectly trained athlete. Jeffries, massively built, with muscles bulging like a weight-lifter, scaled fifteen stone, six pounds (216 pounds), to the challenger's thirteen stone, six pounds (188 pounds). Corbett was attended by George Consodine, Gus Ruhlin and Leo Pardello, while the champion's cornermen were Bill Brady, Tommy Ryan, Jack Jeffries (his brother), and Ed Dunkhorst. Brady, trying one of his psychological tricks, protested about the tape on Corbett's hands. He was satisfied when Jim lifted a section of the tape to show there was no hidden horseshoe.

From the opening bell Corbett's darting left jab, fast footwork, tight defence, and spoiling tactics whenever the champion got close bewildered his former sparring partner. For round after round Corbett's unerring left shot home. When Jeffries crouched, the challenger would straighten him up with a left feint for the head, followed by a right hook or uppercut. If Jeffries tried a lead, his rival would slip the blow and counter with lefts and rights to the head. On the rare occasions when the champion did land a punch, Corbett was moving away and its force was minimised.

In the sixth round Corbett rattled the titleholder with seven successive left jabs without taking a single blow in reply. The fight was so one-sided that Jeffries' supporters were worried he had no answer to the older man's skill. Corbett's fans' only concern was whether he would be able to keep up the excellent work without running out of steam.

'By the sixth round,' said Jeffries later, 'I bitterly regretted not having trained faithfully. I had chased him for miles around the ring without landing a solid blow. And, all the while, he was piling up points.'

As is ever the case when the underdog is doing well, the neutrals in the crowd cheered lustily at Corbett's success. The former champion acknowledged the applause by bowing as he returned to his corner after each round. The one thing Jeffries had going for him was his dogged determination to land a decisive blow. He did hurt Corbett with the occasional body dig, but not enough to slow down his gallop. If he would just stand still for a minute, then we'll see who is best, the frustrated titleholder seemed to be thinking. The dancing master was in no mood to oblige his old campmate by playing his game.

'I was in an out and everywhere those first rounds,' recalled Corbett, 'feinting and sidestepping with all my old skill. Never before had I such marvellous judgement, such accurate timing. ... As the rounds went on, the audience grew resigned to losing their wagers on Jeffries. But, as many told me afterwards, they felt it was worth it, seeing me win back my old championship.'

In the ninth round Corbett surprised his opponent by switching his usual left jab to a hook. Two hard lefts to the jaw staggered Jeffries and almost put him down. The challenger followed up his advantage, rushing forward and having the better of the exchange that followed. It was Corbett's best round so far.

He resumed his jabbing tactics in the tenth, landing with almost monotonous regularity. The blood flowed from the champion's nose and mouth. Jeffries kept moving in, trying for a finisher, but the alert challenger either blocked the punches or slid smoothly out of range. 'The crowd was with me almost to a man,' said Corbett, 'and they rose and cheered me till the walls rang. As I went to my corner I felt no fatigue, no pain of any kind.'

Round after round, the pattern was repeated: Jeffries chasing, Corbett making him miss and doing all the scoring. Once, in the fifteenth round, Jeffries connected with a heavy right swing to the challenger's head. Corbett looked set to fall, but he recovered quickly and came back with a volley of hooks, jabs and uppercuts that reminded the Boilermaker who was master.

Jeffries now began to stalk his rival without rushing in and wasting his strength. All the time he was on the lookout for the opportunity to connect with the one punch that would matter. The pace of the fight slowed.

In the eighteenth round Corbett, his confidence sky high, adopted an aggressive approach, moving in and landing fast combinations. The concerned cries of his cornermen – 'Not yet', 'Wait', 'Be careful, Jim' – could be heard above the crowd's chant of 'Corbett, Corbett'.

The frustration in Jeffries' corner erupted into a blazing row at the end of the nineteenth round. Tommy Ryan, a better fighter than a corner strategist, urged the champion to box. Bill Brady, white with indignation and anxiety, ordered the big fellow to wade in and go all out for a knockout. He knew Jeffries had no chance of matching the challenger's skill. Brady ordered Ryan to leave the corner. When Tommy refused, the manager threatened to get the police to remove him. Ryan relented. Now in total command, Brady told Jeffries, 'Your only chance of winning is to knock him out. He'll grab the title for sure if you don't mix with him.'

Gentleman Jim, though forging further and further ahead on points, accepted the wisdom of his friends' advice to be cautious when, in the twentieth round, a huge swing missed his chin by a whisker. Inevitably, the pace had begun to tell on the ever-mobile challenger. Though he continued to outwit the ponderous Jeffries, his footwork had slowed and he was taking more punches from the desperate champion.

Nevertheless, Corbett was convinced he had the championship in the bag. Having won every round to date, he knew he could not lose on points unless in a 'robbery'. Over-confidence prompted him to defy logic and go all-out to put Jeffries on his back. 'Even if I should not succeed in knocking him out,' he said, 'just to have him groggy at the end of the twenty-fifth round would be a nice topping-off after so far outpointing him. It would be quite dramatic, I thought.'

While resting in his corner after the twenty-second round, he began to plan what he would do when he was champion again. 'I sat there on my stool, puzzling over the choice of a road manager, planning out a new play, and I was actually deciding what size type I would use on the big posters that would proclaim me "Champion of the world again!" '

The vivid pictures were still occupying Corbett's mind when the bell rang for the twenty-third round. He took up the story in *The Roar of the Crowd:*

> Brady and Delaney kept yelling to Jeffries, as they had since the sixteenth round, 'The only way you can win, Jeff, is by a knockout.' An encouraging admission, I thought, that they had already lost. As he

had done ever since the middle of the fight, Jeff was trying to rough me around, swinging madly. I just relaxed and danced here and there, often letting my hands hang idly at my sides. All the while I was seeing those wonderful posters and electric lights. And I was waiting for the twenty-fourth ...

The next thing I saw was not the electric lights, but flashing stars and a hand holding smelling salts under my nose. I was in my corner, sprawled out on a stool. A cousin of mine, Tom Corbett, whom I hadn't seen for years, was bending over me, kissing me on the cheek. The crowd was standing up and cheering. It sounded like music to my ears. I straightened myself to get up so the referee could hold up my hand. But I felt a little hazy, and I saw my seconds looking at me peculiarly. 'What is it?' I asked. 'Jim,' they said sadly, 'you were knocked out.' And, from that day to this, I don't remember ever being hit. I don't remember being on the floor at all.

What had happened was that Corbett had come out for the twenty-third round fast and aggressively, feinting, sidestepping and throwing a series of jabs. Jeffries concentrated on his target, mindful of what he had to do to save his title and his unbeaten record. He saw an opening and crashed a hard left hook into the challenger's body. Corbett fell back against the ropes. The champion followed up his advantage with a stiff left to the face. Then, feinting to throw a right, he crashed home a terrific left hook to the jaw. The same punch that had missed hundreds of times caught Corbett as he came back off the ropes, increasing its impact. Gentleman Jim dropped like a wet rag, and never moved while Charlie White counted to ten.

The crowd applauded Jeffries' dramatic escape from the jaws of defeat, but showed great appreciation for the challenger's gallant effort. The result was a bitter disappointment to Corbett and his supporters. Having gained an unassailable points lead, all he had to do was stand on his feet for another seven minutes and he would have been heavyweight champion of the world once again. He had given one of the finest exhibitions of sheer science ever seen in the ring, but had finally lost out to brute strength.

'Jeff, you're the luckiest man in the world to have won tonight,' said Corbett when the winner called to his dressing room. According to Corbett, Jeffries didn't answer, but 'just stood in front of me, like a bad boy with his head bashfully hanging down'.

Years later, when Jeffries was interviewed by Nat Fleischer, then sports editor of the *New York Telegram,* he admitted he was surprised by Corbett's speed, but never lost faith in his ability to wear him down. 'Corbett was a master boxer,' he said. 'He knew every trick and angle. He was as game as he was scientific and, even though he was past his prime then, he cut a terrific pace while his stamina lasted.'

The finishing punch, however, was no accident, insisted Jeffries. He said it was normal for him to start slowly, gradually softening up his opponent until he could apply the finisher. 'I knew Corbett was tiring fast, but I could keep going indefinitely. In the twenty-third round, I figured I would fake a left lead, make him jerk his head back and then, as his head bobbed forward again, I would let fly with the KO punch. It all worked out as I planned.'

Fleischer believed that, had Corbett's reactions not slowed at that late stage of the fight, he would have been able to avoid the finishing blow. Considering his age handicap, it was the greatest performance of his career, said the renowned writer and historian.

CHAPTER 20

A double dose of scandal

The world loves a gallant loser. Corbett's popularity soared to unprecedented heights because of his brave bid to regain the title. Wherever he went, he was greeted as if he was once again king of the heavyweights. 'When I entered Rector's, Martin's, or any place on Broadway, the diners would applaud and frequently cheer me, an unusual tribute for a defeated man,' he said. 'I believe I was more popular than I had ever been as champion.'

The acclaim was short-lived. Within three months of his loss to Jeffries, he plunged from hero to villain.

Two events shaped the dramatic fall from grace of Gentleman Jim. His victory over Kid McCoy was widely believed to have been faked, and his wife, Vera, started proceedings for a divorce. She accused her husband of adultery, cruelty, and being 'anything but a gentleman'. To make things worse, both boxers' wives backed the stories of the fight fix. Vera later retracted, once she had patched up her differences with Corbett, but Mrs McCoy remained adamant that a fight deal had been done.

A match between Corbett and McCoy was a 'natural' for New York. Each had a big following in the metropolis and the rivalry was fanned by widely-reported insults exchanged by the pair. The mutual dislike was genuine, even though McCoy had acted with admirable sensitivity at the time of Corbett's parents' tragic deaths, refusing to claim the forfeit due when the fight was cancelled.

Their feud came to a head when the pair bumped into each other in the bar of the Gilsey House, New York, in September 1898. In what the hard-to-shock *Police Gazette* described as 'a disgraceful affair', Corbett berated his rival for calling him a monkey. This was prompted by Jim's fondness for dressing up in a 'monkey suit'. 'You're a fine-looking fellow to be calling someone else a monkey,' said Corbett. The Kid retorted that 'Gentleman Jim' was a misnomer, as evidenced by Corbett's ill-mannered treatment of Sharkey and Fitzsimmons. A scuffle between the pair resulted in Corbett being kicked in the groin. He was laid up in bed for several days as a result.

McCoy, born Norman Selby in Rush County, Indiana, on 13 October 1872, was one of the most notorious characters ever to pull on a boxing glove. Even though he was a highly talented fighter, he couldn't resist trying to pull a fast one on gullible opponents. The numerous stories told about his trickery, mostly apocryphal, are a treasured part of boxing folklore. Once, it was said, he filled his mouth with loose teeth and, at an opportune moment in the fight, spat them out. While his horrified rival stopped to apologise for the damage he had done, McCoy promptly delivered a knockout punch on his unguarded chin. On another occasion, when facing a shifty boxer who fought in his bare feet, the Kid had one of his seconds scatter thumb-tacks on the canvas to upset his rhythm. Before facing Tommy Ryan, he told the world welterweight champion he was ill and hadn't been able to train properly. Ryan took it easy on him, only to find McCoy suddenly springing to life and battering him to defeat in fifteen rounds. Most despicable of all his tricks was the time he sent a telegram to Peter Maher just before they fought. The message said there had been a sudden death in Maher's family back home in Ireland. By the time the distraught Maher discovered it was a hoax, it was too late. McCoy scored a fifth round knockout.

A specialty of the Kid's armoury was the 'corkscrew' punch. This was a blow delivered with a last-minute twist of the wrist, aimed at ripping open his opponent's skin. The odd thing was that McCoy didn't need to resort to such cruel tactics. He won most times on merit. After capturing the world middleweight title in 1897 by knocking out Dan Creedon, within the next two years he faced – and beat – many top heavyweights, including Gus Ruhlin and Joe Choynski, despite conceding considerable weight. Because there was some confusion with a lesser-known fighter named Peter McCoy, also known as Kid McCoy, a newspaper sub-editor wrote the headline, 'Choynski is Beaten by the Real McCoy'. The term grew into popular usage in describing something which is the genuine article.

The Kid fought, on and off, for twenty-five years. He finally hung up his gloves for good at the age of forty-three, ran a saloon and a gym, acted in movies and worked as a salesman and a detective. His love life was even more bizarre than his ring antics. As well as enjoying numerous affairs, he was married eight times. Two of the women he married twice. In 1924 he was convicted of manslaughter after shooting the woman he was living with. Sentenced to twenty-four years in prison, he served seven before he was released on parole. On 18 April 1940, McCoy committed suicide.

Demands for the antagonists to settle their differences in the ring resulted in a match being arranged for 30 August 1900 at Madison Square Garden. It was the last major contest permitted under the Horton Law, which had governed boxing in New York state since 1896. This had allowed fights with no limit to the number of rounds, decisions by referees and the posting of forfeits and side-bets. There had been such an outcry over the levels of corruption in the sport, with regular accusations of fixed fights to facilitate gambling interests, that reform was demanded. The Horton Law was replaced by the Lewis Law, which restricted contests to 'members only' clubs, where they could be more strictly supervised, but there were still too many loopholes. In 1911 the controversial Frawley Law was enacted. Contests in New York were limited to ten rounds and referees were barred from giving points verdicts. The only way a champion could lose his title in a 'no decision' fight was by knockout. When a bout went the distance, it was left to designated pressmen at ringside to give their opinions as to the 'winner', though these 'newspaper verdicts', as they were known, had no official status. Finally, in 1920, the Walker Law (sponsored by New York's famous Mayor Jimmy Walker) specified fifteen-round fights to a decision and supervision by a commission. The rest of the United States adopted the system and it served as a pattern for boxing authorities across the world.

As it happened, the Corbett vs. McCoy fight served up the type of scandal that had led to the cries for reform of the old Horton Law. Rumours of a fix were rampant in the run-up to the affair. The betting favoured Corbett. To win $60, one had to lay down $100. A rumour that the fighters had privately agreed to split their share of the gate fifty-fifty, instead of the official seventy-five per cent to the winner and twenty-five per cent to the loser, caused a fall-off in wagers. With the persistent talk of a fraud, the attendance at the fight was disappointing. The $35 box seats were not filled and the total receipts reached only $56,000. The fighters' share was $33,810.

On the morning of the fight George Siler, who had refereed Corbett's bout with Fitzsimmons, disclosed in the *Chicago Tribune* that there were lots of ugly rumours of a 'fix'. He had been told by a wellknown fight manager, whom he did not name, that it had been arranged for McCoy to get knocked out. Siler did not say if he believed the stories, but he had heard that Corbett had not been taking the best care of himself for the last couple of days. 'In fact, it was given to me confidentially that he imbibed too freely last night and retired at a late hour a little under the influence,' said Siler. It was just one of the many unsubstantiated stories flying about town.

However, most people were convinced the contest was on the level. As with Corbett's controversial second fight with Tom Sharkey, they didn't believe either man would sully his reputation and jeopardise his place in ring history by being involved in a fake fight. With two such skilled practitioners of the Manly Art of Self-Defence in opposition, there was lively debate as to who would prove the master. Though Corbett had all the physical advantages – he was two inches taller and, at 190 pounds, twenty pounds heavier – he was seven years older than McCoy.

By fight time, the odds on a Corbett victory were two to one on. He entered the ring to a tremendous reception. McCoy's welcome was somewhat more subdued. The referee, Charlie White, threw two sets of gloves into the ring, one owned by Corbett and the other sponsored by the Garden club, and asked the participants to make a choice. The Kid picked the club gloves, while Corbett preferred his own. When the referee called the fighters to the centre of the ring to shake hands, McCoy snarled and turned his back. Jim shrugged his shoulders, laughed and walked back to his corner. His seconds were George Consodine, who had succeeded Bill Brady as his manager, Leo Pardello, Tommy 'Spider' Kelly and Fred Stone, the noted comedian and useful amateur boxer. Looking after McCoy were his brother, Homer Selby, Philadelphia Jack O'Brien (who would win the world light-heavyweight title from Bob Fitzsimmons four years later) and Bobby Burns.

The fight opened at a lively pace. Corbett, backed to the ropes, neatly blocked a right aimed at his head and rammed a couple of stiff jabs into his opponent's face. In the second round the Kid connected with a hard left hook and ducked a countering left. After a clinch, Jim opened up with a left and right to the head and sent

McCoy's head jerking back with a succession of jabs. The spectators enjoyed the cut-and-thrust exchanges, while noting that Corbett had the better of the opening rounds. Jim admitted afterwards he was learning that 'McCoy was far more clever than Fitzsimmons'.

Spectators were astonished to find both men abandoning their cultured styles in the third round and engaging in a prolonged slugging match. A somewhat affronted Corbett later observed that it was 'pretty scientific slugging'. It seemed to him that the Kid had suddenly thrown caution to the wind and 'fought like a crazy man'.

McCoy tried repeatedly for his rival's body, but was unable to penetrate his tight defence. Corbett used his reach advantage to pick off the Kid with left leads. Just before the end of the fourth round, a Corbett barrage to the body left his opponent looking hurt and weak as he stumbled back to his corner.

Jim, eager to follow up his advantage, started the fifth round with a rush. He missed with a right uppercut, leaving himself open to a solid jab to the mouth. Corbett stormed in and it was give-and-take for a few seconds, with Jim landing the more effective punches. On breaking from a clinch, Corbett sank home a terrific left to the body, causing his opponent to stagger back, grimacing in pain. As he sank to the floor, Corbett hooked him rapidly to the head with a left and right. At 'eight' McCoy made a feeble effort to rise, but the effort was too much. Charlie White tapped Corbett on the shoulder and said, 'You win.'

Jim had learned the value of the 'solar plexus punch' from Bob Fitzsimmons and emulated it to dramatic effect.

Many spectators were not convinced the knockout was genuine. They felt McCoy, had he wished, could have risen before the referee got to 'ten'. The ringside reporters were divided. The *New York Times* was satisfied that McCoy went down under merciless punching for a clean knockout. The savagery of the fight contradicted the rumours that it was pre-arranged, or, if it was, McCoy took needlessly severe punishment. George Siler, writing in the *Chicago Tribune*, took the opposite view. It was hard to believe the men were not acting, he said. 'At the end, one had the same feeling as a person coming away from a clever but decadent play – he wants to take several long breaths of good, fresh air and a drink of cool, clear water to take the taste out of his mouth.' James J. Jeffries, in the same paper, said the Kid was 'fairly and decisively defeated on his merits'.

The controversy lasted for a long time. Alexander Johnson, in *Ten and Out, the Complete Story of the Prize-ring in America*, published in

1927, observed that McCoy 'dropped to the floor and gave an excellent imitation of a man in distress'. Samuel Hopkins Adams, the novelist and historian, who was at the fight, was even more scathing: 'While the house shrieked and McCoy writhed on the floor in a touching representation of *The Dying Gladiator*, the referee tolled out ten with his arms and it was all over. Eighty-thousand-odd happy suckers, including world champion Jeffries and my humble self, departed in the fond illusion that we had witnessed one of the great events in ring history. So we had, but what we had been watching was not a supreme fight. It was a supreme fake.'

Adams, in an article entitled *There's No Fraud Like an Old Fraud*, published in *Sports Illustrated* in 1958, quoted George Consodine as saying that McCoy had confessed to him that he had accepted $5,000 to throw the fight. But, as $5,000 was the loser's official share of the purse, it seems an odd co-incidence that the bribe figure was exactly the same. To further debunk the story, Consodine was in London, not New York, at the time the scandal broke; and, in any case, he was Corbett's manager, not McCoy's, as Adams believed.

Whatever doubts there might have been about McCoy's performance, most experts believed Corbett was innocent of any wrongdoing. William Naughton, in *Kings of the Queensberry Realm*, written two years after the event, said it might have been true that McCoy had sold himself to some bookmaker, but 'there is no gainsaying the fact that the punch that finally sent McCoy to the floor was a wicked one'.

Corbett, in *The Roar of the Crowd*, gave his side of the story:

> This accusation hurt me more than anything that had ever been said about me or done to me in my life, for I certainly saw no evidence of McCoy's reported efforts to 'lay down'; and he fought very hard in the fight. And I knew that I gave to the public the best that was in me. Ever since I started in boxing it had been one of my aims, in addition to making something of myself, to elevate the sport; and I believe I have a host of supporters who will substantiate me in that claim. I had bluffed my opponents sometimes, but it was beyond me ever to descend to fixing a fight.

Charlie White, years after the fight, told Nat Fleischer he was convinced there was nothing crooked about it. As referee, he was no more than two feet away from the fighters when the left to the stomach put McCoy down and out. 'The wallop was hard enough to take the fight out of any man,' he said. Corbett had proved himself the better man and had given his rival 'as fine a licking as any chap ever got in the ring'. If there was anything phony about the fight, concluded White, 'McCoy alone was accountable for it. I'll stake my last dollar that Jim Corbett, who got an undeservedly raw deal from the press, was not to blame in any respect.'

For the first week after the fight, mutterings of a fraud were no more than that. No-one came forward with any conclusive evidence. It looked like the controversy might die away until, on 9 September, the bombshell dropped. The *New York World*'s front page headline read, 'Corbett Runs Away – McCoy Fight Fixed.'

The previous day, it was reported, Jim had disappeared from his New York home. At two o'clock that afternoon, he sailed for England on board the Cunard liner *Campania*, along with his manager George Consodine. Also on board was the beautiful Marguerite Corneille, a vaudeville singer, whose friendship with Corbett was no secret. Jim left two notes, one to his wife and the other to D. J. Tobey, a friend and business associate, to be delivered after the ship was at sea.

Immediately she got the message Vera rushed to her husband's Broadway saloon. She startled customers when she burst in, agitated and confused, demanding to know where he was. John Consodine, brother of Corbett's manager, was asked to confirm or deny that Jim had gone away. He said he knew nothing. Vera quizzed every bartender and waiter in the place, without getting any satisfaction. She went straight home and sent a message to her lawyer, asking him to draw up papers for a divorce on the grounds of cruelty and desertion.

By that evening Vera had calmed down enough to agree to be interviewed by a reporter from the *World*. She charged that Corbett, aware of the growing disclosures about his contest with McCoy, had fled rather than face the music. 'The fight was a fake,' she said, 'as every sporting man in town knows. It was fixed up right here in this very room in which we are sitting.'

Where her version of a pre-arrangement differed from the others was that Corbett was the one who had agreed to lose. Half an hour before the fight, she said, Jim had a change of heart and 'gave the Kid the double-cross'.

As to her husband's deserting her, she said she wasn't sorry to see him go. 'I will get a divorce purely on the grounds of cruelty,' she said. 'For five years I have endured his treatment. He struck me. He stuck a lighted cigar against my cheek and was mean to me in other ways. I called a policeman once on the street to protect me. Gentleman Jim he was called, but never was a name more mis-applied. Mr Corbett and I have not lived together since a short while after his fight with Jeffries. We spoke to each other and he came here sometimes to attend to business matters. We had separated several times before, but each time he had begged to be taken back. Now we are separated for good.'

Kid McCoy was furious when he heard of Vera's story. In a letter to the editor of the *World*, he dismissed the fraud accusation as nonsense. They were 'simply the utterances of a jealous woman'. Her motive was 'pure malice and spite to revenge herself on Corbett, who she admits has deserted and mistreated her. The old saying "Hell knoweth no fury like a woman scorned" seems to be applicable in this instance'.

The Kid insisted that neither he nor any representative had entered into negotiations to get Corbett to lie down. 'I cannot see where either of us could have gained any prestige or money by being defeated,' he said. 'I fought a bad and wrong kind of fight, by smothering up and not being the aggressor. It was my intention to tire Corbett out and, when he was in that condition, to beat him. I was in good condition and unhurt up to the time I received the hard punch in the stomach, a spot where it does not take a very hard punch to incapacitate one from being able to fight for the few seconds allowed to recover. I want to state now, as I did immediately after the contest, that I was defeated fairly and squarely, and have no-one to blame but myself. I still believe I can beat Corbett and hope some time in the near future to have another chance to prove it.'

Looking back, a century later, it is impossible to say with any degree of certainty that there was nothing crooked about the affair. No film appears to have been made of the fight, and Siegmund Lubin, an enterprising Philadelphia moviemaker, only added to the confusion by releasing a 'reproduction', in which actors attempted to follow the newspaper descriptions of the action. Anyone who accepted this as a realistic re-enactment would have been convinced of a fraud, for the players were not trying too hard.

The fact that McCoy was the underdog makes it unlikely that gamblers offered him a bribe to lose. The odds would not have made the investment worthwhile. If the favourite, Corbett, had lost, such an arrangement would have made more sense. The other suspicion is that Gentleman Jim wanted to be sure of victory and paid his opponent to lie down. But, for the same reasons given for his other suspect fight, against Sharkey, Corbett simply had too much to lose by getting involved in any shady deals. As for Vera's allegation of a fix, McCoy probably hit the nail on the head by putting it down to the rantings of a jealous woman. At the time of her husband's desertion, she was prepared to say anything to cause him damage.

The headline in the *World* of 11 September added another sensational chapter to the running story: M'COY AND CORBETT BOTH SUED FOR DIVORCE. The report stated that Julia E. Selby, after learning that the Kid had instigated divorce proceedings, brought a counter suit against her husband. She obtained an order for his arrest after telling a court she believed McCoy intended to dispose of his property and leave the country. He had taken jewellery worth $10,000 belonging to her, she said. She accused her husband of adultery with two young actresses, Beulah Cameron and Lilly O'Neill. To conduct her case, Julia hired Howe and Hummel, the same attorneys who were to represent Mrs Corbett in her action.

In her suit for absolute divorce, Vera Corbett named Marguerite Corneille as co-respondent. She had learned that her husband had disposed of all his property before leaving the country. She asked for liberal alimony. In papers submitted in the case she alleged that Corbett had several times threatened to kill her and tortured her by holding a lighted cigar to her face. On one occasion, he had threatened her with a pistol, saying 'I'll kill you'. Her life was saved by George Consodine and Vance Barton, who took the gun from Corbett.

'Shortly after we married,' she said, 'I discovered his love was shallow and that I was married to a human brute.'

Emanuel Friend, counsel for Corbett, said he had been retained by the former champion to look after any suit his wife might bring. 'I saw Corbett the night before he sailed,' said Friend, 'and he was on the verge of nervous prostration. He needed a rest and went away to get it.'

When the *Campania* docked at Queenstown, in Ireland, a correspondent for the *New York World* was waiting to quiz Corbett. After exchanging a few pleasantries, with the former champion saying he had enjoyed the voyage immensely, the newshound went straight for the jugular: 'Do you know that Mrs Corbett is reported to have followed you, and that she has threatened to shoot Miss Corneille because she is on the same ship as you?'

'Oh, that's ridiculous,' replied Corbett. 'It's false. I'm sorry for Miss Corneille. I never met her until this ship was sailing. I am travelling all alone under the name of George Francis. I occupy a stateroom entirely separate from Miss Corneille's. She has rooms with her mother. When I was introduced to her on starting, I was told her name was Mrs Martin. Consodine is travelling as Mr Martin. He has a stateroom to himself.'

Asked why they registered under assumed names, he said it was 'to avoid being interviewed in New York and to keep our departure quiet'. On being told of Vera's divorce action, he said, 'No, I don't believe that's possible. She was probably irritated by hearing certain reports and therefore acted hurriedly and made wild statements, for which she is sorry by now.' When he learned that Mrs McCoy was also suing for divorce, he said with a laugh, 'Well, that's news indeed.'

The *World* man, keen to add to his hot story, informed the former champion, 'Your wife and Mrs McCoy have issued formal statements that your fight with Kid McCoy was a fake and that he lay down.'

'Oh, that's rich,' said Corbett. Told that Vera claimed the Tom Sharkey fight was also faked, he growled, 'Another lie. I never faked a fight in my life. These stories about fakes are started by soreheads in New York.'

'Your wife says you took $200,000 with you and that you have run away to dodge the disgrace of being in New York now,' said the persistent newshound.

'I'm dodging nothing,' barked the tetchy ex-champion. 'As for the money I've got with me, that's my business and nobody else's.'

Asked if he wished to make a 'complete statement about your fights and put yourself right in the eyes of the American people', Corbett said his character was well known and he didn't need a statement to back it up. He would stand on his record.

On how long he intended to stay in Europe, he said, 'I don't know. Consodine and I have had this trip planned for some time. I'll do some work over here if I can find anyone to put on the gloves with me. Maybe Mitchell will do it. Nothing has been arranged. When I go back to New York, I will fight Jeffries for the championship. That will be my last battle.'

Consodine corroborated everything Corbett said. He said Jim was on a pleasure trip, needing a rest after training continuously for a year and a half and fighting two hard battles.

Marguerite Corneille could not be located by the reporter. Her mother gave nothing away. 'My daughter is indisposed,' she said. 'She is in our stateroom. She has come to Europe on professional business only. Any story that there is a relationship between her and Corbett is a pure invention. My daughter is travelling in my stateroom and is under my constant care and watchfulness.'

Readers of the *World* were left in little doubt as to Corbett's real reasons for making the trip. The reporter had done his job well. He had managed to elicit, through his hard questioning and the less than convincing answers, that Gentleman Jim was fleeing from his wife to enjoy a European fling with his lover. The excuses given for Corneille, Consodine and himself all travelling under assumed names stretched credulity too far. If Jim had only met Marguerite for the first time just before they sailed, why would she pretend to be Consodine's wife? The 'Mr and Mrs Martin' cover was an all-too-transparent pact between Corbett, his manager, his lover and her mother. If, in the interests of decorum, Jim and Marguerite chose not to share the same stateroom, they knew they could make up for lost time once they were ashore.

The pretence that there was nothing between them was kept up on their arrival in London. Corbett and his manager moved into the Hotel Cecil, while Corneille was booked into another West End hotel. Whether the couple managed to evade the ever-vigilant press and spend some time together is not known, but Corbett was adamant that he and his wife understood each other. 'If I had eloped with Miss Corneille,' he said, 'I certainly would not leave her to go to a separate hotel as soon as I arrived here.'

At any rate, the affair did not survive more than a couple of weeks in Europe. On 23 September, Corbett was back on the *Campania*, en route for home. The *World* correspondent was again waiting at Queenstown to interview him. Although Jim was evasive in his answers, he said he was returning home to sort out things with Vera. It seemed that he had a guilty conscience about deserting his wife, and was ready to dump Marguerite and go back to her. He said he did not blame Vera for her reaction to the reports that he had eloped with Corneille. 'The people who hang about my wife put those lies in her mind,' he said, 'and naturally she believed them. Corneille is nothing to me, never was and never will be. My intention is to see Mrs Corbett when I reach New York and convince her of that fact. There is no-one living like her.'

His lawyer in New York made public a telegram Jim had sent from London to Vera: 'Stories about woman false. Come over here quick, darling. Will prove it. Love you only. Jim.'

George Considine tried to convince Jim that his wife would not have said the nasty things about him if she cared for him. He reminded him of how Vera had screamed as he was leaving home for the McCoy fight, 'I hope he hits you on the head and kills you.'

Back on American soil, Corbett told reporters that he had returned to fight all the charges made against him. He intended to sue the newspapers which had printed untrue stories. The only baggage he carried off the ship was a small hatbox, no doubt a 'sweetener' gift for his mistreated wife. Meanwhile, Vera's counsel, Abe Hummel, stated that divorce papers would be served on Corbett the following day. Mrs Corbett had told him that 'this late-day repentance of my husband's may fool the public, but it can't fool me. Under no circumstances will I ever live with him again. Protestations and promises from his glib tongue will not avail. I am through with him'.

At the same time that Hummel was making the announcement to the press, a smiling Corbett, in full evening dress, strolled into Rector's restaurant on Broadway. On his arm, constantly glancing up and gazing lovingly into his eyes, was Vera.

Newsmen, delighted at the kiss-and-make-up angle on the saga, were assured that Gentleman Jim had gone on 'a bit of a spree' after quarrelling with his wife. It was a reckless act, he conceded. He had too much wine at a party celebrating his win over McCoy, and Consodine had shipped him off to Europe without him realising it. As to Miss Corneille, the stories put out were 'absurd'. Her presence on the ship was a complete surprise to him. He had explained everything to his wife. Vera said they had both made mistakes, but matters had now been straightened out. The divorce action would be dropped, she added. After dinner, the couple went to Koster and Bial's Music Hall. Their box, next to the stage, was the most conspicuous they could find. They wanted to show the world that, whatever their differences in the past, true love had won out.

Within a year, the incorrigible philanderer was caught up in another love scandal that threatened to wreck the patched-up marriage. He was named as a co-respondent in a divorce action taken by the bandleader and celebrated trombonist Frederick Innes. Jim was one of four men alleged to have been romantically involved with Innes' wife, Georgie.

When Mrs Innes heard that papers in the suit had been filed in the New York Supreme Court in June 1902, she set off immediately for Pittsburgh, where Corbett had a stage booking. Jim then called his lawyer, Emanuel Friend, asking him to represent him. Corbett insisted, none too convincingly, that he had never set eyes on Georgie Innes until that very day, and couldn't understand why he had been named in the suit.

Frederick Innes, in his complaint, said he had been married to the former Georgie Mundy for nine years. Early in 1901 the couple lived at the Hotel Navarre in New York. Corbett also stayed there, and Innes alleged that, while he was away on the road with his band, a romantic friendship developed between his wife and the former champion. Georgie angrily denied that there was anything between her and Corbett, and put the accusations down to her husband's 'insane jealousy'. Though it was true that she and Corbett stayed at the same hotel, Mrs Corbett was always with him, she said. All she had was a 'bowing acquaintance' with the couple.

Strangely, and unwisely as it turned out, the musician's lawyers decided not to pursue the accusations against three of Georgie's supposed lovers, but rested their case on her alleged affair with Ernest Crowhurst, sports editor of a Philadelphia newspaper and one-time press agent for Innes. Thus Corbett, along with Howard Flannigan and Wybert Phillips, got off the hook. The jury found Mrs Innes not guilty of misconduct with Crowhurst, but decided her husband was guilty of a romantic liaison with a Mrs Katherine Wenzel (or Thayer), as Georgie had charged in her counter suit.

Vera Corbett showed remarkable tolerance over her husband's latest straying from the nest. There was none of the histrionics exhibited at the time of the Corneille affair. Though it is highly unlikely she accepted his innocence plea, she let the matter blow over. Shortly afterwards the couple purchased a handsome Queen Anne-style house at 221–4 Edgewater Avenue (later renamed Corbett Road) in Bayside, in the borough of Queens, New York City, where they would spend the rest of their days together.

CHAPTER 21

Jeffries again – and George Bernard Shaw

In the three years after his controversial victory over McCoy, Corbett's only ring appearance was a three-round exhibition bout in Detroit in December 1902 with Tommy Burns, a future world heavyweight champion. It was generally assumed that he was so sickened at the fall-out from the scandal, particularly what he considered the unfair way the press had covered his alleged role, that he was finished with fighting.

He devoted most of his time to stage work, his act consisting of an amusing monologue and tales about his life and boxing career, plus a dexterous display of bag-punching. Although frequently quoted as saying he would like another go at James J. Jeffries' title, most experts figured he was just looking for publicity. He was now going on thirty-seven, and his chances of defeating the champion, nine years his junior and in the prime of his fighting life, were considered remote.

It was Jeffries' total supremacy over the current heavyweight crop that stirred up interest in a possible re-match with Corbett. The Boilermaker had, quite simply, run out of decent opponents. Since his epic come-from-behind knockout over Corbett, Jeffries had beaten Gus Ruhlin in five rounds and again bested the man from whom he took the world title, Bob Fitzsimmons, this time in eight rounds. Big Jeff was getting tired of fighting and had several times talked about packing it in. A timely challenge from Gentleman Jim made him think again.

James W. Coffroth, who ran the Tijuana racetrack in Mexico, had begun to promote boxing events in San Francisco. He figured that a world heavyweight title contest between the two local rivals would be a popular attraction at the Yosemite Athletic Club, where he had already staged successful shows. He called the two fighters together and an agreement was signed for the fight to take place at the club on 14 August 1903.

Coffroth was the first of the big-time fight promoters. Previously, it had been largely up to boxers and their managers to agree terms, then invite clubs to bid for the staging of the bout. Now the pattern was changing. Promoters secured the agreement of the principals, arranged the venue and paid the fighters either an agreed sum or a percentage of the profits. Coffroth, born in California, had begun work as a clerk in the Surrogate Court in San Francisco. A great boxing fan, he would travel east to watch big fights and became friendly with New York promoter Jim Kennedy. The two began to stage contests on the west coast. Their first major venture was the Jeffries vs Ruhlin title fight in 1901. The bout earned its place in history when Ruhlin's manager threw in the sponge, the first time this action was used to signify a fighter's surrender. When his partner died in 1903, Coffroth continued as a solo promoter for another twelve years.

A meeting between Corbett and Jeffries to discuss details of the fight blew up into a row over Corbett's insistence on wearing hand bandages. He had used them for several years, he argued, and it was more or less standard practice for fighters by then. Jeffries was adamant that nothing should be worn under the gloves. His stance was understandable. He believed Fitzsimmons had dipped his bandaged fists in plaster of Paris the night before their second meeting, so they were like concrete in the fight. Jeffries' face had been ripped to shreds before his great strength enabled him to overcome Ruby Robert.

Rumours of the use of plaster of Paris was a recurring theme in fight controversies for many years, most notably when Jack Dempsey slaughtered big Jess Willard to take the world heavyweight title in 1919. The Manassa Mauler was such a lethal puncher, however, that any illegal 'top up' was unnecessary. The same went for Fitzsimmons. Besides, hitting with rock-hard fists would probably cause as much damage to the offending boxer's hands as to his opponent's face or body.

En route to California to commence training, Corbett stopped off in Chicago. He told reporters, 'I am leaving here as an ex-champion. When I return, I will again be the champion heavyweight of the world.' In San Francisco, where he might have feared some lingering resentment over 'deserting' his home town to live in New York, he got a prolonged standing ovation when he performed his monologue act at the Orpheum Theatre.

Jim went into training at Croll's, in Alameda, across the bay from San Francisco, with his usual vigour. It was noticeable, however, that the years had slowed his reactions. His chief sparring partner, Yank Kenny, a big but notoriously slow heavyweight, surprised the ex-champion by getting through his once impenetrable defence with relative ease. Jim's other sparmate, Sam Berger, was a smart boxer and it was not a matter of concern that he could land punches often, but it was unthinkable that Kenny should look so good against the master craftsman. Corbett's timing was way off, but he put this down to his three-year absence from the ring. Part of the problem could have been his deteriorating eyesight. His wife had noticed how he squinted when he read the newspapers and advised him he might need glasses.

A big boost to Jim's confidence was the arrival of Tommy Ryan as his trainer. The volatile former world welterweight and middle-weight titleholder had been Jeffries' tutor, but defected to the enemy camp after a row with the champion over some trivial issue. He told Corbett he would work with him for nothing just to get back at the Boilermaker. Jim welcomed him with open arms. Not only was Ryan a master strategist, but he was able to provide first-hand information on Big Jeff's current state of mind and body. Since Tommy had worked with Jeffries on perfecting his crouching style, he now instructed Corbett on how best to deal with it. Jim normally worked out problems his own way, but he listened intently when Ryan showed him how to hold his right hand in such a way that, when Jeffries swung, Corbett would turn to his left and catch the blow with his hand. He practised the move until both men were satisfied he had it perfected.

Jeffries did his training at Oakland under the careful eye of Billy Delaney, Corbett's one-time tutor. The fact that both fighters had trainers who had worked with the opposition seemed to even things up, but the champion gained a considerable advantage when Bob Fitzsimmons arrived on board. The Englishman had never forgiven Gentleman Jim for the insults of bygone years and vowed to help Jeffries finish off the arrogant Californian's fighting career. Fitz joined Delaney, Jack Jeffries and Joe Kennedy in the titleholder's corner.

Corbett, seconded by Ryan, Yank Kenny, his brother Tom Corbett and Sam Berger, looked very confident and in excellent physical shape when he ducked between the ropes at the Yosemite Club. But he couldn't ignore the stark reality that he was fighting a man nine years younger and thirty pounds heavier. Nor could he forget that he had outclassed Jeffries for twenty-two rounds in their first meeting and still got knocked out. Still, a repeat of that performance would make him champion once more, for this time the fight was limited to twenty rounds.

In his corner, waiting for referee Eddie Graney to call the competitors to the centre of the ring for their last-minute instructions, Corbett felt, if anything, too relaxed. He wished he was even a little bit nervous. On the way to the ring, he had walked behind Jeffries, in the shadow of his huge back. 'It seemed like a man-mountain or a big elephant leading a parade,' he said later. 'He looked so big that it struck me as funny, and I began to laugh.' The champion, in contrast, was so uptight that he was trembling. He was so pre-occupied with his own thoughts that he seemed not to notice Corbett's entry to the ring. Gentleman Jim walked across to his rival's corner, slapped him on the back and greeted him with a hearty 'Hello Jeff'. They shook hands.

When a photographer asked the fighters to adopt a sparring pose in the centre of the ring, Jeffries seemed to have difficulty finding the chalked line where he was to stand. Corbett bent down to push his feet into position, then advised the champion on the proper stance. Psychologically, all the pre-fight points had been scored by Corbett, as usual. He was the master and Jeffries was the nervous, uncertain pupil.

The day before the fight, Jim had discussed with his brother Harry the likely tactics of the champion. 'There is only one way Jeffries can fight me,' he said. 'If he boxes, he will be outpointed and he can't afford to try that game. So he'll tear into me from the tap of the gong, using that left if he can, but chiefly roughing me, pushing me, and bearing down on me to tire me out, taking all the advantage he can of his strength and youth.'

The prognosis was spot on. Jeffries went all out for a quick win, blasting away with both fists at every opportunity and roughing up his opponent in the clinches. Corbett was less the dancing master than usual, being content to slip punches, take them on his arms, roll with them or duck away. He suffered no damage in the lively opening round and went to his corner smiling.

Early in the second round, Gentleman Jim got the chance to try the strategy he had worked out with Ryan on how to defend against the champion's famous left hook to the body. He saw the blow coming and dropped his right hand to catch it in his glove. Unfortunately, his old sense of timing was no longer there. The punch ripped into his side with tremendous force, sinking him to the floor. He felt that every rib on his right side must be broken. Luckily for him, the referee was an old pal from schooldays and gave him the benefit of a slow count. By the time Graney reached 'nine' – Corbett later estimated he was down for seventeen seconds – Jim was back on his feet. He hung on desperately until the end of the round.

The writing was on the wall. As his cornermen sponged him down and furiously fanned him with a towel, Corbett cursed himself for following Ryan's advice instead of relying on the instincts that had served him so well throughout his career. At the gong, he found he was unable to stand up straight because of the terrible pain in his side. He was forced to adopt a crouch in a bid to protect his ribs. His neck muscles were also sore from the effects of the fall, and he could not pull his head away from punches like in the past.

In the circumstances, all he could do was to try to beat Jeffries at his own game. He chose to slug it out. It was a hopeless strategy. Big Jeff was made of too stern stuff to be bothered by what the weakened challenger could throw at him. Corbett then tried a verbal assault. He taunted his opponent, telling him how poor he was and that 'you couldn't put me out in a thousand years'. It didn't work. Five times over the next few rounds Corbett hit the floor. Only his fighting heart kept him going. He continued to hook and jab mechanically, but there was nothing behind his blows.

There was some brief encouragement for the former champion in the seventh round, when Jeffries stood off, as if he was feeling the pace of the fight. Corbett, seeing his chance and ignoring his aching body, launched a spirited counter attack that roused his near-silent supporters to a cheering frenzy. Jeffries retreated, more surprised than hurt by the punches he had to take. The crowd was on its feet, some leaping up on seats, in a heartfelt longing for a major upset. A Corbett victory would have been the most popular in San Francisco's sporting history.

'You've got him licked, Jim,' said an elated Ryan when he put the water bottle to the challenger's lips. Corbett knew better. Though he had landed at will in the seventh round, he could see how little effect the punches had on the California Grizzly. 'I might as well have been slapping him,' he said later.

Jeffries perked himself up and won the eighth and ninth round. Corbett weathered the attacks as best as he could, but he was tired and sore. The end came in the tenth round. The champion feinted with his right, then tossed his favourite left hook to Jim's body. Corbett managed to turn away so that the punch missed his damaged ribs, but it caught him right in the pit of his stomach. He doubled over in agony and fell to the floor. Up at 'nine', he was again caught with a terrific left to the body, followed by a right to the jaw. As Graney tolled off 'seven', Ryan threw in the sponge in token of Corbett's defeat.

Pulling himself together, Jim walked over to his conqueror and told him, 'Jeff, this is my last fight. I'm never going to try it again. You're a wonderful man and I've got nothing but admiration for you. Good luck.'

Although he meant it when he said he had quit the ring for good, Corbett found it hard to get rid of the old bug. It bit again in July 1904, when he signed to fight Philadelphia Jack O'Brien over six rounds in his opponent's home town. O'Brien, who would win the world light-heavyweight title a year later by knocking out a forty-two-year-old Bob Fitzsimmons, wanted Corbett to weigh in at no more than twelve stone, seven pounds (175 pounds), the light-heavyweight limit. This was rejected out of hand by Jim, whose natural fighting weight was around ten pounds heavier than O'Brien's demand.

Although the fighters eventually came to terms, the mayor of Philadelphia threw a spanner in the works by refusing permission for the bout to take place. An attempt was made to switch it to St Louis, but it fell through.

By September Corbett had lost interest in the ring and returned to the stage in the American melodrama *Pals*, in which he had the leading role. It opened in Trenton, New Jersey, before going on the road. Jim played one of a pair of ex-Harvard chums who quarrel after both fall in love with the same girl. His former friend turns out to be a nasty piece of work who tries every mean trick to break up Jim's romance. To no one's surprise, the play ends with a fist fight between the two rivals, with the hero winning out. The *Milwaukee Free Press* noted that Corbett's experience in vaudeville had helped to give him 'ease, spontaneity and geniality'.

As for boxing, Jim accepted the reality that his glory days were history. Like John L. Sullivan before him, and those who followed, he had learned the hard way that even the greatest fighters must ultimately accept that time does not stand still. Though a relatively young man in terms of normal life expectancy, as a fighter he had nowhere left to go. He did not want to end up like so many former champions, a human punchbag for ambitious youngsters ready to make a name at the expense of a faded legend.

Unlike other great fighters, however, Corbett wasn't going to slip quietly out of the limelight, nostalgically poring over the pages of his scrapbook, and enjoying the occasional appreciation of the fans when he was introduced as the 'former heavyweight champion of the world'.

For the thirty years he lived after his last fight he remained a popular public figure, working regularly to support a comfortable lifestyle for Vera and himself at their home in Bayside. As well as acting on stage and screen, he appeared regularly in vaudeville, took off on lecture tours, contributed a ghosted newspaper column, did radio broadcasting and lent his name to advertising companies.

An example of his earning capacity outside boxing was a contract he signed with theatrical impresario Oscar Hammerstein, grandfather of the famous songwriter, in 1906. For a week's engagement, Corbett was guaranteed $750, which was big money for the time. Interestingly, the contract was included in a collection of boxing memorabilia up for auction in 1997 and made $500.

On 8 January 1906, Jim opened on Broadway in a stage adaptation of one of Bernard Shaw's early novels, *Cashel Byron's Profession*. The 'profession' of the central character was that of a pugilist, so what better casting than to get a fighter, and a famous one at that, to play the part. Corbett had already appeared in a pirated version of Shaw's work five years earlier, but he relished the chance to perform at that hallowed temple of the arts, Daly's Theatre.

Asked in his dressing room if the high-bred audience would frighten him, he said, 'If a fellow can keep his head in the ring, with a lot a madmen yelling at him, he ought to be able to keep it at Daly's.' During the first act, Corbett stripped to the waist, bringing audible gasps of appreciation from the female playgoers. Later he evoked more than a few tears when he told his leading lady in a tender moment, 'If I can't have the satisfaction of marrying you, I may as well have the satisfaction of saying I'd like to.' The final curtain came down to spirited applause.

The rather flimsy story was of a young prize-fighter (Byron) who encounters a high-class lady (Lydia Carew) at an English country house. She mistakenly thinks he is a professor of athletic culture and becomes interested in him, as he does in her. When she discovers his true vocation she breaks off the budding romance. Later they are reconciled and get married. The hero is accepted into society and becomes a Member of Parliament.

It was not a work for which Shaw is best remembered. Initially, he feared the novel would not find a publisher, as rejection slips by the dozen dropped through his letterbox. It eventually found its way into circulation through the back door of the tightly-knit British Socialist press and American pirate publishers. It was Corbett's impersonation of Byron on stage that brought the melodrama to prominence, if not critical approval. Later, Shaw would be acclaimed a genius when his play *The Devil's Disciple* was produced in New York.

To many, it seemed an odd contradiction that Shaw, a renowned pacifist, was a lover of boxing. But he was always quick to explain that his attraction to the sport was based on artistic merit. 'My interest is purely scientific,' he said, 'I hate the sight of blood'. As a young bohemian in London he had taken boxing lessons in a Haymarket gymnasium from 'Professor' Ned Donnelly and, in 1883, entered the English Amateur Boxing Association championships; but he was refused permission to compete because of his lack of experience. Over forty years later, Shaw formed a close and lasting friendship with Gene Tunney, an intellectual who astonished the game's purists by taking the world heavyweight title from the great Jack Dempsey and beating him again in the return match.

In the Broadway production of *Cashel Byron's Profession*, Corbett found that the critics were kinder to him than they were to the play. Perhaps it was out of respect for his wide popularity, but the general feeling was that he had done his best to lift a dire drama. Once his initial shyness wore off, observed the *New York World*, the former world champion equipped himself well. At times he let his words run together, but if the rest of the actors had performed half as well, the play would have been twice as successful, said its observer. The drama itself was 'a dreadful waste of words … a long-winded, actionless stretch of narrative put in the mouths of a collection of puppets.'

The *New York Sun* was gushing in its praise of the fighter, describing him as 'a sincere, intelligent and amusing actor'. Its critic wrote: 'The devotee of the Drama with a capital D no doubt had occasion to sniff, for realism mingled with make-believe in a manner that might well have dispelled the atmosphere of legitimate art. Most of the fun of the performance turned upon the fact that the protagonist was, in fact, a redoubtable fighting man. But the wonder was that Mr Corbett obtruded his personality so little – or, to put the case more fairly, that he succeeded so well in creating the illusion of impersonation. To say that he is a consistent and finished actor would perhaps be stretching the truth. But this much is certain, he conducted himself with the same scrupulous intelligence and skill that gained him his prominence in the prize-ring. No prizefighter was ever more neatly created in the image of Shaw's sincere and downright hero; and to his native advantages he added a surprising degree of histrionic spontaneity and address.'

The paper noted that Jim's 'most beautiful grin' captivated the females in the audience just as it did the heroine in the play.

The *New York Herald* refused to take the affair seriously. Adopting the style of a fight report, its headline read, 'Corbett knocks out Bernard Shaw', followed by 'Wins Readily in a Lively Three Rounds Go at Daly's, Gets the Decision Easily'. To another critic, from the *New York Press*, Corbett's acting, while not doing justice to the author's intent, was a revelation. 'The prizefighter takes all the sting out of Shaw's cynicism, and robs his most captious comment of its sharpness. There is a keen relish in the rollicking vigor of Corbett, and instead of being an object of ridicule he has become a welcome addition to the ranks of stellar players.'

A practical approach was taken by the *New York American*, which hired a fighter, Philadelphia Jack O'Brien, to cover the play. O'Brien, who had won the world light-heavyweight title from Bob Fitzsimmons the previous year, wrote that, while it had been his ambition to knock out Corbett in the ring, he felt unqualified to knock his histrionic abilities. Corbett was a natural born actor, he said. In his role as Byron he showed 'the humiliation that a pugilist is confronted with when he attempts to lead a quiet social life'. O'Brien thought the society lady should have known immediately that her acquaintance was a prizefighter by the way he shifted his feet and clinched his hands. The reviewer admitted he missed the last act as he had to attend another engagement, but it was 'dollars to doughnuts from the way he was progressing with the love affair that he captured her'. O'Brien, like most well-known boxers of the period, supplemented his ring earnings by appearing on the stage. His 'other engagement' was at a nearby burlesque house.

The *Daily Tribune* dismissed Shaw's play as 'a skit'. Margaret Wycherly, 'an inconsequential actress of a sentimental order', appeared as Lydia Carew, while 'Mr Corbett received much applause from his friends'. The inference was that neutral observers were not so ready to show appreciation of the boxer's thespian qualities.

If he didn't win the unstinted approval of the critics, he certainly won over his leading lady. 'Mr Corbett is one of the finest actors I ever met,' Margaret Wycherly told writer William O. Inglis. 'He has great intelligence and tact, and he brings out every detail in a character. And he is so considerate of his company.'

Box office takings for *Cashel Byron's Profession* were poor. The noted critic Brooks Atkinson, in his book *Broadway*, wrote that 'the play collapsed – under the weight of Corbett's acting, someone said. In the last act, Corbett was on his feet, but Shaw was flat on the canvas'.

A somewhat more successful theatre vehicle for Jim was *The Burglar and the Lady*, which ran for three seasons (1906–'07–'08). The melodrama was later turned into a movie, with Corbett again in the lead role. Some prim distributor, carrying decorum to the extreme, thought it more proper that it be called *The Lady and the Burglar*.

But none of the later stage dramas equalled the popularity of *Gentleman Jack*, which ran at the height of Jim's fighting fame. Even then his appeal had been as a celebrity rather than as an actor. His appearances were mostly an excuse for audiences to see Gentleman Jim Corbett in the flesh. Alan Woods, of the Department of Theatre at Ohio State University, wrote that Corbett's initial image as a dandified bank clerk was carefully cultivated by his manager-producer, William A. Brady. He proved a competent actor and was perceived by his audiences as 'a modest, virtuous, decorous, and clean-living young man who happened also to be a superb fighter'.

Woods, in his article, *James J. Corbett: Theatrical Star*, published in the *Journal of Sports History* (Summer 1976), observed that 'the masterfully developed public image Brady created for Corbett provides a clear (and early) example of the commercial business that American entertainment became in the modern era. Corbett was packaged and sold to the public as a commodity. ... While he certainly was not the first professional athlete to be sold to a mass audience (and was far from the last), Corbett's marketing succeeded on a larger scale than any earlier efforts, thus making a major step in the American commercialisation of both sport and theatre.'

Miriam Allen De Ford, in her book *They Were San Franciscans,* wrote that Corbett, as early as 1905, 'anticipated Orson Welles by advocating Shakespeare in modern dress, though he never (perhaps fortunately) got the chance he wanted, to play an up-to-date *Hamlet*'. (His one stab at a Shakespearean part was in 1899, when he played Charles the Wrestler in a charity presentation of *As You Like It* at Larchmont, New York.)

CHAPTER 22

'The black boy with the yellow streak'

White America was outraged when, on 26 December 1908, Jack Johnson, a superb black fighter from Texas, took over as king of the world's heavyweights. It wasn't just that sport's premier prize had slipped out of white hands for the first time: it quickly became clear that Johnson intended to use every moment of his tenure to get even for the years he had been ignored and humiliated.

Having pursued Canadian Tommy Burns half-way around the world before finally cornering him in Sydney, Australia, he teased and tormented the titleholder for fourteen rounds before the police, fearing a riot, insisted that the slaughter be halted. Johnson proceeded to rub his critics' noses in the dirt by parading around in expensive clothes, driving fast cars and, worst of all, escorting beautiful white women. It might have been all right for Gentleman Jim Corbett to strut around like a proud peacock, but black men should know their place. When Johnson refused to conform, the white establishment began a frantic campaign to get him removed from the heavyweight throne.

As none of the existing white contenders looked capable of worrying Johnson, a desperate cry went out to James J. Jeffries to come out of retirement and regain the title for the white race. The Boilermaker, now a contented rancher, had no need or desire to give up his quiet life in the country for the hellish task of getting back into shape, while carrying the awesome responsibility of fighting the white man's war. The persuaders didn't let up, reminding him that is was his duty to 'wipe the golden-toothed smile off the nigger's face'.

Even Corbett got in on the act, vowing that if no-one else would try, he would come back himself. The idea was ludicrous, for Jim was now in his mid-forties.

While his name was being bandied about, along with scores of other 'white hopes', Corbett cashed in on the publicity by taking off for a theatrical tour of the British Isles. His monologue act was booked for Dublin, Belfast, Manchester and London. He arrived in Queenstown, County Cork, on 5 July 1909, on board the ill-fated *Lusitania*. (Six years later, the Cunard liner was sunk by a German submarine off the Old Head of Kinsale, on the southern Irish coast, with the loss of 1,200 lives. The outrage was a major factor in America getting involved in World War One.)

Corbett appeared on stage twice nightly during a week-long run at Dublin's Theatre Royal, telling 'true and humorous stories of his travels and experiences'. He had his first-night audience eating out of the palm of his hand after telling them that he had, that very day, visited the house at Islandbridge where his mother was born. The *Irish Independent* noted that the former champion, 'who looked anything but a bruiser' in his close-fitting evening suit, had 'a pleasing personality, spoke with the voice of a romantic actor, and the smile of an auctioneer'. Most of the stories he told were against himself, and the theatregoers laughed with him. 'There was no swank or bounce about the man,' said the reviewer.

If Gentleman Jim did have any hidden pretensions, he was brought down to size by the *Irish Times*. Its representative relegated Corbett's performance to second place in the review, giving priority to a 'daring' acrobatic act by the Banzai Family from Japan. In just seven lines, the paper said that the pugilist entered gracefully into his role as raconteur, and 'entertained his audience highly by his pithy anecdotes'. At least he earned prominence over Miss Fanny Elton's banjo-playing, the Seven Du Cos Perezoffs' comic juggling, and Mr Walton's Dexterous Dogs, who all got a mention.

A Dublin *Evening Mail* reporter who secured an interview with Corbett found, not the 'bent-nosed, toothless pugilist' he expected, but a handsome man with 'the mild eye of a browsing milch cow, a calm, deliberate, unprovocative gaze, and as modest as a daisy'. The newsman, obviously one for the colourful phrase, fired what he called 'leading questions' at the visitor. 'What's the matter with pugilism today?' was his opening gambit. 'The trouble is that there are no good heavyweights,' replied Corbett. Tommy Burns was too small, Philadelphia Jack O'Brien had just been beaten by a middleweight (Billy Papke) and Johnson had only one hand and a good uppercut. If Jeffries got fit, he should win back the title, he said.

'Tell me,' said the *Mail* man, 'do you believe in niggers?' Corbett wondered if the next question would be, 'Do you believe in fairies?'

'Well,' he said, 'don't ask me if I believe in the brotherhood business. But I don't think you often get a dead-game nigger. Peter Jackson was an exception. Weight for weight and cleverness for cleverness, I back the white man all the time.'

The tone of the conversation, viewed from today's perspective, is blatantly racist. But it must be considered in context. Few in those days believed it offensive, let alone incorrect, to suggest that the white man was his black counterpart's superior physically, intellectually, and every other way. Black people, whatever they might have thought privately, didn't have the clout to make an issue of such slurs. With one notable exception – Jack Johnson.

The world heavyweight champion revelled in his elevated position. He mocked white society and tortured his white opponents before dispatching them when he was tired of his cruel games. At last, Jeffries yielded to the frenzied calls to come out of retirement and salvage the pride of the white race. The challenge for Johnson's title was set for Independence Day 1910 at Reno, Nevada.

Corbett was brought on board to advise Jeffries on tactics, as well as act as chief of propaganda. 'Take it from me,' he would say to the newspapermen, 'the black boy has a yellow streak, and Jeff will bring it out when he gets him into that ring.'

Johnson reacted angrily to the comment, stating that he would fight Corbett for nothing just to show he was no 'faker'. Jim kept the row on the boil by saying, 'I only wish the big stiff had been champion ten years ago. I would have considered him easy picking.' Corbett, who topped up his earnings by reporting on the fighters' preparations for the *Chicago Tribune,* was none too pleased to discover that John L. Sullivan had been hired to do a similar job for the *New York Times.* 'What the hell do you want?' he barked, when his old enemy called to watch Jeffries in training. Heated words were exchanged and for a while it seemed as if they might resort to fisticuffs. Finally Sullivan roared, 'If you're running the camp, I don't want to see him.' He then turned on his heel and left.

Walter Kelly, a vaudeville artiste and uncle of the yet unborn Grace Kelly, witnessed the incident. 'I had a lump in my throat as I watched John L. drive away,' he said. 'He was leaving the camp of a heavyweight champion without even the tribute of a handshake or a goodbye. For some reason, it just didn't seem right.'

Peacemakers managed to entice Sullivan back the next day, and great play was made of the old enemies shaking hands, posing for pictures and drinking a glass of wine together. Probably the only film footage ever taken of Corbett and John L. together shows them playfully squaring up. Jim, smiling broadly, grasps his old rival in a hug. Despite the staged reconciliation, Corbett and Sullivan never really buried their differences.

The weather was hot and sticky on the day of the fight, but announcer Billy Jordan and other ring luminaries wore their customary stiff collars, watch-chained waistcoats, suits and hats. By pre-arrangement, Johnson and Jeffries did not shake hands. The omission of such a fundamental ritual, the very expression of sportsmanship and fair play, was a clear indication of the symbolic importance of the match.

Right from the start, it was clear that the old and tired Jeffries was no match for the sharp-hitting, defensive genius who faced him. Johnson, in between dishing out steady punishment, used every opportunity to taunt the Boilermaker and ridicule his hopeless efforts. As early as the second round, after foiling a Jeffries attack, he said, 'What's the rush, Jim, I've got all day.' An infuriated Corbett heard Johnson comment during the next round, 'Come on now, Mr Jeff. Let me see what you got. *Do* something, man. This is for the cham-*peenship.*'

Almost as interesting as the fight itself was the verbal battle between Corbett and the champion. Randy Roberts, in his excellent study *Papa Jack: Jack Johnson and the Era of White Hopes*, said that Corbett was ' the most vocal racist in Jeffries' corner. He hated all blacks, but Johnson more than the rest. And he had a theory that blacks became useless fighters when enraged. But they did not have the desired effect. Instead of making Johnson angry, the insults seemed to have a calming effect. When Corbett said something, Johnson replied politely and smiled.'

Arthur Ruhl, who covered the fight for *Collier's*, also noted that Johnson's retorts were well-mannered, quiet and generous. He had 'the good sense or cleverness to keep the respectful ingratiating ways of the Southern darkey'. Corbett grew increasingly infuriated as the fight wore on. In the twelfth round, Johnson looked over his opponent's shoulder and called to Corbett, 'I thought you said you were going to have *me* wild.'

By now Jeffries was suffering way beyond the call of duty. His mouth was cut inside and out, and his nose was broken and bleeding. Even Johnson's body was smeared with his rival's blood. It was obvious that the champion could have ended matters at any time, but he wanted to make Jeffries, the symbol of white supremacy, suffer. 'How do you feel, Jim?' he would ask. 'Did that one hurt?' Finally, in the fifteenth round, a battery of punches sent the Boilermaker sagging to the floor. Up at 'nine', he was subjected to a further blistering attack that left him draped over the bottom rope. Tex Rickard, who doubled as promoter and referee, got to 'seven' before he yielded to the crowd's screams of 'Stop it, don't let him be counted out.'

First into the ring to congratulate Johnson was John L. Sullivan. Though he regarded the black champion with undisguised odium, it was the lesser of two evils that Johnson won rather than Corbett's man. Billy Delaney, Jeffries' trainer, was also quick to give credit where it was due and shook the champion's hand. When Johnson went to his victim's corner to see how he was recovering, he was brushed away by Corbett and Philadelphia Jack O'Brien.

In a terrible sequence to the fight, whites went on the rampage in the Deep South after hearing the result and nine blacks died in bloody riots. The film of the bout caused further disturbances when it was shown, and it was banned in Britain for fear of similar violent outbreaks. White society had to wait another five years before Johnson, weary of exile in Europe after fleeing from a jail sentence, finally lost the world title to Jess Willard in Havana, Cuba. Whatever justification Johnson might have felt for his avenging mission against white injustice, there can be no doubt that his behaviour did no good at all for the cause of black fighters. Not until the great Joe Louis came along in the 'thirties did a black heavyweight take his well-earned place on the championship throne. Louis' impeccable behaviour during his record twelve-year reign did much to dispel the prejudices nurtured during the Johnson era. His brilliant performances in the ring won him countless admirers from all sides. Black fighters, no longer denied their rights, have dominated the heavyweight division ever since.

If Corbett never attempted to hide his relief that he had been born white, he didn't object to parodying a black man on stage. He 'blacked up' to act as interlocutor in George Evans' *Honey Boy* minstrel show, which opened at New York's City Theatre on 13 August 1910.

By this time the legitimate theatre, vaudeville, opera and concert halls were facing growing competition from movie houses. Since the first American cinema had opened its doors in Los Angeles in 1902, moviegoers had flocked to see such productions as George Melies' fantastic *Trip to the Moon*, Edison's action-packed *The Great Train Robbery*, and the Kalem Company's biblical epic *Ben Hur*. By 1907, America had upwards of 3,000 nickelodeons (so-called because the entry fee was five cents). Many of the movie houses were primitive in the extreme. All anyone needed to set up in the business was a projector, a vacant store or shed and some chairs. In warm areas, a building wasn't even needed. The machine could be set up in the open and, once darkness fell, the show began in the 'airdomes'.

'The Nickelodeon's five-cent admission was not as cheap as it sounds,' wrote Kevin Brownlow in *Hollywood: the Pioneers*, 'but it offered in one programme the same kind of fare as vaudeville, the same thrills as melodrama, potted culture from art galleries and the legitimate stage, action from the ballpark and boxing ring, together with glimpses of foreign countries which could only be duplicated by travel. And on top of all this, topical items of sensational journalism, such as the Stanford White murder case.'

The movie screen promised new opportunities – and bigger pay-days – for popular stage performers. Corbett was among those who jumped on board, although he continued with his vaudeville work when he wasn't filming. Once again, he proved how adaptable he was to change. In around a dozen feature films, shorts and serials in which he appeared between 1913 and 1930, he often took the starring role. In others he played a supporting part or made a cameo appearance. His name on the cast always guaranteed extra revenue at the box office.

Corbett the movie actor made his first appearance in *The Man from the Golden West*, which was released in September 1913. The one-time bank clerk was well cast as a banker who lends money to a prospector planning to deposit his gold in Jim's establishment. The treasure is stolen en route to the bank, but Jim sets off in hot pursuit and manages to catch the crooks and recover the gold. In the meantime, a business associate, who has forged bonds to cover his financial ruin, kills a detective who arrives to question him. Somehow, Jim gets the blame for the shooting, is arrested and sent to Sing Sing. He escapes and later proves his innocence with a photograph of the victim's eye, which shows a reflection of the real culprit. The storyline might have been ridiculous, but there was enough drama and lively action to satisfy most moviegoers. Basically, it was standard unsophisticated fare for a largely undemanding audience.

Many of the films in which Corbett appeared had the scripts written specially for him. For instance, in the serial *The Midnight Man*, a story about New York's high and low life, he had plenty of opportunities to display his boxing and other athletic skills. Shown in eighteen episodes over as many weeks, it held picturegoers in suspense until the next part revealed how their hero had escaped some terrible fate. The titles of the chapters, such as *Blazing Torch*, *The Death Ride*, *A Fight to the Finish*, *Jaws of Death*, and *Hurled from the Heights*, indicate the exciting exit scenes. The *San Francisco Examiner*, reporting capacity houses at every showing at the Frolic, praised Corbett as 'polished in manner and a finished actor'. The serial shared the bill with *The Man in the Moonlight*, a romantic comedy starring Monroe Salisbury, a newsreel of current events, the Frolic Orchestra, and 'a surprise comedy'.

In the movie version of *The Burglar and the Lady*, Corbett's earlier experience of playing the same part on stage, as a gentleman crook who was really a detective, came in useful. It gave his acting 'a finish and polish that would otherwise be lacking', said *Motion Picture News*. The comedy *The Beauty Shop*, however, failed to impress *Variety*, which complained that everyone – Corbett, his co-stars and the writers – all tried too hard to be funny. Raymond Hitchcock and Billy B. Van, in the main roles, were more suited to burlesque, while Corbett, wearing a wig and heavy moustache as a Spanish inn-keeper, was not presented in a favourable light. The trade paper, trying not to be too unkind, said that 'what Corbett does here will never be held for or against him'.

Making movies and mixing with many of the big names in the fledgling industry enabled Jim to expand his circle of friends. He relished being accepted into the tight circle of film makers and performers, just as they welcomed the great sporting hero who was now one of their own. John Ford, who directed Corbett in *The Prince of Avenue A*, told of lining up his two children, Patrick and Barbara, to meet the former champion after building them up with the story of Gentleman Jim's conquest of John L. Sullivan, 'You'll be able to say that you shook the hand that shook the man who shook the world.'

Stars of the stage, too, found Corbett an agreeable companion. Sir Harry Lauder, the famous Scottish comedian, would arrange a meeting whenever they were booked in the same American city. Lauder, of 'Roamin' in the Gloamin' ' and 'Stop Yer Ticklin', Jock' fame, regarded Jim as being 'in a class by himself, both as a fighter and as a personality'. He thought *The Roar of the Crowd* was 'a ring classic of the first water', and it held his 'breathless attention' for many weeks.

Writer P. G. Wodehouse was also a big fan. He admitted to a boyish enthusiasm for the American fighters of Corbett's era, such as James J. Jeffries, Tom Sharkey and Kid McCoy. His fictional account of 'The Debut of Battling Billson', a chapter in *He Rather Enjoyed It,* is one of the classic uses of a boxing theme in humorous literature. Wodehouse once carried a letter of introduction to Corbett, but he was disappointed to find Gentleman Jim was elsewhere when he thought they might meet. 'I did not get to know him till a good many years later, when he was a charming old gentleman and one of Broadway's leading actors,' he said.

Mark Twain, too, was an unabashed admirer. He wrote that Corbett had 'a fine face and is modest and diffident, besides being the most perfectly and beautifully constructed human animal in the world'. The author once offered to spar with the ex-champion, but Jim declined, saying, 'Don't you have fame enough? You might knock me out with an accidental blow. Then my reputation would be gone and you would have a double one.'

One famous personage who did entice Jim to 'put up the dukes' was Maurice Barrymore. The actor was a useful amateur boxer and, according to Bill Brady, equipped himself pretty well in sparring sessions 'as long as Jim remembered not to put on too much pressure'. Lionel Barrymore, one of Maurice's celebrated offspring, remembered calling at the Lambs Club, an exclusive Manhattan establishment for members of the theatrical profession, and seeing his father and Corbett 'standing among a group of courtiers at the bar, the champion holding a conspicuous glass of milk in a hand that seemed fashioned for the playing of a violin'.

It was probably Maurice Barrymore who got Jim into the Lambs Club. At first, the elitist club didn't want to know him. Brady, already a member, recalled the toffee-nosed committee members getting into a tizzy because they feared he would bring 'Jim Corbett, the prize-fighter' on board. When Corbett did apply for membership, his credentials were considered so impeccable that he got more endorsements than anyone else in the club's history. Indeed, he was eventually appointed to the board of directors.

Membership of another actors' club, the White Rats, cost Corbett dearly. Though really nothing more than a social group, the Rats organised a strike in 1900 for better salaries and working conditions for all vaudevillians. But they didn't have the muscle to make it succeed. The strike was failing when some members sold out, leaving a legacy of bitterness and recriminations. Corbett, who retained his membership, still had his Broadway saloon at the time. He was virtually put out of business cashing so many worthless cheques and making cash advances to fellow members.

While Jim was lauded by his fellow actors as a considerate and generous man, he didn't have the same regard for struggling play-wrights, judging by what happened to one aggrieved dramatist. In April 1909, Lillie Krebs, from St Louis, Missouri, sued him for $10,000, the amount she claimed she lost because Corbett had withheld a manuscript she sent him. As a result of his tardiness, or lack of interest, she had missed an opportunity to sell it to someone else, she said. The judge, hearing the case in Krebs' home town, threw out her claim because she failed to support it with sufficient evidence.

CHAPTER 23

Gentleman Jim and the Empress of Sex

Two of Corbett's greatest ring rivals took the fatal count within four months of each other. Bob Fitzsimmons went first, in October 1917, succumbing to lobar pneumonia at the age of fifty-four. In February of the following year, John L. Sullivan suffered a massive heart attack and died. He was sixty.

Gentleman Jim once again raised doubts on the appropriateness of his nickname by shunning Fitzsimmons' funeral, and turning up at Sullivan's only after a last-minute change of heart. Not even at the final salutes to two of boxing's great names, it appeared, was he prepared to forgive and forget. Though he sent a message of condolence, which was read to the 3,000 friends and admirers of Ruby Robert gathered at the funeral service in the Moody Tabernacle in Chicago, he declined to make the trip from New York in person. A short time later, probably suffering pangs of conscience, Corbett was among many famous boxing personalities who attended a memorial service for Fitz at the Campbell Funeral Church on Sixty-Sixth and Broadway. He even got up to pay a few hollow-sounding compliments to his old adversary, praising his courage in the ring and his capacity for friendship. The following year, Jim stood alongside Julia Fitzsimmons, Bob's widow and third wife, and laid a wreath on his conqueror's grave.

When Sullivan passed on, Corbett sent a floral horseshoe, but pleaded that a theatrical engagement prevented him from being present at the funeral in St Paul's Church, Boston. After being advised by friends that it would be seen as a discourtesy to miss the

185

great man's final send-off, he suddenly showed up to take his place as an honorary pallbearer.

Since he got off so lightly in the Frederick Innes divorce action in 1902, Corbett's name had not been linked to any woman apart from his wife. He and Vera lived a life of apparent tranquillity in their comfortable Bayside home, with not another breath of scandal to feed the avaricious gossip mongers. It was, therefore, the juiciest titbit of all when, in 1919, Gentleman Jim was seen around town in the company of the voluptuous 'Empress of Sex', Mae West.

There is no proof that the pair were ever more than, in the classic Hollywood cliché, just good friends. At the time they met Corbett was fifty-one years old, twice West's age. But if reputations count for anything, their relationship was more than platonic. Jim was a very well preserved middle-aged man and he would not have considered himself too far 'past it' to turn down an invitation, if it came, from the platinum blonde to 'come up and see me'. For an egocentric such as he, it would been immensely flattering to be wooed by the woman who was every red-blooded male's greatest desire.

As for Mae, she made a lifetime hobby out of attracting prize-fighters to her bed. One would-be lover summoned to her mirrored bedroom, and dismissed as not living up to expectations, caustically remarked, 'With her it came through loud and clear that you could be a combination of Einstein and Cary Grant, but you would mean nothing if a well-built fighter with a crooked nose, cauliflower ears, and the IQ of an ape appeared.' Corbett didn't fit the pugilistic stereotype, but he was certainly on Mae's favoured list.

Never one to deny her voracious sexual appetite, West had wooed and discarded scores of men since first becoming the target of reformers and the censor's office for her provocative stage performances. Throughout her long career in the theatre, in films, on radio and television, she continued to provoke controversy with her frank sensuality. Draped in feathers, furs and diamonds, she usually portrayed women who accepted their lives of dubious virtue with flippant good humour. Her Broadway debut, in a play un-ambiguously called *Sex*, earned her a six-day prison sentence, but she emerged a national figure. In movies such as *Night After Night* and *She Done Him Wrong*, she so outraged the powerful League of Decency, set up to campaign against sexual frankness in movies, that her later scripts were butchered.

According to one of West's biographers, Maurice Leonard, she picked up with Corbett just after she dumped her previous lover, the accordionist Guido Diero. Her affair with Diero had lasted several weeks until she went down with influenza. Guido never left her side, lavishing every care upon her, but his gentleness had the opposite effect to what he expected. 'Men should be men in Mae's book,' wrote Leonard. 'They were sex objects and their ability to transport her sexually was all that mattered. If she had wanted a nurse she would have hired one.'

In *Mae West: Empress of Sex*, Leonard continued, 'When she was on her feet again she fell straight into the arms of heavyweight boxing champion James J. Corbett, whom she had seen fight in the ring. He was much more satisfactory and their relationship was sustained, on a casual basis, over several years.'

West herself didn't admit to a love affair with Gentleman Jim, merely to a friendship. She recalled her great delight in seeing Diero's reaction when he found out who was her new escort. In her autobiography *Goodness Had Nothing To Do With It* (that was the answer she gave to a character in one of her films who remarked, 'Goodness, what beautiful diamonds'), she coyly refrained from calling Diero by his full name, simply referring to him as 'D'. She described how, while playing Newark, New Jersey, she would regularly come back to her hotel around three o'clock in the morning to find Diero had been lying awake in bed, waiting to hear the elevator door open.

One evening Diero called to the theatre where Mae was appearing and was surprised to see her walk through the stage door with a man 'with a very adoring look on his face'. Not recognising her companion as Corbett, Guido went to her dressing room and demanded to know who he was. 'Just a friend who took me to the theatre,' replied West. The musician noticed a derby hat and overcoat hanging on her chair. Flying into a rage, he accused her of lying and swore to find her new boyfriend and punch him on the nose. 'You'll be sorry,' she advised him.

'There was a knock on the door,' recalled Mae. 'D. opened it. "Pardon me, I left my hat and coat here." And in walked James J. Corbett, ex-Heavyweight Champion of the World, whom I had met at a prizefight and whom I knew for many years after that. D. punched no noses that night.'

West's statement that she had met Jim at a boxing match is probably more accurate than Leonard's assumption that she had actually seen him fight. His last bout was in 1903, when Mae was just eleven. In a more recent biography, *Becoming Mae West*, author Emily Leider said the pair appeared on the same bill in Newark, along with Minnie Palmer's Four Marx Brothers, although she did not say this was their first meeting. It is possible, of course, that Mae had seen Jim box, as she was often taken to fights in her growing-up years by her father, a former professional fighter known as Battling Jack West. Boxing was a popular topic in the West household, and she would certainly have heard about Gentleman Jim.

If Corbett did share Mae's bed, he was only one of an impressive line of famous fighters she numbered among her 'conquests'. Max Baer, one of Jim's successors as world heavyweight champion, was one, and Joe Louis was widely believed to be another. In his autobiography, *Joe Louis: My Life*, he tells of meeting 'this real good-looking white woman with blonde hair' in a car showroom. The salesman who had been discussing a possible deal with Louis was called away by the woman. When he returned, he told the fighter, 'The lady has already purchased the car for you.' Joe, then a young black heavyweight making his way towards the world title, was mindful of the damage caused by Jack Johnson in his associations with white women, and was worried about bad publicity if he took the car and the news got out. 'But what the hell can you do when the lady is insistent and charming as hell?' he said. He took the car and promised his secret benefactor two tickets for his upcoming fight with Max Baer.

For five years after that, Louis got a new Buick every year at Christmas. 'The lady was a very important white woman and I was a very important black man' was all he would say. She taught him the meaning of discretion, and neither ever talked about their meetings. If Mae was the mystery woman in Joe's life, it would be in keeping with her reputation for keeping secret the names of her lovers, whenever possible. But Maurice Leonard said he had little doubt she was the famous blonde who bestowed gifts on the 'Brown Bomber'.

Another heavyweight champion, Jack Dempsey, was a bit more wary when he got into a clinch with the sex goddess. They planned to do a movie together called *Daredevil Jack* and, during rehearsals, she urged him to be more aggressive. 'Hold me tighter, Champ, I won't break,' she chided him. The film project fell through and, despite Mae's fondness for Dempsey, there is no record of them ever having an affair.

She did shack up for a time with Johnny Indrisano, a Boston fighter who appeared in one of her movies, *Every Day's a Holiday*. He taught her boxing exercises to keep fit and even showed her how to jab. She admitted to an affair with William 'Gorilla' Jones, who held the National Boxing Association version of the world middle-weight title. Jones lived rent free in a house owned by the actress, and she employed his mother as a maid. Speedy Dado, a Filipino who was recognised as world bantamweight champion, but only in the state of California, was another of her lovers.

West successfully sued the scandal magazine *Confidential* over an article it printed alleging a lasting affair with Albert 'Chalky' Wright, who held the world featherweight title from 1942 to '44. While the story was almost certainly true, it was another thing proving it. Wright used to take her to the fights in Pasadena, California, every Tuesday and Friday, and she would give him $100 to $200 betting money. Mae took over his management and, on his own admission, helped him throughout his life. She even came to the rescue of his brother Lee when he was arrested for shooting another boxer. 'Chalky' was supposedly employed by West as her chauffeur. Asked by a friend why he didn't wear a uniform, he admitted the job was a front. 'I'm not the chauffeur, I'm the *man*,' he said.

West remained a sexual icon, if a much-parodied one, throughout her life. She recognised the humorous side of her public image, and was always ready to enjoy a laugh at her own expense. In August 1980, a week before her eighty-seventh birthday, she suffered a stroke and fell out of bed. True to character, she issued a press release stating that she had been having a pleasant dream when she took the tumble. 'How bad can a dream about Burt Reynolds be?' she quipped.

Three months later, she returned from hospital to her Hollywood home to die. She was laid to rest in a large mausoleum at Cypress Hills cemetery in Queens, New York. As well as holding the remains of her parents, brother and sister, the two-storey crypt was the last resting place for, among others, the Polish pianist and statesman Jan Paderewski – and James J. Corbett.

Of all former fighters, no one put his fame to better use than Gentleman Jim. Apart from his long and profitable career on stage and screen, he was always willing to try his hand at something new – if the money was right. He backed and trained promising fighters, was a part-owner of several racehorses, wrote and lectured on health matters, lent his name to advertisers, and was a popular broadcaster.

For many years, he penned a newspaper column for King Features Syndicate. As well as pontificating on current and past boxing, he commented on baseball, answered readers' queries, advised on self-defence for citizens and doled out health tips. One of his physical training routines was designed to prevent constipation. The set of exercises was complemented by a bottle of pills. If the physical jerks didn't work, the pills did the trick!

However, it was as a boxing columnist that he attracted greatest attention – for all the wrong reasons. He hardly ever picked a winner. Strangely, for someone so well versed in all aspects of the game, he couldn't seem to miss going for the wrong guy. Forecasting fight results is not an exact science, but most experts, by the law of averages, come out right more often than not. Corbett took the top prize for classic clangers.

His predictions that both Tommy Burns and James J. Jeffries would whip Jack Johnson could be put down to his well-documented racial bias, but it is hard to see his logic in tipping Georges Carpentier to topple the much-bigger Jack Dempsey, or in suggesting that brittle-chinned Britisher Bombardier Billy Wells could withstand the heavy weapons of Gunboat Smith. Fighters were filled with horror when they saw that Corbett favoured them to win. Usually, it was the kiss of death.

His choice of the top ten heavyweights, up to Dempsey's time, also provoked a storm of controversy. He had Peter Jackson and James J. Jeffries joint best, followed by, 2: Bob Fitzsimmons, 3: John L. Sullivan, 4: Frank Slavin/Jack Dempsey, 5: Sam Langford, 6: Jack Johnson, 7: Jess Willard, 8: Tom Sharkey/Harry Wills, 9: Charlie Mitchell/Kid McCoy, 10: Jake Kilrain.

Few agreed, either, with his choice of Kid Lavigne as the best lightweight, or Mickey Walker as the outstanding welterweight. Not surprisingly, Corbett reserved special admiration for boxers in his own mould, those who favoured science over strength. He was especially taken with the Australian featherweight marvel Young Griffo. Though he never won universal recognition as a world champion, and often entered the ring intoxicated, Griffo dazzled American audiences with his brilliant technique. Corbett, in a rare show of modesty, said, 'In my time I have been credited with a degree of skill, but I could never hold a candle to Griffo.'

Another boxing master, Tommy Loughran, who was world light-heavyweight champion from 1927 to '29, greatly impressed Gentleman Jim. In 173 fights, Loughran only scored seventeen knockouts. He relied on speed and craft to beat his opponents, many of them much bigger and heavier than himself. Corbett, who had only 25 contests, told the Philadelphian he envied him because he could do things in fights that he (Corbett) was only able to practice in the gym. 'I enjoy seeing you fight,' he said, 'making all those movements. I can appreciate them. But other people sitting there watching wouldn't know what you're doing.'

In defence of his wayward predictions, Jim pleaded that his syndicated newspaper articles were not written by him at all, but by his ghost-writer. He never saw the pieces until they were published, he said, and therefore could not take responsibility for what appeared in print. It was a rather lame excuse, for he must surely have been consulted before any words were written in his name.

Gene Fowler, one of his 'ghosts', told an amusing, if apocryphal, story of how Jim advised all his friends to bet on Dempsey to beat Gene Tunney in their first fight in Philadelphia. The renowned sports journalist, not wishing to spoil Corbett's reputation as a false prophet, wrote down that Tunney was too fast for the ageing Dempsey and would win a clear decision. Fowler didn't believe the words he put in Corbett's mouth, but thought that Jim would again be proved wrong. When the published forecast proved to be spot on, Corbett flushed up with pride and told everyone who would listen how his logic had worked out. 'By the time he got back to New York,' said Fowler, 'Gentleman Jim believed that he really *had* chosen Tunney to win.' Tunney's manager, Billy Gibson, was reportedly so upset at learning that Corbett had picked his man to win that he offered Jim $1,000 if he would change his mind and go for Dempsey.

Corbett, however, resented the accusations that he was a bad tipster. If confronted, he would go to great pains to list all his predictions and show that he had chosen more winners than losers.

Ever on the lookout for a 'white hope' to knock the hated Jack Johnson off the heavyweight throne, Jim gave his support to several young prospects he thought might do the job. In 1910, he backed Miles McLeod, a 28-year-old giant from Albany county, Missouri. Standing six feet, six inches and weighing 270 pounds, McLeod had spent his youth on a farm, never drank or smoked, and swore by the benefits of fresh air and plenty of hard work. He promised to knuckle down to hard training under Corbett and to learn what tricks were needed to whip Johnson. 'If Mr Corbett says I ought to be able to lick Johnson, I'll sure enough lick him,' he said. He never got that chance, no doubt fortunately for himself. Indeed, little more was ever heard about Miles McLeod.

While threatening to make Johnson's 'square nose even flatter' if they met, Jim backed Al Palzer, one of the better 'white hopes'; Edward Marsh, a truck driver with inflated pugilistic ambitions; and Warren Barbour, the millionaire amateur champion of America. In his first venture as a boxing manager, he looked after Bobby Waugh, from Fort Worth, Texas, for a year, but the youngster failed to live up to his promise.

Tom Cowler, another of Corbett's protégés, looked like he might go places. The American-based Englishman accompanied Jim to Australia in March 1915, but the former champion was adamant that he was not Cowler's manager. He was merely advising him, and it would not be fair to label him a 'white hope' until he worked his way up a bit. Corbett was booked for a four months' theatrical tour of the Tivoli circuit by Hugh D. McIntosh, who built the famous Sydney Stadium at Rushcutters Bay for Tommy Burns' world heavyweight title defence against Bill Squires in August 1908. It was also the venue, on Boxing Day of that same year, where Burns was finally cornered by Johnson and made to pay dearly for his years of dodging him. McIntosh not only promoted the Burns-Johnson fight, but also refereed it.

Jim had to cut short his tour 'down under' on hearing that his 'favourite' brother, Tom, had died. Tom, youngest of the six Corbett boys, was just thirty-seven when he succumbed to pleurisy at his home, 1464 Sixth Avenue, San Francisco, on 16 April 1915. He had taken over the thriving Corbett bookmaking business on the death of his brother Harry in 1907. An enthusiastic hunter, Tom headed off almost every weekend on shooting trips, but also accompanied Jim on many of his American theatrical tours. He was survived by his wife, Margaret, and two children, Katherine, aged four, and Margaret, two.

In the meantime, Cowler, who weighed over 200 pounds, proved too big and strong for his three Australian opponents. But he was shown up badly when he returned to the States and was beaten by Battling Levinsky, Jack Dillon, Fred Fulton, Frank Moran and Billy Hicks. Nat Fleischer described him as 'a respected trial horse', which wasn't much of a compliment. The Englishman's one claim to fame was in holding Johnson to a ten-round draw in Mexico in April 1919. Johnson was no longer world champion, having lost the title to Jess Willard four years previously, and it's likely he took Cowler lightly. When they met again two months later, it was a different story. The Britisher had only his courage to commend him as he took a systematic battering before being stopped in the twelfth round. Gentleman Jim had lost interest in him by then.

Too old for active service in World War One, Corbett did what he could to help the cause, principally with charity performances or in propaganda work. In August 1917, the US Government appointed him chairman of the War Department Committee on Athletic Instruction. Serving alongside him were his former ring rival Kid McCoy, his one-time trainer Mike Donovan, Professor Richard Nelligan, of Amherst College, Massachusetts, and Robert Edgren, sports editor of the *New York Evening World*. The committee's aim was to gather together famous fighters to teach boxing to soldiers. Such ability could be useful in close combat with the enemy, it was thought.

The *Chicago Sunday Tribune* reported in July 1918 that Jim had joined a cast of 150, headed by Frank Tinney, in a revue called *Doing Our Bit*, at the Palace Theatre in Randolph Street. According to Jack Dempsey, Corbett made a film with Charlie Chaplin, Douglas Fairbanks and Dempsey called *All Good Marines*. The reference appears in the Manassa Mauler's autobiography *Dempsey*, which was written with the aid of his daughter Barbara Piattelli Dempsey. It was 'one big mêlée', he said. 'Naturally, we all thought of it as a Classic.' The title suggests a propaganda 'short', but efforts to trace a film of this name proved fruitless.

His date of birth might have ruled him out of active involvement in the war, but Corbett prided himself on his high level of physical fitness. He slept eight hours, exercised regularly, played tennis, climbed mountains, took three to four spoonfuls of olive oil daily, drank lots of water, and limited his smoking to six cigars a day. To prove his theory of how clean living could combat the effects of ageing, he announced that he would make a comeback to the ring at sixty. He would go into intensive training for a year, then take on a teenage opponent. While not expecting to win, he would show that the only advantage of youth was endurance. Fortunately, he didn't carry out his promise.

When Corbett's vaudeville act had run its course, he switched, with success, to the lecture platform. He made his debut in this new role at Detroit, Michigan, in 1925, and continued entertaining audiences for the next five years. His talks on physical culture, manliness, and sportsmanship were full of good common sense. He philosophised and advised on the benefits of clean living and regular exercise, and wound up his talks with amusing tales of his experiences in and out of the ring.

For each location he tailored his talks to give a local angle. If he was in Boston, for instance, he would have a complimentary tale to tell about that city's favourite son, John L. Sullivan. If it was Philadelphia, a mention would surely be made of Jack O'Brien, and so on. 'Jim was a great entertainer,' said Nat Fleischer. 'He always picked his spots and judged his hearers before he went into verbal action, and had something new and fitting for every burg where he was billed.'

One of his stories that went down well everywhere was of the time President William McKinley and himself were booked into the same hotel in Hamilton, Ohio. The president was due to give a speech in the town, while Corbett was there on a theatre booking. Jim was just about to leave for his performance when he was invited to the president's suite. After a chat, Corbett begged to be excused because of his urgent engagement. McKinley accompanied him to the hotel lobby, which was packed with people.

Corbett took up the tale: 'Young folks were in the majority. They didn't seem to know anything about the President being in their midst, but they did know about me, and rent the air with cries of "Corbett, Corbett". I bowed and we strolled to the hotel door, where we overheard a couple of kids arguing. "I tell you that the big feller is Corbett and the feller with him is his sparring partner, Con McVey." McKinley's face was a study in mirth as he listened to that enlightened conversation. As we shook hands in parting he remarked, "We live and learn, Mr Corbett. I never before realised how much more popular a champion boxer is than a mere President." '

When he told a similar story to British audiences, the central character became the diminutive English music hall comic Little Tich. Renowned for his funny dance with great flap boots almost as big as himself, Tich, whose real name was Harry Relph, met Corbett in London. As they stood talking outside the Horseshoe pub, on the corner of Tottenham Court Road, a woman in a passing carriage cried out to her companion, 'Oh, look, there's the world heavyweight champion.' Gentleman Jim took off his hat, bowed to the two women and retorted, 'Who do you mean, ladies, me or my little pal here?'

Another popular yarn concerned Jim's late father and Steve Brodie, who boasted about his famous feat of jumping off the Brooklyn Bridge. Pat Corbett scornfully retorted, 'Sure any damned fool could do that. From the fuss that was made over you, I'd be thinking that you jumped *over* the bridge. Now that would be something worth hollering about.'

Corbett is also credited as being the originator of the much-repeated lobster joke. Lunching in New York's famous Romano's restaurant, Jim was served a lobster with only one claw. When he queried this, the waiter told him it had been in a fight with another lobster. 'Take it away,' growled Corbett, 'and bring me the winner.'

Jim's fighting days were just a distant memory when, in 1925, he was persuaded to put on the gloves again – to face Gene Tunney.

Sports writer Grantland Rice arranged for the two boxing masters to spar for three rounds, each of two minutes' duration, for Sportlight Films. Tunney, who would beat Jack Dempsey for the world heavyweight title a year later, was delighted with the idea. He had long admired Gentleman Jim and had been inspired to emulate his scientific approach to the sport. Just as Corbett had used advance planning and skill to outfox the stronger, harder-hitting John L. Sullivan, so too would Gene's sharp mental powers and well-rehearsed moves overcome the tearaway Dempsey.

The filmed sparring session was staged on the top of the Putnam Building in midtown Manhattan. Tunney, eager to pick up any tips he could from the old master, stepped into the ring in his boxing trunks. Corbett, now aged fifty-nine, said he would rather wear his long white trousers. 'I had a pair of good-looking legs in the old days,' he told Rice, 'but they don't look so good now.'

'Corbett was brilliant,' wrote Rice in his autobiography, *The Tumult and the Shouting*. 'He feinted with his left – then punched with his left. A left feint … a left hook; a right feint … a left jab; a right feint; a right cross. He still had bewildering speed! He mixed up his punches better than practically any fighter I've seen since – with the possible exception of Ray Robinson.'

After the session, Tunney said to Rice, 'I honestly think he's better than Benny Leonard. It was the greatest thing I've ever seen in the ring. I learned plenty.'

At almost sixty, concluded the writer, Corbett was 'still the master'.

CHAPTER 24

The fatal count

Up to the beginning of 1932, Corbett had little to worry about in terms of his health. There had been a bad scare twenty years earlier when his appendix burst suddenly. It was feared he might not live, but, heartened by over 5,000 goodwill messages from all over the world, he recovered well after an emergency operation at the Jefferson Hospital in Philadelphia. Later, he said he enjoyed reading his premature obituary notices in the newspapers.

Back in 1902 Jim had undergone an operation to remove a cancerous growth on his tongue, caused by excessive smoking. Though he cut down on cigars, he refused to give up them up completely. That same year he sued a West Virginia newspaper, the *Wheeling Telegraph*, for stating that he had insulted women passengers on a train by refusing to stop smoking until the conductor threatened to have him ejected.

By the time he reached his mid-sixties, he was still active and the years had not hampered the ease and grace of his movements. But, during 1932, while riding on the New York subway, he was suddenly doubled over by an intense, shooting pain which temporarily paralysed his left side from the neck down. He managed to get off at the next station and stood, leaning against a pillar, gasping for breath. After assuring a helpful bystander he was fine, he called a cab to take him home. His physician, Dr G. Willard Dickey, entered into a conspiracy with Jim's wife to keep the truth from him. Corbett was told he was suffering from a heart ailment. In fact, he had cancer of the liver.

An operation gave him some relief, but he went steadily downhill. Even though he must have known how ill he was, his pride would never let him admit it. He would go to great lengths to hide his condition from others. One night he took his wife to a boxing show and, ascending a flight of stairs, his step faltered and he paused for an instant. A young man seized his arm to assist him, but Jim said, 'Please don't do that. I'm perfectly all right.' Later he told Vera he regretted his remark and worried that he had hurt the man's feelings.

Fight fans had always marvelled at how well he had kept his age. They would cheer loudly as the still slim, immaculately groomed ex-champion, his good mop of black hair showing only traces of grey, would duck nimbly between the ropes when introduced at a tournament. By 1932, however, his deterioration was all too clear.

At Madison Square Garden that year, Joe Humphreys, the veteran announcer, spotted Jim in the crowd and called for silence. 'I want to present to you an old and beloved friend, who has been having a tough battle lately. I want to present to you the greatest of them, now, and yesterday, and forever – Jim Corbett. Stand up there, Jim.'

The recipient of the thunderous applause stood up, pale and tired looking, and waved his hand in appreciation. It was the first time he hadn't been able to bound up onto the ring apron and take his bow from centre stage.

Corbett's last appearance at a boxing tournament was in the summer of 1932. The occasion was the opening of the Jamaica Arena, not far from his home on Long Island. He helped promote amateur boxing there, not for his own financial gain, but merely as a public service. Always ready to show his social consciousness, he had two years earlier agreed to act as chairman of the special Emergency Employment Committee of the Borough of Queens set up at the beginning of the depression.

By early 1933 his health had reached a critical stage. It was clear that the end was not far off. His once athletic frame was reduced to a skeletal ten stone (140 pounds). A headline in the *San Francisco Chronicle* of 8 February announced, 'Jim Corbett Waging His Last Fight'. It was followed by 'Doctor Gives Up Hope for Former Champion, Near Death'. The conspiracy between Vera and Dr Dickey to keep from Jim the fact that he was dying of cancer held firm. The newspapers, too, were kept in the dark. They reported that heart trouble had brought him down.

Confined to bed, he was allowed few visitors, although there was a constant stream of callers and hundreds of telephone messages. On 10 February he sat up to hear the radio account of the Primo Carnera vs. Ernie Schaaf contest from Madison Square Garden. He didn't think much of the fight and expressed doubt that either heavyweight was of championship calibre. He was not to know the tragic outcome of the bout. Schaaf lapsed into a coma and died five days after his knockout defeat. Carnera went on to win the world title from Jack Sharkey four months later.

On 16 February, five days after he had received the last rites of the Catholic Church, Corbett surprised his wife by getting out of bed, walking around the house, and smoking a cigar. It was his last defiant act in the face of death. Around 1.30 pm on 18 February, he passed away so peacefully in Vera's arms that she didn't realise he was dead. He was aged sixty-six.

The only other persons present at his death were John Kelleher, an old friend from Boston, John's brother Dennis, who had once been Jim's sparring partner, and Joe Smollen, a neighbour in Bayside. 'There was absolutely no pain at the end,' said John Kelleher. 'He had been sleeping since early morning, when the doctor gave him a sedative. Suddenly we noticed his lips were twitching. Mrs Corbett put her arms around him. Then he relaxed. That was all.'

There had been no time to call Jim's physician before he died, and he had refused to have a nurse. Dr Dickey later issued a formal statement that the cause of death was 'carcinoma of the liver, with metastasis in adjacent organs'. Asked by reporters why he had said earlier that Corbett's condition was due to a heart ailment, he said it was to spare his patient, whom he knew was an avid newspaper reader. 'His unusual reserve of vitality was amazing to us all,' he said. 'His persistent determination to fight to the end was only overcome by the seriousness of the disease.'

The death certificate described him as 'retired actor'. There was no mention of the sport to which he owed his fame. Whether this was Jim's dying wish, or Vera's or the doctor's decision, it indicated that, right to the end, he was something of a snob.

For the two days before the funeral, Bayside had to organise special traffic controllers to handle the crowds who came, in limousines and broken-down jalopies, but mostly on foot, to look upon Gentleman Jim for the last time. They paid their last respects as he lay, first in bed in his old rose-coloured dressing gown, his rosary wound around his left hand, and later in his 700-pound bronze coffin.

The weather on 20 February, the day of the funeral, was in keeping with the sombre occasion. A cold rain beat down steadily on the 2,000-plus mourners huddled in the streets around St Malachy's Church, on West Forty-Ninth Street, Manhattan. Only those with special tickets, around 700, were allowed into the little building known as 'the actor's church' because it was where many members of the theatrical profession worshipped. Corbett himself had often attended Mass there. Father John Hayes, a young priest from Jim's local Sacred Heart Church in Bayside, celebrated the solemn high requiem Mass, assisted by Father Patrick Gallaher and Father Thomas Best, both of St Malachy's. Father Hayes was a good friend of the Corbetts and had been a regular visitor to Jim's bedside during his last days.

A long list of honorary pallbearers from Corbett's friends among sportsmen, actors, politicians and businessmen had been drawn up, but in the end there were so many that none at all was asked to serve.

'Familiar figures of the stage and screen, gray-haired veterans of the fight game, a handful of them survivors of Corbett's own days as the heavyweight champion and conqueror of the mighty John L. Sullivan; younger men with the battered features of their fistic profession, promoters and champions, sports magnates and old friends, all mingled in the silent gathering,' wrote Alan Gould, sports editor of the Associated Press news agency.

Among the old fighters paying their last tributes as the funeral cortège moved off to Cypress Hills cemetery were Jack Skelly and Jack McAuliffe, both of whom had fought in the New Orleans three-day fistic carnival when Corbett took the title from Sullivan. Benny Leonard, ranked with Jim among the scientific boxing masters, was there. So was Johnny Dundee, the Italian-born featherweight king with the incongruous nickname 'the Scotch Wop'. Reigning world heavyweight champion Jack Sharkey, just three days after attending the funeral of his protégé Ernie Schaaf, arrived from Boston with his manager Johnny Buckley. William A. Brady, who had managed Corbett as a fighter and as an actor, was another mournful figure.

Baseball paid its tribute through the presence of Charles A. Stoneham, president of the New York Giants. Jim had been a regular rooter of the Giants at the Polo Grounds. Boxing and wrestling promoter Jack Curley attended, as did William F. Carey, president of Madison Square Garden, and James J. Johnston, the

Garden's matchmaker. The New York State Boxing Commissioner, Brigadier John E. Phelan, was present, as was Police Commissioner Edward P. Mulrooney.

From the theatrical world came George M. Cohan, Fred Stone and scores of Jim's old actor pals from the Lambs Club. Famous screen stars William S. Hart and Edward G. Robinson were among the early arrivals. Harry Fairbanks talked to fellow mourners about his days touring with Corbett when Harry was a member of the Gotham Comedy Quartet.

Surprisingly, no member of Corbett's own family attended the funeral. He was survived by his brother Joe and three sisters, Katie (Mrs Jack McEnerney), Theresa (Mrs John Boyd) and Esther, who was unmarried. For whatever reason, none made the trip from San Francisco. While the overland 2,500-mile journey would have taken several days, it was known for several weeks that Jim was dying, so there had been ample time to make travel arrangements. Perhaps there had been a falling out between Jim and his relatives – his divorce and well-publicised romantic adventures would not have sat well with his staunchly Catholic family – but contemporary newspapers gave no clue to the reasons why his brother and sisters stayed away. All that was reported was that they were 'unable to make it'.

Jim's widow, who had collapsed after taking a last look at his body that morning, rallied bravely and was escorted to and from the services by the Kelleher brothers. Two cars banked high with flowers accompanied the funeral procession. Among the offerings which most affected Vera was a wreath with a large red-winged 'O', representing the Olympic Club of San Francisco, from where Corbett had set out on his boxing career.

Although Jim was hardly a paragon of the Catholic church's strict code on moral behaviour, he remained a devout and practising Catholic throughout his life. Nevertheless, he had insisted on being laid to rest in the non-sectarian Cypress Hills cemetery, so that Vera, a non-Catholic, would eventually lie alongside him. With this in mind, he had bought their place in the expensive mausoleum some years earlier.

All over the world, newspapers gave generous amounts of space in paying tribute to the departed champion. In Paris, where boxing was hugely popular, veteran sportsmen gathered to discuss 'the first man to use scientific boxing'. His death was a topic in London clubs, restaurants and the old pubs on the Strand which were the centre of the capital's life in Corbett's heyday. Old timers recalled his last visit to London in 1909, and spoke of how he antedated Gene Tunney as 'a boxer who had read a book and knew his Shakespeare'. Berlin newspapers emphasised his gentlemanliness and reported his career in detail, ranking him among the best fighters in history. Nowhere was his death felt more profoundly than in Ireland, where the *Sunday Independent* made it the lead news story and devoted most of its front page to the popular Irish-American.

Whatever Corbett's impact on society at large, it was, of course, as an outstanding ring champion that he was best remembered. He would have been especially gratified by the accolades from those who followed him as world heavyweight titleholders. Gene Tunney said that, 'besides bringing a charming personality and a gracious manner to what was considered a brutal calling, he brought the keenest and most analytical fighting brain that ever graced a prize ring'. Corbett had been Tunney's boyhood idol.

Jack Dempsey said he had lost a friend and, although he had never seen him fight, he was convinced there never was a greater boxer. 'As a gentleman there was none finer,' he said. 'As a champion, he was all by himself.' Jim's former two-time conqueror, James J. Jeffries, said the finest thing anyone could say about him was that he was 'a good winner and a good loser'. Mr and Mrs Corbett had spent a day at his home the previous year, he recalled, and Jim appeared to be in good health, though he didn't have the same rugged physique as when they fought thirty years ago.

'There were just prizefighters before Corbett,' said Jess Willard. 'He put the game on a different level. He put science into fighting.' Even Jack Johnson put aside the enmity that had existed between them at the time of Johnson's fight with Jeffries to pay tribute to 'the first man to use scientific boxing'. Max Schmeling sent a cablegram from Germany to his manager, Joe Jacobs, telling of his grief at hearing the news. 'I had the pleasure of meeting him when I was training at Kingston for my bout with Jack Sharkey and on several other occasions. He took the trouble to show me some of the punches that made him famous, and which he thought I might use. But none but a Corbett could perfect the punches he used.'

Few outlined Corbett's impact on boxing better than his former manager, Bill Brady. 'Boxing owes him a debt it can never repay,' he said. 'Before he came on the scene, boxing was not quite respectable. He brought some education, brain power and talent to the ring ... the sport became legitimate and grew in popularity, whereas before his day boxing was an outlaw sport whose exponents had to hide away from the authorities when a match was planned. As a matter of fact, there was no boxing before Corbett's time. It was simply knock-down-and-drag-out fighting, the bar-room type of fighting. He, in my humble opinion, was largely responsible for the transition, if he was not altogether responsible for it.'

The leading newspapers devoted generous column inches to the flood of accolades. Amid the eulogies, however, there some frank appraisals of a man who wasn't without his faults. Several sports writers who had followed Corbett's career from the early days expressed the opinion that Corbett's greatest victory was over his own temper. The mellowed character of his later years contrasted with the 'acerbity and self-assertiveness' he often showed during his prime, said the New York *Evening Post*.

As a boxer, there was no-one better at the art of feinting than Corbett, wrote Paul Gallico in the New York *Daily News*. Jim would complain while watching fights during the 1920s that feinting was a lost art. He had tried to pass on his knowledge to young boxers, but they hadn't the patience to learn, he moaned. According to Gallico, Corbett could feint with his arms, with his legs – even with his eyebrows!

The New York *Herald Tribune*'s editorial writer found it hard to believe that, up to his fatal illness, the 'trim, youngish-looking fellow, swinging along with his cat-like steps, was really an old man'. Even when his friends began to notice his deterioration, he would brush it off in his husky baritone voice with a cheery 'Oh, I'll be all right, boys'.

Whether he left his widow 'all right' was another story. Exactly how much financial comfort she inherited remained something of a mystery. Jim was said to have considerable life insurance, real estate and other assets. Like most investors, he suffered losses in the 1929 stock market crash. Some estimates of his total earnings from boxing, acting, lecturing, his newspaper column, and other activities were as high as $4,500,000. In his will, filed for probate a month after his death, he left his estate, estimated then at up to $100,000, to his widow. The following year, however, the estate was officially appraised in Queens Surrogates Court, New York, at $4,534.43. After funeral expenses and other bills were paid, Vera was left with just $2,769.52.

Undoubtedly, Corbett earned well throughout most of his adult life. It was said that he was not accustomed to saving money, and thought about financial security only in his latter years. But he wasn't a big spender either. Unlike John L. Sullivan, no one caught Gentleman Jim going into a bar and ordering 'drinks for the house'. He may have taken a heavier blow in the Wall Street Crash than he was prepared to admit. That old pride would have kept up the façade that the Corbetts were doing just fine, thank you.

To outward appearances, at any rate, the couple had enjoyed a comfortable lifestyle in the stylish Bayside neighbourhood which also included the homes of film comedian W.C. Fields, actress Marie Dressler and Broadway producer John Golden.

Walter Judd, one-time treasurer of the Bayside Historical Society, who had lived in the area since 1911, remembered the Corbetts fondly. They lived in 'a nice, comfortable house, nothing fancy', kept a servant, and their green La Salle car was much admired as it stood parked in the driveway. One of Gentleman Jim's few extravagances was his clothes, said Judd. 'We would see him walking to the train every day wearing pearl-grey spats, a Chesterfield coat with a velvet collar, grey gloves and a silver-topped walking stick. He was quite a striking figure.'

Though he had no children of his own, Jim was at his happiest when he was surrounded by noisy, boisterous youngsters. Neighbours noted how he loved to play baseball with local kids every Sunday. On regular train trips to Manhattan, he would patiently answer questions from young people anxious to know more about the well-dressed elderly man their parents called Gentleman Jim.

Vera, who survived her husband by twenty-six years, would take offence any time stories were printed that Jim had left her financially insecure. 'It isn't fair to a great man to let people think he didn't leave me well provided for,' she told one reporter. 'Long before he died, much of the property was in my name. Even to his dying breath, he thought of me.'

But, in her widowhood, she certainly struggled to maintain the good standard of living they had enjoyed. There was some relief when, nineteen years after Jim's death, she was named a beneficiary in the will of his long-time friend John Kelleher, who had been at his death bed. The bequest gave her an income of $100 a month. That same year, Vera gave an interview to the Brooklyn *Sunday News* in which she reminisced about her life with Gentleman Jim. She recalled how John L. Sullivan had never forgiven Jim for beating him. Yet, whenever Corbett stopped in Boston on his theatrical tours, he always placed a wreath on Sullivan's grave in Old Calvary cemetery. As an actor, she said, Jim's favourite role was in *Cashel*

Byron's Profession. Off stage, he got great pleasure from reciting, with emotion, *Over the Hill to the Poorhouse.* 'Jim had a little bit of the ham in him,' said Vera. 'He was very fond of poetry – I think the Irish are like that.' She smiled at the memory of Kate Corbett, who always carried a vast collection of clippings about her famous son, in case anyone wanted information about him. 'Jim's was a wonderful family,' said Vera. 'It was like a circus when they got together.'

Vera was in her eighties when she died at home on 10 September 1959. Since her husband's death, she had shared the house with her sister, Mrs Ada Parkhurst, who survived her. During her latter years, Vera, once regarded as 'the most glamorous woman in Bayside', had enjoyed entertaining neighbours and a few close friends with colourful stories about her life with Jim. Every Saturday she would faithfully carry flowers to his burial place in Cypress Hills cemetery.

Now, at last, she had re-joined the man she always called 'the Mighty One'.

Epilogue

A favourite pastime with boxing buffs is the harmless, if futile, exercise of comparing great fighters of different eras. In their wishful dreams, they transport themselves to some imaginary arena and settle down to enjoy the true 'battles of the century'. They cheer lustily as Jack Dempsey slugs it out with Mike Tyson, John L. Sullivan tries to pin a haymaker on Floyd Patterson's vulnerable chin, Bob Fitzsimmons manoeuvres his way in close to plant his favourite solar plexus punch in Evander Holyfield's belly, and James J. Corbett feints and fiddles in a bid to bamboozle Joe Louis.

Boxing is the most unpredictable of all sports, so even the most detailed study of respective strengths and weaknesses cannot find a sure winner of these fantasy fights. History has shown, over and again, how a single pay-off punch in a late round can wipe out a huge points lead. A moderate fighter can catch one of the legends on a bad night and score a massive upset. Perhaps a great champion grows complacent, lacks motivation, or is thinking too much of how he'll spend his money, and gets knocked out by a fired-up challenger. These are just a few of the countless possibilities to be taken into account when debating the fights-that-might-have-been.

Assuming both contestants are in their prime and fully geared up for the big occasion, now comes the next question: in what period should the dream fight take place? An old-timer, without the benefits of vastly improved standards of coaching, physical and mental conditioning, dietary control, and all the other aspects of modern preparation, would face huge disadvantages if he stepped straight out of history to face a champion today. On the other hand, would today's giants have the will and endurance to survive the long, gruelling battles of the past? Would Evander Holyfield or Lennox Lewis have the stamina and unquenchable spirit to keep going for twenty-three rounds, as did Corbett and Jeffries, or, more emphatically still, the mind-boggling sixty-one rounds endured by Gentleman Jim and Peter Jackson?

Boxing experts enjoy drawing up ratings of the heavyweight greats, assessing them on such attributes as boxing ability, punching power, defensive skill and endurance, then balancing these against weaknesses like inadequate size and strength, doubtful punch resistance, lack of dedication, inability to adapt. Most have Muhammad Ali, Joe Louis, Jack Dempsey and Rocky Marciano around the top of the pile, with Corbett, at best, struggling to get into the top ten.

Nat Fleischer, who wasn't a great Ali fan, rated Jack Johnson as the best all-rounder among the heavyweights. In his top ten, Johnson was followed by Jeffries, Fitzsimmons, Dempsey, Corbett, Louis, Sam Langford, Gene Tunney, Max Schmeling and Rocky Marciano. In a detailed breakdown of fighting abilities, *The Ring*'s founder considered Corbett the best pure boxer and the fastest of the big men. It has to be said that Fleischer rarely gave credit to the fighters of his latter years.

Corbett disagreed with Fleischer's high ranking of Johnson. 'He was an excellent, clever boxer, but I always thought he lacked guts,' he told Nat in an interview. 'I'm sure he would never have stood up against the great Jeffries who fought me when I lasted twenty-three rounds. The Jeffries of those days would have stopped Johnson within fifteen rounds.'

Though, on another occasion, Corbett had said Peter Jackson was the greatest fighter he had ever seen, he told Fleischer that he rated Jeffries the best heavyweight, with Fitzsimmons next. 'Jeffries had everything that goes to make a great fighter except cleverness,' he said. 'In a way he was what you might call clumsy, but he made up for his clumsiness with powerful fists, a tremendously powerfully built body, speed to burn, stamina and courage.'

In the passing of time, *The Ring*'s all-time heavyweight ratings has inevitably got a bit more crowded. In 1987, the magazine, then under the editorship of Nigel Collins, awarded points in ten categories: punching power, defence, hand speed, determination, durability, footwork, cut resistance, natural ability, quality of opposition and historical impact. When the points were totalled up, Muhammad Ali came out tops, followed by Johnson and Louis. Corbett only made it to fifteenth place. His best individual mark, not surprisingly, was for historical impact.

Long-time *Boxing News* editor Gilbert Odd, the doyen of British boxing writers up to his death at the age of ninety-three in 1996, awarded Gentleman Jim ninth place in his list of twenty-five heavyweight champions. He saw Corbett as a 'good, English-style boxer' who came into prominence at the right time to beat the ageing Sullivan. He should not have lost to Fitzsimmons, and he made two great comeback efforts, concluded Odd.

Others were less complimentary. Herbert G. Goldman, in the December 1989 issue of *Boxing Illustrated*, slotted Corbett into a derisory thirty-fourth place in his all-time top hundred heavyweights, behind such *immortals* as Ernie Terrell, Paulino Uzcudun and Pinklon Thomas. Two years earlier, the public was given its say by *Boxing International*. Corbett got just 426 votes, earning him a poor seventeenth place. Louis polled best, followed by Ali and Marciano. Surprisingly, when the voters were split into age categories, Corbett's best showing was among the under-twenties.

Most scathing of Corbett's critics was the late Jim Jacobs, the former handball star who made a life-time hobby out of hunting down, purchasing and restoring old fight films. Founder, along with Bill Cayton, of The Big Fights, Inc., Jacobs watched the great names in action hundreds of times over, and formed the opinion that the old-timers were, with the exception of Johnson, decidedly 'ordinary'. Corbett, he said, 'with his stiff-armed jabs, would not be good enough today to win an amateur championship'.

During the 1960s someone came up with the bright idea of leaving the ultimate decision up to a computer. It turned out to be a bit of a farce. The simulated tournament was the brainchild of Murray Woroner, who, no matter what the critics felt, made a tidy profit out of the venture. Tons of information, including results and blow-by-blow accounts of the top heavyweights' fights, were fed into the computer. Announcer Guy LeBow did the fictional commentaries, which were broadcast by 380 radio stations across the United States. Corbett made a quick exit, suffering a seventh round 'knockout' by Jack Dempsey. The Manassa Mauler reached the final, when he was flattened in the thirteenth round by Rocky Marciano. It was good fun while it lasted, but no-one could take seriously a tournament that had Max Baer outscoring Jack Johnson, and Muhammad Ali losing on points to Jim Jeffries.

The nearest comparisons to Corbett among the heavyweight kings, in terms of technical skill, were Johnson and Tunney, most experts agree. Among the champions themselves, Johnson considered Corbett too clever for Tunney and also fancied him over Louis and Dempsey. Gene, for his part, wasn't overly impressed by Johnson. He felt Corbett's class might overcome the deadly punching, but slow moving Louis in a fifteen-rounder. Gentleman Jim was 'fleet-footed, brainy and quick in his reflexes – an all-round dangerous opponent', said Tunney. Jeffries rated Corbett above Johnson, but it is common for fighters to pick someone they beat, rather than someone who beat them. It makes them feel good.

In the final analysis, there are just too many imponderables to come to a definitive decision as to who was the greatest. It must be admitted, however, that the odds favour the moderns. After all, athletes are running faster and jumping higher than ever, world records in all sports are being continually smashed, and levels of fitness and mental preparedness are improving all the time. Modern fighters probably have too much of everything for the old-timers. But the arguments will go on for as long as boxing itself continues, maybe even beyond.

As to James J. Corbett, it is unquestionable that, as an exponent of pure scientific boxing, he was one of the greatest the game has seen. His footwork and defensive ability were so highly developed that he emerged from a tough, brutal profession without a single facial blemish. Even in the fights he lost, his opponents bore much more signs of punishment at the end. And, it must be remembered, Jim was largely self-taught. He had no role model to study, whereas the likes of Tunney learned from him. Had Corbett come along in a later era, who knows what heights of brilliance he might have achieved?

Whatever his technical mastery, however, it is clear that Corbett's lack of a big punch would have proved a major handicap against the all-time top heavyweights. With just ten knockouts from twenty-five professional fights, he was one of the lightest hitters among the heavyweight kings. His size, too, would be a disadvantage against the much bigger, heavier and more powerful heavyweights of the modern era. He fought at a time when in-fighting or combination punching were unknown. Doubts about his ability to absorb heavy punches also must come into the reckoning. While his courage and stamina are beyond question, his two knockout defeats by Jeffries and his sudden downfall against Fitzsimmons show a definite weakness. The fact that Fitz, a middleweight, was able to knock him out with a single body blow is the most damning indictment. Could he possibly have withstood the deadly digs of a Louis, a Marciano or a Tyson?

Corbett's great achievement was as an innovator. He revolutionised boxing with his scientific approach, born out of necessity. Other heavyweights with his weakness as a puncher would accept that the path to the top was too full of obstacles and would go for another line of work. Jim wasn't prepared to give in so easily. He had the foresight, backed by an indomitable will, to show that highly developed technical skills could compensate, to a large degree, for lack of power. When unexpected pitfalls threatened his progress, he turned them to his advantage. Against Joe Choynski, his most effective weapon, the left jab, was rendered almost useless because of the pain from his damaged knuckles. So he improvised. He introduced the left hook, with significant success.

Corbett's ability as a body puncher is rarely credited. Although he used the tactic primarily to protect his delicate hands, he could hurt and slow down an opponent with well-placed body shots. In the art of feinting to create an opening, no boxer in history did it better than Gentleman Jim. He was also one of the first fighters to use psychology as a weapon, not only to boost his own confidence, but to upset and sow doubts in the minds of his opponents.

Ultimately, Corbett deserves his place among the all-time greats for his mastery of the Noble Art of Self Defence. There have been more dynamic punchers, more durable battlers, maybe even more technically proficient boxers, but he was the one who showed there was a way to success other than through brute strength. To reach the peak of his profession required immense self-belief and a dogged refusal to listen to those who thought the task was beyond him.

Without that cockiness in his make-up, the dream would never have become a reality. He would probably have stayed in his secure bank job until he earned his pension. He would never have stuck the tremendous demands of the fight game, or beaten the 'unbeatable' John L. Sullivan to become heavyweight champion of the world. He would never have revolutionised boxing by turning a primitive test of strength and bravery into a performance of grace and beauty.

If that same arrogance carried over into his private life, it is hardly surprising. While many people resented his elegant dress code – who did this *prize-fighter* think he was? – and his haughty, opinionated manner got under many a skin, those who loved and understood him accepted his vanity as part of the man. You took him as he was or you left him

On finding an outlet through the boxing ring for his desire to show off, he continued on his giant ego trip for most of his life. Putting on a performance of one sort or another kept him in the limelight and he loved it all, the recognition, the applause, the roar of the crowd. He hoped he wouldn't be forgotten. He hasn't been.

Appendix 1

Gentleman Jim: the movie

In 1942 Hollywood marked the fiftieth anniversary of Corbett's famous victory over John L. Sullivan to win the world heavyweight title by putting his colourful life on screen in *Gentleman Jim*.

Corbett, who died nine years before the film was made, would probably have been pleased with the Warner Brothers production, even if the facts weren't always allowed get in the way of telling a good story. He would surely have enjoyed Errol Flynn's portrayal of him as a jaunty, devil-may-care dude utterly convinced he will win both the title and the girl. And he does. Of the sixty movies in which Flynn appeared, *Gentleman Jim* was his favourite.

Director Raoul Walsh made a good stab at evoking the lively, rumbustious San Francisco of the late nineteenth century as a colourful background to the success of the Golden Gate city's favourite fighting son. The readiness of the Corbett family to get involved in brawls at the drop of a shillelagh was a bit over the top, even allowing for Hollywood's fondness for stage Irishry, but it added to the general good-humoured tone of the movie.

Alexis Smith played the female lead, as the fictional Victoria Ware, a beautiful but haughty society lady who pretends to be put off by Corbett's cocksure manner, but whose secret admiration eventually turns to love. Alan Hale was altogether too carefree a character as Gentleman Jim's father, revealing none of the dark moods that haunted the real Pat Corbett. But then, no one claimed this was how it really was. As Harvey Marc Zucker and Lawrence J. Babich summarised it in *Sports Films: a Complete Reference*, 'If you don't mind Hollywood taking liberties with some facts, *Gentleman Jim* is certainly the most thoroughly enjoyable boxing biography ever put on screen'.

It was the realistic fight scenes that really got moviegoers cheering. The battle on the barge between Corbett and Joe Choynski was especially well staged, and the enactment of Jim's conquest of Sullivan (played with rip-roaring gusto by Ward Bond) captured well the excitement and drama of the great occasion. The most memorable scene, though entirely fictional, is when John L. arrives unannounced at Corbett's victory party. The celebrations give way to silence as the crowd wonders if Sullivan is about to seek revenge for his defeat. Instead, he unwraps his championship belt and hands it to Jim, telling him to take good care of it. 'Maybe you're bringin' somethin' new to the fight game, somethin' it needs, and never got from fellers like me,' he says. If the real Sullivan had put it as eloquently as that, it would have earned its place among the great boxing quotations. Instead, it was just the imagination of a Hollywood scriptwriter at work. In the film,

211

Sullivan tells Corbett he is the fastest thing on two feet. 'Sure, 'twas like trying to hit a ghost,' he says. (While Bond's Sullivan delivers his speech with a thick Irish brogue, as if he had just stepped off the immigrant boat, Flynn speaks in his normal cultured English accent. Maybe no one told him Corbett was every bit as Irish as John L.).

The choice of Tasmanian-born Flynn, son of a one-time professor of biology at Queen's University, Belfast, was an inspired piece of casting by Raoul Walsh. Though better looking than Corbett, Errol was about the same height and weight, was quite well built, and had done a bit of amateur boxing in New South Wales. So he at least looked the part, more so than many of the Hollywood hams whose portrayals of boxers make genuine fight fans squirm. Flynn also picked up some of Corbett's arrogance, believing he could do the boxing scenes better than his stand-in, Freddie Steele, the former world middleweight champion. The publicity department at Warner Brothers put out a fanciful story that Flynn had won an Olympic Games boxing gold medal in 1932. The records do show that E. Flynn was a winner in Los Angeles that year, but it was a welterweight named Eddie Flynn, unrelated to the actor.

For a while, it looked as if *Gentleman Jim* would never get made, at least with Flynn in the starring role. Far from being fighting fit, Errol was a physical wreck at the time shooting began. A notorious heavy drinker and womaniser, he had a mild heart condition and suffered from recurring bouts of malaria and tuberculosis. He found the six weeks of intensive physical training under Mushy Callahan, one-time holder of the world junior welterweight title, too much. He twice collapsed at the Warner Brothers studio gymnasium and had to be taken home. During filming, only one minute of boxing action could be shot at a time. Flynn was too exhausted to go any longer. The constant stoppages drove Ward Bond mad, but the former college football star could do nothing about it. One thing that impressed Callahan, who had worked with Errol on an earlier movie with a boxing background, *The Perfect Specimen*, was his enthusiasm to get the job done right.

'Errol tended to use his right fist,' said Callahan. 'I had to teach him to use his left and to move very fast on his feet. I had to turn him into Corbett. Luckily he had excellent footwork. He was dodgy and could duck faster than anyone I saw. By the time I was through with him, he'd jab, jab, jab with his left like a veteran.'

Despite all the problems, *Gentleman Jim* turned out to be a commercial and critical success, even if one scribe was unkind enough to suggest that Flynn's feet were more mobile than his features. If the critic had done his homework, he would have found that Errol didn't even deserve that back-handed compliment. The close-ups of Corbett's fancy footwork, showing only the bottom half of his body, were actually a cut-off Billy Conn, the former world light-heavyweight champion. Conn had led the great Joe Louis a merry dance for thirteen rounds in a 1941 heavyweight title fight before the Brown Bomber caught up with him.

The generally up-beat movie, a pleasant change from the normal Hollywood depictions of boxing's seamier side, still crops up from time to time in TV schedules. It gets a two-star rating in *Halliwell's Film Guide*, indicating 'a good level of competence and a generally entertaining film'. *The Time Out Film Guide*, while pointing out that the film may not be all that historically accurate, praises it as 'lavish, lustrous ... Hollywood at its cavalier best, with a perfectly judged performance by Flynn, brash yet engaging, as the social-climbing Corbett'.

Mike Tyson, a keen student of boxing history when he wasn't devouring opponents in the ring, said *Gentleman Jim* was the best boxing movie he ever saw. While enjoying Flynn's portrayal of the first of the Queensberry rules heavyweight champions, Iron Mike thought Ward Bond was 'incredible' as the bellowing, bullying John L. But then he would, wouldn't he?

Appendix 2

Statistics and ring record

Born in San Francisco, California, 1 September 1866. Died in New York, 18 February 1933.
Height: 6ft 1in. Weight: 178–190 lb. Reach: 73in. Chest (normal): 38in. Chest (expanded): 42in. Waist: 33in. Biceps: 14½ in. Neck: 17in. Wrist: 6½ in. Calf: 14½ in. Ankle: 8¼ in. Thigh: 21 in. Fist: 12¾ in. Forearm: 11½ in.

Key to boxing record. W: won. L: lost. D: drew. NC: no contest. KO: knockout. Dec: decision. Disq: disqualification. Exh: exhibition.

Amateur bouts (dates and venues unknown)

Billy 'Forty' Kenealy, W4; Dave Eiseman, W2; 'Capt.' James Dailey, W2.; Mike Brennan, W3; 'Professor' John Donaldson, W4; Martin 'Buffalo' Costello, W3; 'Prof.' William Miller, W6; Tom Johnson, W4; Bill Hayes, W3; Joe McAuliffe, W4; Frank Glover, W2 ; Joe Choynski, W1 (*Some reports say this ended in 'no decision'*); Joe Choynski, W3.

Amateur bouts (dated)

1886
Billy Welch, L dec. 4, San Francisco.
Billy Welch, W ko1, San Francisco.

1887
27 August: Jack Burke, D 8, San Francisco.
(In many so-called amateur bouts, Corbett's opponents were paid, and Jim himself often got 'expenses')

Professional record

1886
3 July: Frank Smith, W dec. 4, Salt Lake City, Utah.
(Corbett boxed as John Dillon)
August: Duncan McDonald, D 8, Evanston, Wyoming.
(Corbett, again claiming to be Dillon, was thought to be Jack 'Nonpareil' Dempsey, and was announced as such. Some accounts say Corbett won on a decision.)

1889
30 May: Joe Choynski, NC 5 (Sheriff stopped contest), Fairfax, California
5 June: Joe Choynski, W ko 27, Benicia, California
15 July: Joe Choynski, W dec. 4, San Francisco
11 Dec.: Australian Billy Smith, W dec. 10, San Francisco

28 Dec.: Dave Campbell, D 10, Portland, Oregon
(Corbett was a clear winner, but had agreed to a draw if he failed to score a knockout)

1890
18 Feb.: Jake Kilrain, W dec. 6, New Orleans
14 Apr.: Dominick McCaffrey, W dec.4, Brooklyn, New York

1891
21 May: Peter Jackson, NC 61, San Francisco
26 June: John L. Sullivan, Exh. 4, San Francisco
(Both sparred in evening dress at Sullivan's insistence)
8 Oct.: Ed Kinney, W dec. 4, Milwaukee

1892
16 Feb.: William Spilling, W ko 1, New York City
16 Feb.: Bob Caffrey, W ko 1, New York City
16 Feb.: Joe Lannon, W dec. 3, New York City
(Above three contests took place on same bill)
2 Mar.: Jim Daly, W dec. 4, Philadelphia
4 Mar.: Tommy Monoghan, Exh., W ko 2, Philadelphia
26 Aug., Jim Daly, Exh., W ko, New York City
7 Sept.: John L. Sullivan, W ko 21, New Orleans
(Won world heavyweight title)
17 Sept.: John L. Sullivan, Exh. 3, New York City

1893
Inactive

1894
25 Jan.: Charlie Mitchell, W ko 3, Jacksonville, Florida
(Retained world heavyweight title)
24 Feb.: Charlie Mitchell, Exh. 4, New York City
12 May: Jim Daly, Exh., Folies Bergères, Paris
(Exhibitions with Daly continued for next seven nights)
7 Sept.: Peter Courtney, W ko 6, Orange, New Jersey
(First motion picture of a fight)

1895
4 Jan.: Con McVey, Exh., W ko 3, New Orleans
27 June: John L. Sullivan, Exh. 3, New York City
30 Sept.: Steve O'Donnell, Exh. 3, New York City

1896
24 June: Tom Sharkey, D4, San Francisco

1897
17 Mar.: Bob Fitzsimmons, L ko 14, Carson City, Nevada
(Lost world heavyweight title)

1898
22 Nov.: Tom Sharkey, L disq. 9, New York City

1899
Inactive

1900

11 May: James J. Jeffries, L ko 23, Brooklyn, New York
(Challenge for world heavyweight title)
30 Aug.: Kid McCoy, W ko 5, New York City

1901

Inactive

1902

8 Dec.: Tommy Burns, Exh. 3, Detroit

1903

14 Aug.: James J. Jeffries, L ko 10, San Francisco
(Challenge for world heavyweight title)

1910

4 Mar.: Jack Dillon, Exh. 3, Indianapolis

Corbett on stage

1890: *Camille.* Corbett played Count De Varville in scene from burlesque version of play on benefit show at Baldwin Theatre, San Francisco.

1891: Toured with George Thatcher's minstrel show, sparring between acts.

1891: *After Dark.* Joined future manager William A. Brady on tour in Dion Boucicault melodrama. Corbett appeared in music hall scene.

1892: *Sport McAllister.* Debut in play, written by Charles T. Vincent, at Bijou theatre, New York City, 26 June.

1892: *Gentleman Jack.* Played title role in play commissioned by Brady and specially written for Corbett by Charles T. Vincent. Debut Elizabeth, New Jersey, 2 October.

1894: *Gentleman Jack.* British tour opened at Theatre Royal, Drury Lane, London, 21 April. Week-long engagements followed in Liverpool, Sheffield, Newcastle-upon-Tyne, Birmingham, Manchester, Leeds, Edinburgh and Glasgow.

1894: *Gentleman Jack.* Irish tour opened at Queen's Theatre, Dublin, 9 July. Further bookings in Belfast, Waterford, Limerick and Cork, plus special one-night engagement in Ballinrobe in aid of uncle's church.

1895: *A Naval Cadet.* Played lead in another play specially written for him by Charles T. Vincent. Debut Lynn, Massachusetts, 25 November.

1898: *The Adventurer.* Played main role in drama by Henry Guy Carleton. After several one-night out-of-town performances, play's first city staging was at Bijou theatre, Milwaukee, Wisconsin, 10 February.

1899: *As You Like It.* Played Charles the Wrestler in charity performance of Shakespeare's play at Larchmont Yacht Club, New York, 24 August. Proceeds went to local St John's Church.

1904: *Pals.* Played main character in light comedy. Debut, Trenton, New Jersey, September.

1906: *The Burglar and the Lady.* Again took main role in play later made into a film also starring Corbett.

1906: *Cashel Byron's Profession.* Played principal role in Bernard Shaw's play. Broadway debut, Daly's Theatre, 8 January.

1908: *Facing the Music.* Headed his own company and took main part in comedy by Charles Henry Darnley. Debut, American Theatre, San Francisco, 15 November.

1909: British and Irish music hall tour. Delivered monologue on his travels and experiences. Tour opened at Theatre Royal, Dublin, 12 July. Went on to Belfast, London, Manchester and Oxford.

1910: *Honey Boy.* Corbett 'blacked up' to act as interlocutor in George Evans' minstrel show, City Theatre, New York, 13 August.

1915: Opened Australian music hall tour in Melbourne in March. Abandoned tour to return home after sudden death of his youngest brother Tom.

1918: *Doing Our Bit.* Joined cast of 150 in revue at Palace Theatre, Chicago, in aid of US war effort, July.

1921: *The 18th Amendment.* Played 'straight man' to comedian Billy B. Van in skit at Moore Theatre, Seattle, Washington, March.

1923: *Ziegfeld Follies.* Appeared in New York show as raconteur.

1925: Retired from vaudeville to do lecture tours, billed as *Memories of an Active Life and How to Keep Young.*

1929: Played 'feeder' to 'blacked up' comedian Neil O'Brien at Orpheum Theatre, San Francisco, October.

Corbett on screen

1894: *Corbett and Courtney Before the Kinetograph* (also known as *The Corbett-Courtney Fight*). Filmed by Thomas Edison for William K.L. Dickson's production company. 750 ft.

Contest between Corbett and Peter Courtney at Orange, New Jersey, on 7 September 1894, was the first fight to be filmed. Corbett won by knockout in sixth round. Each round was filmed on a separate reel for showing on Kinetoscope machines.

1897: *The Corbett-Fitzsimmons Fight.* Filmed by Enoch Rector for Thomas Edison's Veriscope Company. 4 reels. 2,880 ft (35mm).

The world heavyweight title fight at Carson City, Nevada, on 17 March 1897 was filmed by Rector in a 63mm format. He used three cameras and exposed a then-record 11,000 feet of film. The film measured over two miles in length and contained over 165,000 individual pictures. It was copied, edited and distributed by Edison's Veriscope company in 35mm. Edison's banner, 'Copyrighted the Veriscope Company 1897', was placed on the edge of the ring and is clearly visible in the film.

Reproductions of Corbett's fights with Fitzsimmons (1897), Tom Sharkey (1898), Kid McCoy (1900) and James J. Jeffries (1900 and 1903), with actors taking the parts of the contestants, were made by Siegmund Lubin. Audiences were not convinced that what they were seeing was close to the real thing and showings were frequently interrupted by cries of 'Fake!', 'Cheat!' and 'Give us our money back!'. By the time of the second Corbett-Jeffries bout, the re-enactment was more professionally done. The reproduction, by the American Mutoscope and Biograph Company, won high praise for its realistic depiction of the actual fight. Shot in a New York studio, under the same conditions prevailing at the original location, the fight scenes were summarised as 'fast and furious'. (The same company released a film in 1899 called *Jeffries vs Corbett* which really had the feathers flying. It was a cock fight between game birds bearing the fighters' names!)

1906: *James J. Corbett and Fred Stone*. Silent. Short.
Film version of burlesque four-round boxing bout between Corbett and Stone, an actor, with proceeds going to Actors' Fair Fund. Sparring match took place on roof of Globe Theatre, New York, where Stone was appearing in *The Old Town*.

1910: *How Championships Are Won – and Lost*. Silent. Vitagraph Company of America. 1,025 ft.
Cast: James J. Corbett, Florence Turner, Professor Cooper, Tom Kennedy.

1910: *Actors' Fund Field Day*. Silent. Vitagraph Company of America. 387 ft.
Film of charity event at Polo Grounds, New York City, on 19 August 1910.
Cast: Eddie Foy, Bert Williams, Marie Dressler, Lew Fields, Marshall P. Wilder, George M. Cohan, Victor Moore, James J. Corbett, Tim Sullivan, Joe Humphreys, Emma Carus, Louis Mann, Terry McGovern, Annie Oakley, Irene Franklin.

1913: *The Man from the Golden West*. Silent. Mittenthal Film Co./Warner's Features. 5 reels.
Corbett's movie acting debut. He plays a bank clerk who single-handedly catches a gang of robbers, but is then wrongly convicted of murder. He escapes from Sing Sing and proves his innocence with a photograph of the victim's eye, which shows a reflection of the real culprit. Corbett was the only cast member named.

1915: *The Burglar and the Lady*. Silent. Sun Photoplay Co./Warner's Features, Inc. Director: Herbert Blache. 5–6 reels.
Corbett plays one of two brothers parted when their parents split up. One grows up in poverty and the other in luxury. The poorer one gains

notoriety as a gentleman crook called Raffles. (Presumably the screenplay was based on one of E.W. Hornung's Raffles stories.) His brother, a clergyman, is in love with the daughter of a wealthy banker. The girl discovers her heart really belongs to Raffles, who robs her father's mansion, then turns himself over to the police and decides to reform for the sake of his loved one.

Cast: James J. Corbett, Claire Whitney, Fraunie Fraunholz, Calvin Reisland, Edward Cecil, Agusta Burmeister.

1916: *The Other Girl*. Silent. Raver Film Corp./State Rights. Director: Percy Winter. 5 reels.

Corbett, as champion fighter Kid Garvey, agrees to teach a clergyman how to box in return for some society introductions. Catherine, a wealthy socialite, falls for him and, though engaged to someone else, she agrees to elope with Garvey. One of her friends, overhearing the plans, locks Catherine in a room and, disguised in a veil, takes her place. Garvey, in his haste, accidentally runs down his girl's fiancé in his car and is taken to the police station. The recovered accident victim then reveals that he really loves someone else, so leaving Garvey free to announce his plans to marry Catherine.

Cast: James J. Corbett, Paul Gilmore, Horace Vinton, Mortimer Martini, Louis Thiel, Rawland Ratcliffe, Henry Redding, Ten Eyck Clay, Mona Ryan, Becky Bruce, Edith Luckett, Frances Thompson, Lizzie McCall, William Muldoon.

1919: *The Midnight Man*. Silent. Universal. Serial in 18 episodes.

At 53, Corbett was a bit old to be a convincing hero in this post-World War 1 cliff-hanger. But he was lively enough to perform feats which would have put younger men to shame. His winning smile and pleasing on-screen personality did the rest.

Cast: James J. Corbett, Orral Humphrey, Sam Polo, Kathleen O'Connor, Joseph W. Girard, Frank Jonasson, Noble Johnson, William Sauter, Georgia Woodthorpe, Joseph Singleton.

1920: *The Prince of Avenue A*. Silent. Universal. Director: John Ford. 5 reels.

Corbett, as Barry O'Connor, is called 'the Prince of Avenue A' because of his foppish appearance. His father, political leader Patrick O'Connor, supports William Tompkins for mayor, but when Tompkins' daughter Mary ejects Barry from a party at their house, the elder O'Connor is enraged. Tompkins, fearful of losing his backer's support, insists that Mary escort Barry to the district ball. When Tompkins' political rival insults Mary at the ball, Barry protects her. This makes her realise that her escort is more than a dandy and the two fall in love.

Cast: James J. Corbett, Richard Cummings, Cora Drew, Frederick Vroom, Mary Warren, George Fisher, Harry Northrup, Mark Fenton, Johnnie Cooke, Lydia Yeamans Titus.

1922: *The Beauty Shop*. Silent. Cosmopolitan Productions/Paramount. Director: Edward Dillon. 7 reels, 6,536 ft.

Corbett was relegated to third place in the cast of this laboured comedy, set in the imaginary kingdom of Bolognia, about a beauty specialist who turns an ugly duckling into a goddess. Corbett wears a wig and moustache for the part of Panatella, an innkeeper. Billy B. Van, Jim's partner in stage sketches, had a leading part.

Cast: Raymond Hitchcock, Billy B. Van, James J. Corbett, Louise Fazenda, Madeline Fairbanks, Marion Fairbanks, Diana Allen, Montagu Love, Laurance Wheat.

1924: *Broadway After Dark*. Silent. Warner Brothers. Harry Rapf Production. Director: Monta Bell. 7 reels, 6,300 ft.

No longer a leading man, Corbett was well down the star-studded list in this Broadway society melodrama.

Cast: Adolphe Menjou, Norma Shearer, Anna Q. Nilsson, Edward Burns, Carmel Myers, Vera Lewis, Willard Louis, Mervyn LeRoy, Jimmy Quinn, Edgar Norton, Gladys Tennyson, Ethel Miller, Otto Hoffman, Lew Harvey, Michael Dark, Fred Stone, Dorothy Stone, Mary Eaton, Raymond Hitchcock, Elsie Ferguson, Florence Moore, James J. Corbett, John Steel, Frank Tinney, Paul Whiteman, Irene Castle, Buster West.

1929: *James J. Corbett and Neil O'Brien*. Silent. Short.

Movie version of Corbett's stage act with comedian O'Brien.

1929: *Happy Days*. Sound. Fox Film Corp. Director: Benjamin Stoloff. 9 reels. 81 mins.

The first 'talkie' in which Corbett appeared, even though he had only a minor part as an interlocutor. The thin plot about a showboat singer who helps out her old friends was mainly a vehicle to parade Fox's leading stars. It is supplemented by well-known vaudevillians performing their acts, plus lots of songs and some lively dancing. Critic Emily Sieger, viewing the film many years later, thought Gentleman Jim looked more like George Burns than Errol Flynn.

Cast: Charles E. Evans, Marjorie White, Richard Keene, Stuart Erwin, Martha Lee Sparks, Clifford Dempsey, Janet Gaynor, Charles Farrell, Victor McLaglen, El Brendel, William Collier Snr, Tom Patricola, George Jessel, Dixie Lee, Nick Stuart, Rex Bell, Frank Albertson, Sharon Lynn, 'Whispering' Jack Smith, Lew Brice, Farrell MacDonald, Will Rogers, Edmund Lowe, Walter Catlett, Frank Richardson, Ann Pennington, David Rollins, Warner Baxter, J. Harold Murray, Paul Page, the Slate Brothers, Flo Bert, James J. Corbett, George MacFarlane, George Olsen and his Orchestra.

1930: *At the Round Table*. Sound. Short.

Corbett's last acting part. Designed to spotlight four popular personalities of the day, it had just two scenes, in a gymnasium and a club dining room. A cub reporter meets the four men and interviews Corbett, of whom he has never heard. The four exploit the newspaperman's innocence in a round of kidding.

Cast: James J. Corbett, Damon Runyon, Mark Hellinger, DeWolf Hopper.

1968: *The Legendary Champions.* Turn of the Century Films Inc. Director: Harry Chaplin. 77 mins.

Documentary on world heavyweight championship boxing from 1892 to 1929. Fascinating footage of legends from John L. Sullivan to Gene Tunney. Includes scenes from the Corbett vs Fitzsimmons title fight in 1897.

Actors' portrayals of Corbett in films

1942: *Gentleman Jim.* Warner Bros. Producer: Robert Buckner. Director: Raoul Walsh. Black and white. 104 mins.

Entertaining biopic, if only loosely based on Corbett's real life.

Cast: Errol Flynn (James J. Corbett), Alexis Smith, Jack Carson, Alan Hale (Corbett's father), John Loder, William Frawley, Minor Watson, Ward Bond (John L. Sullivan), Madeline Lebeau, Rhys Williams, Arthur Shields, Dorothy Vaughan (Corbett's mother), James Flavin, Pat Flaherty, Wallis Clark, Marilyn Phillips, Art Foster, Edwin Stanley, Henry O'Hara, Frank Mayo, Carl Harbaugh, Fred Kelsey, Sammy Stein, Lon McAllister.

1945: *The Great John L.* (retitled in Britain as *A Man Called Sullivan*). United Artists. Director: Frank Tuttle. Black and white. 96 mins.

Biopic of the Boston Strong Boy moved through the locales of London, Paris and New York, but lacked the charm and entertainment value of *Gentleman Jim.* Handsome, muscular Greg McClure, who had been a Warner Brothers extra, got his big chance in the title role, but didn't have the star quality to carry the picture. At least, unlike the Corbett movie, which ended with Jim's triumph over Sullivan, *The Great John L.* showed the Bostonian's downfall due to women and drink. However, he picks himself up and becomes a proponent of clean living. The part of Corbett was taken by a young Texan called Frank McCown, who had won some amateur bouts and had played George Raft's fighter in *Nob Hill.* McCown later became better known as Rory Calhoun. John Indrisano, a former welterweight contender, masterminded the fight sequences as technical advisor.

Cast: Greg McClure, Linda Darnell, Barbara Britton, Lee Sullivan, Otto Kruger, Wallace Ford, George Mathews, Robert Barrat, J.M. Kerrigan, Joel Friedkin, Simon Semenoff, Frank McCown (Rory Calhoun), Harry Crocker, Fritz Feld.

1947: *Vigilantes of Boomtown.* Republic. Producer: Sidney Picker. Director: R.G. Springsteen. Black and white. 56 mins.

Western, from the Red Ryder series, set in Carson City at the time of the Corbett vs Fitzsimmons fight. Ryder (Allan Lane) is on hand to see that a bank robbery doesn't take place while the championship bout has diverted attention. A plot to stop the bout going ahead by kidnapping Corbett goes wrong when Ryder is taken hostage instead. He just makes it back to town in time to thwart the robbers. One reviewer thought Corbett might have wished he was kidnapped – then he wouldn't have lost to Fitzsimmons.

Cast: Allan Lane, Bobby Blake, Martha Wentworth, Roscoe Karns, Roy Barcroft, Peggy Stewart, George Turner (Corbett), Eddie Lou Simms, George Chesebro, Bobby Barber, George Lloyd, Ted Adams, John Dehner (Fitzsimmons), Earle Hodgins, Harlan Briggs, Budd Buster, Jack O'Shea, Tom Steele.

1953: *City of Bad Men.* 20th Century Fox. Producer: Leonard Goldstein. Director: Harmon Jones. Technicolor. 82 mins.

Three notorious outlaws accept the positions of deputy sheriffs in Carson City at the time of Corbett vs Fitzsimmons. They plan to steal the takings of the fight. One of the gang, Brett Stanton (Dale Robertson), has a change of heart after meeting up again with his former girlfriend, Linda Culligan (Jeanne Crain). In a gunfight with his companions, he kills them both and returns the money to Carson City. He marries Linda and stays on as deputy sheriff. The hackneyed Western is lifted by the atmospheric background of the big fight.

Cast: Jeanne Crain, Dale Robertson, Richard Boone, Lloyd Bridges, Carole Mathews, Carl Betz, Whitfield Connor, Hugh Sanders, Rodolfo Acosta, Pasquel Garcia Pena, Harry Carter, Robert Adler, John Doucette, Alan Dexter, Don Haggerty, James Best, Leo V. Gordon, Gil Perkins (Fitzsimmons), John Day (Corbett), Richard Cutting, Douglas Evans, Kit Carson, Tom McDonough, Charles B. Smith, Harry Hines, Jane Easton, Anthony Jochim, Leo Curley, George Melford, George Selk, Charles Tannen, Gordon Nelson, Barbara Fuller, Harry Brown.

Corbett honoured

Elected to *The Ring* magazine's Boxing Hall of Fame in 1954, the inaugural year of the awards.

Inducted into the International Boxing Hall of Fame, based at Canastota, New York, in 1990.

Enshrined in the Bay Area Sports Hall of Fame, San Francisco, in 1982.

Plaque installed on a boulder outside 221–4 Corbett Road, Bayside, Queens, New York, by the Bayside Historical Society, in 1971. It stated that Corbett had lived there (it was formerly Edgewater Avenue) from 1902 to his death in 1933. The stone was chosen from nearby excavations by the then owners of the house, Mr and Mrs Thomas Claro, who enthusiastically supported the project. On 7 October, the day of the dedication, a nostalgic link was provided by the master of ceremonies, Walter S. Dayton, whose father had sold the house to Gentleman Jim in 1902. But the most enjoyable aspect for the large crowd gathered for the ceremony was the opportunity to hear the voice of the man they were honouring that day. Tapes of Corbett's radio broadcasts, reminiscing about fighters and other famous sports figures, were relayed to the crowd.

Tree planted in his memory at Crocheron Park, New York, in May 1933.

A US Liberty ship, the *James J. Corbett*, carried troops and cargo during World War 2, and was later used in conveying supplies to Europe under the Marshall Plan.

A plaque in front of a fire station in Carson City, Nevada, designates the building as being close to the site of the arena that hosted the Corbett vs Fitzsimmons fight in 1897. It was dedicated by the Nevada State Historical Society.

San Francisco, sadly, appears to have neglected its famous fighting son. The only reminder that Corbett was born there is a wall plaque inside the Olympic Club, in Post Street. Corbett Avenue, in the Haight Ashbury district, is apparently named after another Corbett.

Corbett memorabilia

Trade in boxing memorabilia, while not the huge business generated in other sports, is growing fast. Famous champions' gloves, dressing gowns, autographed photographs, letters, fight tickets, programmes, and various other ring souvenirs change hands for high prices at boxing auctions, at gatherings of fight fans, or through collectors' regularly issued newsletters and catalogues.

Most valuable of the Corbett mementoes are the gloves he wore in beating John L. Sullivan for the title. They sold for $41,250 at a public auction in San Francisco in 1992. A much-sought programme for the Corbett-Sullivan fight went for $14,000 at *The Ring*'s 75th anniversary weekend in Atlantic City, New Jersey, in 1997. A full ticket for the 1892 bout fetched $3,200. The Corbett vs Fitzsimmons programme from 1897, regarded as 'a beaut' by collectors, sold for $4,100 several years ago, and would be worth considerably more today.

Although Corbett was quite generous with his autograph (the rarer the signature of a famous person, the more valuable it is) his signed photograph, even with a fold mark, fetched $400 in 1998. A 1906 contract between Corbett and theatrical impresario Oscar Hammerstein, signed by both, was up for auction at a minimum bid of $500 in 1997.

The value of Corbett books depends on which edition is on offer, and whether they bear his signature or not. His signed autobiography, *The Roar of the Crowd*, fetched $316 at the auction of Nat Fleischer's collection in 1997. Unsigned, it can be found for around $40. More valuable is the green-covered first edition from 1925. The red-covered copy was brought out the following year. Fleischer's own work, *Gentleman Jim*, was on offer at

$45 in 1998. The much-rarer *Life and Battles of James J. Corbett,* published by Richard K. Fox in 1892, would not be sold for less than $575.

At *The Ring* magazine auction of memorabilia, conducted by Mastro and Steinbach in Atlantic City in 1997, a framed autographed studio portrait of Corbett was sold for $1,600. A 19th century hand-carved cane bearing pictures of Corbett, Sullivan and Charlie Mitchell fetched $2,400. A bound lot of the *New Orleans Item* covering the Corbett-Sullivan bout went for $420. A framed advert from the 1920s showing Corbett endorsing Lucky Strike cigarettes was sold for $500. A hand written letter by Corbett went for $350. A small illustrated pennant of Corbett the stage actor fetched $375. Pins bearing the images of Corbett and Sullivan were snapped up for $220.

Many of Corbett's personal trophies were stolen from their New York home in 1916. Vera, his widow, said she later donated his remaining trophies to the Olympic Club in San Francisco, but there is no sign of them today.

Even the boxing boots worn by Errol Flynn in *Gentleman Jim* took on some value over the years. The leather boots, which the actor presented to the US Navy's 6th Fleet boxing team aboard the USS *Saratoga* in 1950, were sold at an auction in Bristol, England, in 1997 for £660.

Other fighting Corbetts

Three talented fighters who were devoted fans of Gentleman Jim took the name 'Young Corbett' in tribute to their hero. Each did him proud by becoming a world champion, or at least gaining a strong claim to a title.

First 'Young Corbett' was George Green, a one-time pupil of Jim's at the Olympic Club in San Francisco. He KO'd Mysterious Billy Smith in twelve rounds on the Carson City bill when Jim lost his title to Fitzsimmons on 17 March 1897. Green claimed the world welterweight title, which had been vacated by Tommy Ryan, on the strength of his win. His somewhat tenuous hold on the title lasted just five months, until he was KO'd in eighteen rounds by Joe Walcott, the 'Barbados Demon'.

Next to call himself 'Young Corbett' was William H. Rothwell, from Denver, Colorado, who caused a big upset by knocking out 'Terrible' Terry McGovern in two rounds to win the world featherweight title on 28 November 1901. To prove it was no fluke, he again beat McGovern the following year, though it took him eleven rounds on this occasion. 'Corbett' relinquished the title to move up in weight, but his goal of winning the lightweight title was wrecked in defeats by Jimmy Britt and Battling Nelson.

'Young Corbett the Third' was born Ralph Capabianca Giordano in Naples, Italy. Raised in California, the tough, hard-hitting southpaw boxed for fourteen years before he got a deserved crack at the world welterweight title. He made the most of his opportunity by outpointing Jackie Fields on 22 February 1933. Within three months he was an ex-champion, after being knocked out in the first round by Irish-born Jimmy McLarnin. 'Corbett' moved up in weight and beat top-notchers Mickey Walker, Gus Lesnevich, Billy Conn and Fred Apostoli, but all in non-title fights. He was KO'd by Apostoli in eight rounds in a middleweight title bid in 1938.

Brothers Harry and Dick Corbett, from Bethnal Green, London, both won British titles between 1928 and 1931. Their family name was Coleman, but they adopted the name of the famed world heavyweight champion.

A black bantamweight calling himself 'James J. Corbett Junior' was KO'd in two rounds by Terry McGovern in a non-title fight in Chicago on 12 December 1899.

Bibliography

Books

American Film Institute Catalog of Motion Pictures Produced in the United States: Film Beginnings, 1893–1910, New Jersey and London, 1995.

American Film Institute Catalog: Feature Films, 1911–1920, Los Angeles and London, 1988.

American Film Institute Catalog: Feature Films, 1921–1930, New York and London, 1971.

Anon., *Life and Battles of James J. Corbett*, (Richard K. Fox, publisher), New York, 1892.

Atkinson, Brooks, Broadway, *London, 1970.*

Batchelor, Denzil, *Big Fight: the Story of World Championship Boxing*, 1954.

—— *Jack Johnson and his Times*, 1956.

—— *The Boxing Companion*, 1964.

Bergan, Ronald, *Sports in the Movies*, London and New York, 1982.

Blesh, Rudi, *Keaton*, 1967.

Blewett, Bert, *The A–Z of World Boxing*, 1996.

Blow, Sydney, *Through Stage Doors*, 1958.

Blum, Daniel, *A Pictorial History of the Silent Screen*, 1962.

Boardman, W.H. (Billy), *Vaudeville Days*, 1935.

Brady, Willam A., *The Fighting Man*, Indianapolis, 1916.

—— *Showman*, New York, 1937.

226

Bromberg, Lester, *Boxing's Unforgettable Fights*, New York, 1962.

Brooke-Ball, Peter, (contributing editors Derek O'Dell and O.F. Snelling), *The Boxing Album*, Leicestershire, 1992.

Brown, Gene, editor, *The Complete Book of Boxing: A New York Times Scrapbook History*, New York, 1980.

Brownlow, Kevin, *Hollywood: the Pioneers*, 1979.

Buchanan-Taylor, W., with James Butler, *What Do You Know About Boxing?*, 1947.

Burchell, R.A., *The San Francisco Irish 1848–1880*, Manchester, 1979.

Cantwell, Robert, *The Real McCoy*, Princeton, 1971.

Carpenter, Harry, *Masters of Boxing*, 1964.

—— *Boxing: a Pictorial History*, 1975.

Chidsey, Donald Barr, *John the Great: the Times and Life of John L. Sullivan*, New York, 1942, London, 1947.

Clark, Norman, *All in the Game*, 1935.

Cochran, C.B., *Showman Looks On*, 1946.

Corbett, James J., *My Life and My Fights*, (edited by Frederic A. Felton), 1910.

—— *The Roar of the Crowd*, (edited by Robert Gordon Anderson), New York and London, 1925.

Corri, Eugene, *Gloves and the Man*, 1928.

De Ford, Miriam Allen, *They Were San Franciscans*, USA, 1941.

Dempsey, Jack, with Barbara Piatelli Dempsey, *Dempsey: the Autobiography of Jack Dempsey*, New York and London, 1977.

Dibble, R.F., *John L. Sullivan: an Intimate Narrative*, Boston, 1925.

Doherty, W.J., *In the Days of the Giants*, New York, London and Sydney, 1931.

Donald, Brian, *The Fight Game in Scotland*, Edinburgh, 1988.

Donoghue, Noel, *Proud and Upright Men*, Connemara, Ireland, 1987.

Donovan, Mike, *The Roosevelt That I Know*, New York, 1909.

Durant, John, *The Heavyweight Champions*, New York, 1973.

Edwards, Billy, *Legendary Boxers of the Golden Age*, Leicester, 1990. (Originally published as *The Portrait Gallery of Pugilists of England, America and Australia*, London and Philadelphia, 1894).

Evensen, Bruce J., *When Dempsey Fought Tunney*, Tennessee, 1996.

Farnol, Jeffrey, *Epics of the Fancy*, London, 1928. (Published in USA as *Famous Prize-Fights, or Epics of the Fancy*, Boston, 1928).

Farr, Finis, *Black Champion: the Life and Times of Jack Johnson*, 1964.

Feistead, S. Theodore, *Stars Who Made the Halls*, 1946.

Fleischer, Nat, *Jack Dempsey: the Idol of Fistiana*, New York, 1929.

—— *The Boston Strong Boy: the Story of John L. Sullivan*, New York, 1941.

—— *Gentleman Jim: the Story of James J. Corbett*, New York, 1943.

—— *Jack McAuliffe: the Napoleon of the Prize Ring*, New York, 1944.

—— *The Heavyweight Championship*, New York and London, 1949.

—— *John L. Sullivan: Champion of Champions*, New York and Toronto, 1951, London, 1952.

—— *50 Years at Ringside*, New York, 1958, London, 1960.

—— and Sam E. Andre, *A Pictorial History of Boxing*, New Jersey and Toronto, 1959, London, 1960.

—— editor, *The Ring Record Book*, New York, 1962.

Flynn, Errol, *My Wicked, Wicked Ways*, 1960.

Fowler, Gene, *Good Night, Sweet Prince: the Life and Times of John Barrymore*, New York, 1944.

—— *Skyline: a Reporter's Reminiscences of the 1920s*, New York, 1961.

Freedland, Michael, *Errol Flynn*, 1978.

Fullerton, Hugh, *Two Fisted Jeff*, Chicago, 1929.

Furniss, Harry, *The By Ways and Queer Ways of Boxing*, 1919.

Gallagher, Tag, *John Ford: the Man and his Films*, California, 1986.

Gee, Tony, *John L. Sullivan: Cradle to Grave*, Essex, 1998.

Giller, Norman, and Neil Duncanson, *Crown of Thorns: the Bitter History of a Century's Heavyweight Championship Boxing*, 1992.

Golding, Louis, *The Bare-Knuckle Breed*, 1952.

Golesworthy, Maurice, *The Encyclopedia of Boxing*, 1971.

Gorn, Elliott J., *The Manly Art: the Life and Times of the Great Bare-Knuckle Champions*, New York, 1986, London, 1989.

Green, Benny, *Shaw's Champions: G.B.S. and Prizefighting from Cashel Byron to Gene Tunney*, 1978.

Grombach, John V., *The Saga of the Fist*, New Jersey and London, 1997. (First published as *The Saga of Sock*, New York, 1949).

Haldane, Robert A., *Giants of the Ring: the Story of the Heavyweights for 200 years*, 1948.

Haldane, Robert A., *Champions and Challengers: 100 Years of Queensberry Boxing*, 1967.

Halliwell, Leslie, *Halliwell's Film Guide* (Fifth edition), Granada Publishing Company, 1985.

Hamilton, Marybeth, *The Queen of Camp: Mae West, Sex and Popular Culture*, 1996. (First published in USA as *When I'm Bad, I'm Better*, New York, 1995).

Heinz, W.C., editor, *The Fireside Book of Boxing*, New York, 1961.

Heller, Peter, *In This Corner*, New York, 1973.

Herbert, Stephen, and Luke McKernan, *Who's Who of Victorian Cinema*, 1996.

Hickey, D.J., and J.E. Doherty, *A Dictionary of Irish History Since 1800*, Dublin and New Jersey, 1980.

Higharn, Charles, *Errol Flynn: the Untold Story*, New York, 1980.

Hugman, Barry J., *British Boxing Yearbook*, 1985 to date.

Inglis, William O., *Champions Off Guard*, New York, 1932.

Isenberg, Michael T., *John L. Sullivan and his Times*, Illinois and London, 1988.

Johnson, Alexander, *Ten and Out: the Complete Story of the Prize-Ring in America*, New York, 1927.

Knebworth, Viscount, *Boxing: a Guide to Modern Methods*, (the Lonsdale Library, Vol. XI), 1931.

Lahue, Kalton C., *Continued Next Week: a History of the Moving Picture Serial*, Oklahoma, 1964.

Langley, Tom, *The Life of John L. Sullivan: the Boston Strong Boy*, Leicester, 1973.

Lardner, Rex, *The Legendary Champions*, New York, 1972.

Lauder, Sir Harry, *Roamin' in the Gloamin'*, 1928.

Leider, Emily, *Becoming Mae West*, New York, 1997.

Leigh-Lye, Terry, *In This Corner*, 1963.

—— *A Century of Great Boxing Drama*, 1971.

Leonard, Maurice, *Mae West: Empress of Sex*, 1991.

Lynch, Bohun, *Knuckles and Gloves*, 1922.

McCormick, J.B., *The Square Circle*, New York, 1897.

MacGreil, Fr. Michael (editor), *Monsignor James Horan: Memoirs 1911–86*, Dingle, Ireland, 1992.

Milefich, Leo N., *Dan Stuart's Fistic Carnival*, Texas, 1994.

Milne, Tom, editor, *The Time Out Film Guide*, 3rd edition, 1993.

Moran, Gerard, *A Radical Priest in Mayo: Fr. Patrick Lavelle, the Rise and Fall of an Irish Nationalist, 1825–86*, Dublin, 1994.

Mullan, Harry, *The Illustrated History of Boxing*, 1987.

—— *The Ultimate Encyclopedia of Boxing*, 1996.

Musser, Charles, *The Emergence of Cinema: the American Screen to 1907*, California, 1994.

O'Connor, Richard, *Bat Masterson*, New York, 1957.

Odd, Gilbert, *Great Moments in Sport: Heavyweight Boxing*, 1973.

—— *Boxing the Great Champions*, London and New York, 1974.

—— *The Fighting Blacksmith: a Biography of Bob Fitzsimmons*, 1976.

—— *Boxing: The Inside Story*, 1978.

—— *Encyclopedia of Boxing*, 1983.

—— *Kings of the Ring: 100 Years of Heavyweight Boxing*, 1985.

Plimpton, George, *Shadow Box*, 1978.

Prestage, Michael, *Celtic Fists*, Derby, 1997.

Preston, Sir Harry, *Leaves From My Unwritten Diary*, 1936.

Rice, Grantland, *The Tumult and the Shouting: My Life and Sport*, New York and Toronto, 1954.

Roberts, James B., and Alexander G. Skutt, editors, *The Boxing Register: International Hall of Fame Official Record Book*, New York, 1997.

Roberts, Randy, *Jack Dempsey: the Manassa Mauler*, Louisiana, 1979, London, 1987.

—— *Papa Jack: Jack Johnson and the Era of White Hopes*, New York, 1983, London, 1986.

Sammons, Jeffrey T., *Beyond the Ring: the Role of Boxing in American Society*, Chicago, 1988.

Sinclair, Andrew, *John Ford*, 1979.

Slide, Anthony, *Early American Cinema*, New York and London, 1970.

Snelling, O.F., *A Bedside Book of Boxing*, 1972. (Re-issued as *The Ringside Book of Boxing*, 1991.)

Sugar, Bert Randolph, editor, *The Ring Record Book*, New York, 1980.

—— *The Great Fights*, New York, 1984.

Sugden, John, *Boxing and Society: an International Analysis*, Manchester, 1996.

Sullivan, John L., *Champion of the World: Life and Reminiscences of a Nineteenth Century Gladiator*, Boston and London, 1892. (Re-issued with an update and afterword by Gilbert Odd, re-titled *I Can Lick Any Sonofabitch in the House*, London and Carson City, Nevada, 1979.)

Suster, Gerald, *Champions of the Ring: the Lives and Times of Boxing's Heavyweight Heroes*, 1992.

Tich, Mary, and Richard Findlater, *Little Tich: Giant of the Music Hall*, 1979.

Tunney, Gene, *Arms for Living*, New York, 1941.

Van Court, De Witt, *The Makers of Champions in California*, USA, 1926.

Van Every, Edward, *Muldoon: the Solid Man of Sport*, New York, 1929.

Waldron, Jarlath, *Maamtrasna: the Murders and the Mystery*, Dublin, 1992.

Walsh, Raoul, *Each Man in his Time*, Toronto, 1974.

West, Mae, *Goodness Had Nothing To Do With It*, 1960.

Weston, Stanley, editor, *The Best of The Ring*, Chicago, 1992.

Wignall, Trevor, *Prides of the Fancy*, 1928.

Wodehouse, P.G., *Wodehouse on Wodehouse*, 1981.

Zucker, Harvey Marc, and Lawrence J. Babick, *Sports Films: a Complete Reference*, North Carolina, and London, 1987.

Articles

Anon., 'The D'Artagnan of the Prize-Ring', *The Literary Digest*, March 1933.

Adams, Samuel Hopkins, 'There's No Fraud Like an Old Fraud', *Sports Illustrated*, May 1958.

Berg, AnneMarie, 'When Corbett Lost His Cool in Carson City', *Highway Patrolman*, Jan.1975.

Brannigan, Johnny, 'Bloodbath on a Barge', *Boxing Illustrated*, June 1991.

Brodhead, Michael J., 'The Great Prize Fight', *Nevada Highways and Parks*, Fall 1973.

Cole, Ed, 'New Slants on Fitz's Victory Over Corbett', *The Ring*, March 1965.

Earl, Phillip I., 'The Fight of the Century', *Nevada* (journal of the Nevada Historical Society), March–April 1997.

Girsch, George, 'Twas a Mighty Rough Week for Gentleman Jim', *The Ring*, Oct. 1974.

Harper, Tro, 'One of the Great Ones', *California Living Magazine*, Aug. 1976.

Maracin, Paul R., 'The Day Corbett Fought Tunney', *Boxing Illustrated*, Sept. 1992.

Moore, Thomas F., 'Stage Center for the Heavyweights', *Sports Illustrated*, May 1965.

Pacini, Le, 'He Left His Fight in San Francisco', *San Francisco Magazine*, Aug. 1966.

Rimler, Walter, 'The Last Fight of Gentleman Jim', *California Living Magazine*, Nov. 1980.

Vogel, Ed, 'The First Punch', *Las Vegas Review-Journal*, Dec. 1996.

Weston, Stanley, 'James J. Corbett: Bringing Science and Sophistication to the Sport', *World Boxing*, Oct. 1990.

Woods, Alan, 'James J. Corbett: Theatrical Star', *Journal of Sport History*, Vol. 3, No. 2, Summer 1976.

Newspapers and periodicals

American

Arizona Republican, 1910. *Asbury Park Daily Press*, 1895. *Baltimore American*, 1905. *Baltimore Morning Herald*, 1894–1900. *Beloit Daily News*, 1925–33. *Boston Herald*, 1892–94. *Boston Post*, 1934. *Boxing Blade*, 1922. *Boxing Collectors' News*, No. 89. *Buffalo Enquirer*, 1896. *California Illustrated World*, 1890. *Chicago Saturday Blade*, 1894. *Chicago Tribune*, 1897–1952. *Colorado Springs*, 1897. *Dubuque Telegraph-Herald*, 1913. *Kansas City Star*, 1897–1903. *Los Angeles Examiner*, 1933. *Louisville Courier-Journal*, 1897. *Milwaukee Evening Wisconsin*, 1889–1912. *Milwaukee Free Press*, 1902–17. *Milwaukee Sentinel*, 1927–33. *National Police Gazette*, 1886–1919. *New Orleans Daily Picayune*, 1890–94. *New Orleans Evening Telegraph*, 1895. *New York Herald*, 1893–98. *New York Journal*, 1895–1903. *New York*

Sun, 1890. *New York Times*, 1892–1933. *New York World*, 1890–1901. *Oakland Morning Times*, 1890. *Olympian* (journal of the Olympic Club, San Francisco) 1994–95. *The Oregonian*, 1890–93. *Philadelphia Evening Bulletin*, 1895–1900. *Philadelphia Inquirer*, 1897. *Philadelphia Item*, 1890–92. *Philadelphia Record*, 1897. *Police News*, 1887–99. *Pony Express*, 1953. *The Ring*, 1958–92. *St. Louis Globe-Democrat*, 1897. *San Francisco Call*, 1886–1917. *San Francisco Bulletin*, 1897–1907. *San Francisco Chronicle*, 1891–1948. *San Francisco Daily Report*, 1889–97. *San Francisco Evening Post*, 1889. *San Francisco Examiner*, 1889–1922. *Sioux City Journal*, 1897–1900. *Sporting Review*, 1895. *Sporting News*, 1944. *The Sportsman*, 1890. *Variety*, 1933. *Vaudeville News*, 1923.

Canadian

Toronto Daily Star, 1910. *Toronto Globe*, 1910. *Toronto Mail and Empire*, 1902–10. *Toronto News*, 1910.

Australian

The Referee, 1915.

British

Black and White, 1894. *Daily Mail*, 1898. *Guardian*, 1993. *Illustrated Sporting and Dramatic News*, 1894. *Licensed Victuallers' Gazette*, 1894–7. *Licensed Victuallers' Mirror*, 1896. *Liverpool Daily Post*, 1894. *Newcastle Daily Journal*, 1894. *Sporting Mirror*, 1894–7. *Spy*, 1894. *The Times*, 1894. *Yorkshire Evening Post*, 1894. *Yorkshire Owl*, 1894.

Irish

Ballinrobe Chronicle, 1894. *Belfast News-Letter*, 1894. *Carberry's Annual*, 1951–2. *Connaught Telegraph*, 1894. *Evening Herald*, 1909. *Evening Mail*, 1909. *Freeman's Journal*, 1894. *Irish Independent*, 1909. *Irish Times*, 1909. *Mayo News*, 1894. *The Nation*, 1884. *Tuam Herald*, 1892–1933.

Videos

History of the Heavyweight Championship, ABC Video Enterprises, Middlesex.
The Heavyweights: the Stylists, Pickwick Video Ltd, London.

Miscellaneous

Typewritten manuscript, Bob Fitzsimmons' account of his conquest of Corbett, Robert Hobart collection, manuscript div., New York Public Library.

San Francisco household census, 1870, 1880.

San Francisco Directories, 1861–2, 1865–6, 1867–8, 1868–9, 1869–70, 1871–2, 1875.

Bob Fitzsimmons, centenary souvenir issue, Lonsdale Sports, London, 1997.

Index

Index